From Du Bois
to Van Vechten

From Du Bois to Van Vechten

THE EARLY NEW NEGRO LITERATURE, 1903-1926

Chidi Ikonné

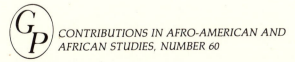

*CONTRIBUTIONS IN AFRO-AMERICAN AND
AFRICAN STUDIES, NUMBER 60*

Greenwood Press WESTPORT, CONNECTICUT • LONDON, ENGLAND

Library of Congress Cataloging in Publication Data

Ikonné, Chidi, 1940-
    From Du Bois to Van Vechten.

    (Contributions in Afro-American and African studies ;
no. 60 ISSN 0069-9624)
    Bibliography: p.
    Includes index.
    1. American literature—Afro-American authors—
History and criticism.   2. American literature—20th
century—History and criticism.   3. Afro-Americans in
literature.   I.   Title.   II.   Series.
PS153.N5I45   810′.9′896073   80-1713
ISBN 0-313-22496-X (lib. bdg.)

Library of Congress Catalog Card Number: 80-1713
ISBN: 0-313-22496-X
ISSN: 0069-9624

First published in 1981

Greenwood Press
A division of Congressional Information Service, Inc.
88 Post Road West, Westport, Connecticut 06881

Printed in the United States of America

10 9 8 7 6 5 4 3 2 1

The following are taken from the James Weldon Johnson Memorial Collection, Beinecke Rare Book and Manuscript Library, Yale University, New Haven, Conn.:

From letters of Langston Hughes to Carl Van Vechten, January 20, 1926, March 26, May 15, June 4 and 24, 1925 with the permission of Donald Gallup, New Haven, Conn. (for Carl Van Vechten) and George H. Bass, Providence, R.I. (for Langston Hughes).

From the letter of Claude McKay to Walter White, September 1, 1931, with the permission of Hope McKay Virtue, Long Beach, Calif. and Carl Cowl Brooklyn, N.Y. (for Claude McKay).

From the letter of Jean Toomer to James Weldon Johnson, July 11, 1930, with the permission of Marjorie Content Toomer, Doylestown, Pa.

From the letter of Carl Van Vechten to James Weldon Johnson, September 7, 1926 with the permission of Donald Gallup (for Carl Van Vechten).

So I lie, who find no peace
Night or day, no slight release
From the unremittant beat
Made by cruel padded feet
Walking through my body's street.
Up and down they go, and back,
Treading out a jungle track.

—Countée Cullen (Heritage)

CONTENTS

PREFACE

The New Negro Literary Awakening took place when there was a great search for artistic and other types of cultural expression in America and many other parts of the world. Consequently, it was not an unalloyed Negro affair.

Unfortunately, while this fact is often acknowledged by both admirers and detractors of this renaissance, there has always been the temptation to exaggerate the influence of whites, such as Carl Van Vechten, upon it and either hastily condemn it as a white man's creation or disregard all its indebtedness to the white world and commend it as an uninfluenced attempt of the Negro to rediscover himself.

A careful scrutiny, however, reveals four facts:

The Literary Awakening was only a moment in a long but continual development of racial pride and self-confidence in literature.

The Literary Awakening was only a component of a larger movement with several aspects (sociopolitical, economic, and cultural) which often interacted with and conditioned each other.

The Literary Awakening had two stages: the essentially Negro self-possessing and Negro self-expressing period before 1926; the publisher/audience-controlled, even if essentially Negro self-expressing, period after 1926.

None of the stages of the Literary Awakening was beyond white influence even if that influence was not the most important single determinant of the trend of black literature.

Since most of the distinguishing features of the second stage of this renaissance had their roots in the first stage, the main focus of the present study is on the period 1903-1926. The dates correspond with the publication of two books, believed to have had tremendous impact on the trend of the Literary Awakening: W. E. B. Du Bois's collection of essays and sketches, *The Souls of Black Folk* (1903), and Carl Van Vechten's novel, *Nigger Heaven* (1926). Many New Negro authors acknowledged Du Bois's book as their source of inspiration; Van Vechten's novel is regarded by many critics as a perverter of young, promising, black writers who, after the success of *Nigger Heaven,* allegedly became "Van Vechtenites" and prostituted their art.

The main difference between the first and the second stages of the renaissance was in the scope rather than in the complexion of the subject matters and the manner in which they were treated. Before 1926 the choice was almost limitless; after 1926 the range of subjects was, to all intents and purposes, compelled by mercenary considerations (of publishers mainly) to be limited to those aspects of Negro life which had proved financially successful. But the end product was from beginning to end expressive of the Negro.

Although none of the aspects of the movement is completely ignored, this study focuses mainly on the literary. Since its principal objective is to determine the nature and effect of each pattern of influence to which this formative stage of the Literary Awakening was subjected, its approach is a combination of textual analysis and historical investigation, with emphasis on primary sources.

Chapter 1, an introduction, reviews the rediscovery and reevaluation of African artistic expression at the turn of the century. It ends with an analysis of representative works about the Negro by white authors between the years 1903 and 1926 and shows their influence on the budding black writers of the period. Chapter 2 examines the "symptoms" of the literary movement before the formal launching of the New Negro literature on 21 March 1924. Without any intention to accord undeserved literary importance to "unknown" authors, it includes in its investigation the works of some lesser-known contemporaries of Paul Laurence Dunbar whose dialect poetry anticipated the Harlem Renaissance use of dialect and the folk language in literature. Chapter 3 analyzes the roles of major black journals in the promotion of the Literary Awakening. Chapters 4 and 5 discuss representative works of the young writers and their indebtedness to extraneous forces. The epilogue summarizes the findings.

This study is by no means a definitive work on what Robert A. Bone describes as the "indigenous character" of the New Negro movement.[1]

It is only a partial response to George E. Kent's call for "a very exhaustive study of all forces operating within the period [Harlem Renaissance], so that properly weighted judgment and completely accurate description can be provided."[2]

Although I am completely responsible for the views expressed in the study, several individuals and organizations have contributed to its existence. George E. Kent opened my eyes to the complexity of the patterns of the Harlem Renaissance. Mercer Cook and the late Léon-G. Damas assisted my understanding of the relationship between the Harlem Renaissance and negritude. The University of Chicago, the American Philosophical Society, and Harvard University (Clark Fund) financed parts of the research on which the work is based. Kenneth Onwuka Dike was an unfailing source of inspiration and strength. Margaret M. Brezicki and her colleagues of Greenwood Press drew my attention to parts of the work that needed polishing or strengthening or both. Carol Thomas assisted in typing the manuscript. Uche, my wife, provided the basic love and support without which the book could not have seen the light of day.

NOTES

1. Robert A. Bone, *The Negro Novel in America,* rev. ed. (New Haven: Yale University Press, 1965), p. 61.

2. George E. Kent, *Blackness and the Adventure of Western Culture* (Chicago: Third World Press, 1972), p. 34.

For my mother, Ekwuluo

From Du Bois
to Van Vechten

INTRODUCTION: NEW VIEWS
ON OLD PREJUDICES

AFRICA AND AFRICAN ART

The emergence of Negro self-confidence in literature and art in the 1920s took place mainly because of the crisis in confidence regarding European and American "civilization." The white man, dissatisfied with his own baby (his un-primitive civilization which could save him neither from emotional desiccation nor from wars and rumors of wars), had, in a desperate volte-face, discovered in the Negro what he thought was the opposite of the product of his own civilization—the "primitive" being, charmingly clothed with unbridled instincts.

Thus, although the New Negro movement had been self-motivated and self-expressing, the white man's interest soon became a part of its impetus and increasingly gained such importance that the movement acquired an appearance of a lost innocence.

Paul Guillaume, Parisian art dealer and editor of *Les Arts à Paris,* remarked in October 1923:

The modern movement in art gets its inspiration undoubtedly from African art, and it could not be otherwise. Thanks to that fact France wields the artistic sceptre, because since Impressionism no manifestation in art could be shown that is not African in its essence. The work of the young painters such as Picasso, Modigliani, Soutine, for example, is to a certain extent, the work of African emotion in a new setting. In the same way the sculpture of Archipenko, Lipchitz and of Epstein is impregnated with Africanism. The music of Berard, Satie, Poulenc, Auric, Honegger— in short, all that which is interesting since Dubussy, is African. One can say as much also of the poetry since Rimbaud up to Blaise Cendrars and Reverdy, including Apollinaire.[1]

Paul Guillaume was one of the sources of influence on European art at the turn of the century. His gallery in Paris, more than any other thing, brought most of the leading artists in contact with the Africanism which later "impregnated" their works. According to a colleague, Albert C. Barnes, Guillaume was known "to the art world as the man who rescued the obscure ancient Negro art from its mere ethnological significance and converted it into a well of unsuspecting spiritual richness from which the whole modern movement in art has drunk deeply."[2] Paul Guillaume himself gave a brief account of his place as a custodian of African "idols and masks"[3] which helped in no small measure to revitalize the modern art which seemed to have "exhausted its energies, and was dying of a slow anaemia."[4] In his one-room apartment near Montmartre he received travellers, explorers, European colonial officers, as well as important African chiefs who had heard of his promotion of African art and had gone to give him their support.[5] Albert Barnes, who describes Guillaume's little room of African and African-inspired art as "the mecca not only of the important creators in France, but in America, Japan, England, and every continental country,"[6] once saw "six chiefs of African tribes there at the same time with four principals of the Russian ballet."[7] Guillaume's main message to his guests was embodied in one sentence which he enunciated at a festival which he organized at the Champs Élysées in 1919: "The spirit of modern man—or modern woman—needs to be nourished by the civilization of the Negro."[8] He did not have to overstress it. What, thanks mainly to his "idols and masks," Picasso and Matisse were doing in painting and the famous French group known as The Six[9] in music, Guillaume Apollinaire and Blaise Cendrars were already doing in poetry. Indeed, Blaise Cendrars's transcription of African legends, tales, riddles, and songs in his *Anthologie Nègre* (1921) reinforced the fumbling interest in African oral literature which had been kindled by such collectors and students of African folklore as René Basset, P.-L. Monteil, Dupuis-Yakouba, Lanrezac, Zeltner and Francois-Victor Equil-becq. Cendrars's book soon became, as Alain Locke points out, "the bible" of what was "a recognized school of modern French poetry."[10]

All this, of course, helped to launch in France, and in Europe as a whole, the vogue of the Negro. Paul Guillaume calls it "a new renaissance," thus comparing the role of the African artifacts in the creation of the vogue to that of classic art in inspiring the Renaissance.[11] Whatever it was, it was further sustained by a combination of other important factors: the flowering interest in Sigmund Freud's analysis of the "civilized" and the "primitive," the works of Leo Frobenius, Maurice Delafosse, and other historians and socioanthropologists who tried to transform the image of Africa with its civilizations from an object of ridicule and contempt to something positive and enviable, the exotic presence of the Senegalese sharpshooters and other blacks in the Europe of World War I, the invasion of Europe by Afro-American music and dance, the award of the enviable French Prix Goncourt to a Negro novel, *Batouala,* by a Negro author, René Maran, in 1921, and the importance of André Gide's *Voyage au Congo* (1927) and *Le Retour du Tchad* (1927)—two of the many follow-ups of René Maran's "véritable roman nègre." The result of all these was the development of an atmosphere in which the smell of negritude or Africanism mingled with the smell of other "isms" even though the Damas-Césaire-Senghor African movement was not born until the middle of the 1930s.

Europe, however, was not the sole creator of this atmosphere which enhanced the universal receptivity to the black-race-motivated art and literature and thereby fostered the emergence of the New Negro literary movement. The works of Franz Boas and several other anthropologists in America strove not only to destroy the idea of the Negro being naturally inferior to the white man but also to win respect for his folk culture. The Association for the Study of Negro Life and History, under the leadership of Carter G. Woodson, dug into the past of the Negro and published its findings in its organ, *Journal of Negro History.* The Pan-African movement, promoted by W. E. B. Du Bois, affirmed the black man's right to a place under the sun. Garveyism and its projection of "black" as a pride-worthy color helped to quicken "the sense of race consciousness and self dignity on the part of the common people among black folks all over the world."[12]

America also had its own Paul Guillaume: Dr. Albert C. Barnes of Merion, Montgomery County, Pennsylvania. Barnes, a close associate of Paul Guillaume, was described as "the first and . . . distinctly the last word in Primitive African Art."[13] Through articles, public lectures, and by throwing the door of his gallery open to the public, he spread the gospel of how "idols made to be worshipped by savages, and masks designed for use in Heathen rites, should have shown the way out of an artistic

impasse apparently hopeless."[14] His foundation offered fellowships to
Aaron Douglas and Gwendolyn Bennett to study in its classes, an indication of his belief in the black man's artistic abilities.[15]

The response to this faith in and promotion of primitive African art
on the part of Albert Barnes and others who, like him, had discovered
it, was overwhelming. Bordering on enthusiasm, it worried Barnes himself, the editors of *Opportunity,* and scholars like Alain Locke, who
feared it was becoming irrational.[16] Whatever it was (irrational, amateur-
ish) by the end of the World War I the interest had spread to all aspects
of Negro life and culture. The returning young American veterans had
not only come in contact with African-inspired art and life in Europe,
they had been frustrated by, and disgusted with Western civilization and
its machine culture. Familiar with and encouraged by Freudian concepts
about the "civilized" and the "primitive," a good number of them and
many of their generation, like their European counterparts, struggled to
escape from the dehumanized civilization into the primitive instinctual
world.[17] The primitive, therefore was in vogue. T. S. Eliot's vision of the
"civilized" world as a "waste land" was acclaimed. René Maran's
Batouala, with its emphasis on the "glorious" life of a primitive Congo
tribe, was presented to the world as "a great novel" by Ernest Heming-
way.[18] *Batouala* was translated into English and "the whole world [was]
reading it."[19] The attempts of Picasso and many other artists in Europe
to capture and glorify "primitive" cultures in their art were applauded
in the United States, even though it was mainly by the young and the
young-at-heart. The sorrow of the non-Negro part of the *métisse cultur-
elle,*[20] exemplified by Van Vechten's character, Mary Love, is a pointer
to how some whites felt at that period:

She had lost or forfeited her birthright, this primitive birthright which
was so valuable and important an asset, a birthright that all the civilized
races were struggling to get back to—this fact explained the art of a
Picasso or a Stravinsky.[21]

It was, indeed, a coincidence that what the Negro had was what was
needed at the time.[22] The atmosphere that sustained the white man's
adulation of the "primitive" Negro was not completely the white man's
creation. As Eugene Holmes argues, even though the "flowering" of the
renaissance "took on a new form and content," it was indeed "a true

renaissance of feeling, a prideful evocation of the dark image of Africa, germinated from a fructified seedbed."[23]

Its voguish aspect (as distinct from the self-expressing trend) may not have stemmed completely from the Negro mass. Langston Hughes, for instance, contends that "the ordinary Negroes hadn't heard of the Negro Renaissance. And if they had, it hadn't raised their wages any."[24] Another eyewitness, Wallace Thurman, describes the patronage of the famous Harlem cabarets as "almost 95 percent white."[25] Yet the Negro was both at the base and at the apex of the renaissance. His music and dance[26] had become, in spite of the protest of intellectuals and classicists, two of the most important elements of the American temperament.[27] It is significant not only that both Paul Laurence Dunbar and James Weldon Johnson had several years before recognized, in their novels,[28] the existence of the New York black Bohemia, a feature of the renaissance, but also that some of the frontline figures of the renaissance were first attracted to Harlem by things over which the white man had only an indirect control. *Shuffle Along,* the musical comedy written and played by Eubie Blake and Noble Sissle, is a case in point. Langston Hughes, who presents it as giving "a scintillating send-off to that Negro vogue in Manhattan,"[29] acknowledges it as the main thing that took him to New York.[30] Arna Bontemps, a participant in and one of the most authoritative chroniclers of the Harlem Renaissance, goes as far as seeing the influence of the "all-black musical comedy" on the poetry of Langston Hughes and of Countée Cullen.[31]

This, however, is not to depreciate the impact the white man's quest for the "primitive" had on the Negro as both a subject and a creator of literature. Even if the black man was not a passive factor in that coincidence, the white man's interest was the most important single part of its evolution. Thanks to the existence of a sympathetic white audience—an audience in search of its own primitive self[32]—there was a proliferation of writings in all the literary genres dealing with the Negro.

The genuineness of these images of the Negro is still an open question. Three things, however, are certain. Firstly, given their motivation—the quest for the instinctive way of life in an anti-instinctive "civilization," those images contained much of the audience's projected wishes, disguised in the color black, to maintain the peace between the ego and superego. Secondly, in order to give the artistic daydream as much illusion of reality as possible (while still maintaining a safe distance between the writer and the reader through the pigmentation of the skin) there were definite attempts on the part of the writers to approach their subjects—even if they were the old stereotypes or the newly developing exotic Negro—in a fresh and more or less serious way. In other words, they tried to give "new views or at least new angles on old prejudices."[33] Thirdly, irrespective of the degree to which the works capitalized on the exotic, they sustained the interest of the audience in the Negro "stuff" and thereby afforded receptivity to the emerging black writers who, essentially working from within, tried to express themselves as best they could, with little or no intention to hurt or please anyone.

A list of white participants in this indirect literary promotion includes, among many others, Carl Sandburg, Sherwood Anderson, e. e. cummings, Ronald Firbank, Waldo Frank, DuBose Heyward, Ridgely Torrence, Marc Connelly, Ernest H. Culbertson, Eugene O'Neill, and Carl Van Vechten. The present discussion focuses on Vachel Lindsay, Carl Sandburg, Ridgely Torrence, Eugene O'Neill, Gertrude Stein, Julia Peterkin, and Carl Van Vechten, whose works are representative of white production in the field of literature about blacks.

VACHEL LINDSAY

A Study of the Negro Race is the subtitle of Vachel Lindsay's poem *The Congo.* His "private letter," which was published in *The Crisis* of May 1915, however, betrays the romanticism of his inspiration, and casts doubt upon the reliability of his study.[34]

The poem begins with a "jungle impression"—the "basic savagery" of the Negro race. The Speaker focuses on "Fat black bucks in a wine-barrel room, / Barrel-house kings, with feet unstable."[35] Their rowdiness furnishes him with a vision. He "SAW THE CONGO, CREEPING THROUGH THE BLACK, / CUTTING THROUGH THE FOREST WITH A GOLDEN TRACK." [LCP, p. 179] An embodiment of the Dark Continent through which the Congo flows, each of the "fat black bucks" carried in him a river Congo with all its attributes: tattooed cannibals, blood-lust songs, tin-pan gongs, blood-thirsty warriors, witch doctors, pygmies, Mumbo-Jumbo, and all other gods of the Congo. The Congo in the "wine-barrel room" is as threatening as the Congo in Joseph Conrad's story, *The Heart of Darkness:*

> Be careful what you do,
> Or Mumbo-Jumbo, God of the Congo,
> And all of the other
> Gods of the Congo,
> Mumbo-Jumbo will hoo-doo you,
> Mumbo-Jumbo will hoo-doo you,
> Mumbo-Jumbo will hoo-doo you.
> [LCP, p. 180]

The second part of the poem continues the vision; but the focus now is on another aspect of blacks—"their irresponsible high spirits":

> Wild crap-shooters with a whoop and a call
> Danced the juba in their gambling hall
> And laughed fit to kill, and shook the town,
> And guyed the policemen and laughed them down
> With a boomlay, boomlay, boomlay, BOOM.
> [LCP, p. 180]

These "high spirits" are manifestations of the optimism which the Speaker sees in the Congo that creeps "through the black":

> A negro [sic] fairyland . . .
> A minstrel river
> Where dreams come true.
> [LCP, p. 180]

The last section, suggested by the sight of "a good old negro" preacher, is a celebration of the "daybreak" on the Congo and the redemption of its men and beasts. [LCP, p. 184]

Lindsay's portrayal of the Negro in *The Congo* was a most useful asset in the indirect promotion of Negro literature. It is also possible that he intended the redemption of the last section of the poem to be an irony, as the following lines seem to indicate:

> Redeemed were the forests, the beasts and the men,
> And only the vulture dared again
> By the far, lone mountains of the moon

To cry, in the silence, the Congo tune:—
Mumbo-Jumbo will hoo-doo you.

[LCP, p. 184]

The peace and silence that reign over a graveyard at the break of day come to mind. One visualizes savages being redeemed by "angels" as savage as the savages themselves. However, the irony is only a whisper in the din of the "boomlay" on earth, and of the "heavenly cry" of "the twelve Apostles," who from their thrones in the sky will the death of Mumbo-Jumbo.

More importantly, Lindsay's perception of Negro traits (both on the Congo and in the United States of America) is questionable. In spite (and, to some extent, because) of his sources of inspiration—the accounts of Stanley and Conrad, Williams and Walker's songs and performance, the dances of Dahomey Amazons which he saw as a boy—his image of Africa is romantic. He has created a few more gods, and a few more traits for African people. He has distorted their traits, and anachronistically furnished them with many things, including "long-tailed coats." Even if his image of Africa is accurate, the facility with which he relates the behavior of blacks in America to the alleged African traits, which are hundreds of years and thousands of miles away, smacks of literary acrobatics. Perhaps, it was this tour de force that W. E. B. Du Bois had in mind when he spoke of the poem's "imperfections of spiritual insight."[36]

The Congo, however, is not the only poem in which Lindsay uses Negro material. Apart from shorter pieces, like *How Samson Bore Away the Gates of Gaza: A Negro Sermon* [LCP, pp. 175-77] and *When Peter Jackson Preached in the Old Church* [LCP, pp. 177-78] , a poem which is "to be sung to the tune of the old negro spiritual 'Every time I feel the spirit moving in my heart I'll pray,' " he has another famous poem on the Negro: *The Booker Washington Trilogy.*

This piece, as its title suggests, has three parts. The first section, *A Negro Sermon,* focuses on Simon Legree, who, ever since he was created by Harriet Beecher Stowe, has come to symbolize the cruel slave master. Here, however, we approach him through the consciousness of a superstitious Negro speaker whose personality, as revealed in his way of talking, is, of course, a projection of his creator's concept of Negroes and their values. Thus we have a superstitious Legree whose "garret was full of curious things: / Books of magic, bags of gold, / And rabbits' feet on long twine strings" [LCP, pp. 161-62] , a monster who "had great long teeth" and "ate raw meat, 'most every meal, / And rolled his eyes till the cat would squeal." [LCP, p. 162] When in the end "he went down to the Devil," he gambled, ate, drank, and lazied with "Mister Devil." [LCP p. 163]

As for Uncle Tom, he is still the faithful slave "who prayed for Legree with his last breath." [LCP, p. 162]

With the conspicuous absence of the slightest awareness, on the part of the speaker, of the book called the Bible, the poem reads more like a story told in a boite de nuit by an ingenious narrator who has thoroughly digested Stowe's *Uncle Tom's Cabin* than like a sermon preached from a Negro pulpit by a Negro folk preacher. But considered simply as a poem, the "sermon," from a stylistic point of view, is better than any of the three parts of *The Congo*. The speaker's voice and the substance of the poem (the call and response) are so synchronized that one automatically calls the other to the consciousness of the reader. In their inseparableness, they are the most successful actualization of Vachel Lindsay's romantic idea of a Negro speaker:

Ideas are raging through the brain of even the duskiest of the Negro leaders [readers?] , and one can handle for such an audience almost any large thought he thinks he understands. He can put it into Negro poetry, I maintain, if he is man enough, and still have it Negro poetry. But he must have his manner bright-colored, full-throated, relaxed and tropical. By manner I do not mean dialect. There are innumerable Pullman porters who speak English in a close approach to the white man's way. But their thoughts and fancies are still straight from the jungle.[37]

Simon Legree—A Negro Sermon is poetry. Whether it deserves the qualificative "Negro" is a different matter, the ineffective use of the folk "call-and-response" format notwithstanding. It takes more than format to make a poem Negro or even Russian, to use another example. Negro idiom normally—and Lindsay is right—is colorful. It is doubtful, nevertheless, that "thoughts and fancies" embodied in it are always "straight from the jungle," irrespective of the speaker's place of birth and training.

The second part of the poem, which pays tribute to John Brown, is an account of the speaker's journey to Palestine, the biblical land of Israel, used here as a symbol for the Christian heaven. It is, therefore, a movement in a direction opposite to his descent to the Devil with Simon

Legree in the first part. The use of the call-and-response pattern is more successful here. The poem, as a matter of fact, can be classed with such spirituals as "Boun' fer Canaan Lan',"[38] and "I heard the Angels Singin' "[39] in which discussions are interrupted by recurring questions. In fact, a short prefatory note under the title of the poem indicates that the piece is "to be sung by a leader and chorus, the leader singing the body of the poem, while chorus interrupts with the question." [LCP, p. 164]

Nevertheless, the poem's second section has much in common with the poem's first part. It has its source in the consciousness of a "Negro" speaker. The naive otherworldly tone of the speaker could have been the voice of the visionary preacher in *Simon Legree—A Negro Sermon.*

The last part of the trilogy is no less visionary. Lindsay himself described it as "a prophecy of a colored Utopia."[40] It is a commemoration of the biblical King Solomon-Queen of Sheba love affair. Once again, the speaker's voice is naive as he paradoxically looks forward to the glorious past when "the Queen of Sheba had four hundred sailors," and did "a cake walk" with King Solomon. [LCP, pp. 170-71] That was in the past; but it will happen again in the future, as the refrain says: "For ten thousand years."

In spite of the speaker's "thoughts and fancies" which are refreshingly innocent and, apparently, "straight from the jungle," for the delectation of those questing for the "primitive" *King Solomon and the Queen of Sheba* is an optimistic poem. Lindsay, no doubt, expected Negro leaders to be grateful for it. Unfortunately for him, however, along with *The Congo,* it was "denounced by the colored people for reasons that [he] can not fathom."[41] W. E. B. Du Bois, for instance, thought it was "nonsense." In his opinion "Mr. Vachel Lindsay knows two things, and two things only, about Negroes: The beautiful rhythm of their music and the ugly side of their drunkards and outcasts." He called this knowledge "little" and "dangerous."[42] When the poet protested he was given a lecture on why his treatment of Negro subjects could not be favorably received by black men and all those who wished them happiness and prosperity there and then:

No colored man doubts your good intentions, but many of them doubt your understanding of their hopes. You look about you and see a black world full of a strange beauty different from that of the white world; they look about them and see other men with exactly the same feelings and desires who refuse to recognize the resemblance. You look forward to a colored Utopia separate and different from the hope of the white man; they have only one overwhelming desire, and that is to share in a common civilization in which all distinctions of race are blurred (or forgotten) by common aspiration and common labor. . . . But somehow we feel (and I say "we" because in this I share the feelings of the colored race), somehow we feel that you do not write about colored humanity as you write about white humanity. . . . Somehow we feel that for you, black men and women are not like others who have been mocked and scorned and wounded, but beings a little different from other sufferers who do not share the same ancestry and the same color of skin.[43]

Nonetheless, Lindsay's interest in the Negro as a subject for literature, like that of several other white poets, his obvious distortion of the image of the black American and of Africa, which he saw dark and unbridled in the Afro-American, helped in creating a wider audience for the Negro "stuff." His conception of Africa would color parts of the works of such New Negro writers as Countée Cullen who owed much of their image of the black continent to exotic literature and films.

CARL SANDBURG

Carl Sandburg's contribution to the receptivity of the New Negro literature was more through his popularization of poetry unrestricted in its choice of subject and manner of treatment than through direct use of Negro material. His titles include *Jazz Fantasia,*[44] *Vaudeville Dancer,*[45] and many other subjects not traditionally regarded as suitable affairs for poetry. Some of his lines overflow themselves and run, in some cases, into as many as four lines on a standard page. This liberative position on poetry accounts for his influence on young black poets, like Langston Hughes, who were looking for flexible forms that they could adjust to their own needs: the expression of their dark selves.
Yet Carl Sandburg also used Negro material:

I AM the nigger.
Singer of songs,
Dancer . . .
Softer than fluff of cotton . . .
Harder than dark earth
Roads beaten in the sun
By the bare feet of slaves . . .

Foam of teeth . . . breaking crash of laughter . . .
Red love of the blood of woman,
White love of the tumbling pickaninnies . . .
Lazy love of the banjo thrum . . .
Sweated and driven for the harvest-wage,
Loud laughter with hands like hams,
Fists toughened on the handles,
Smiling the slumber dreams of old jungles,
Crazy as the sun and dew and dripping, heaving life of the jungle
Brooding and muttering with memories of shackles:

> I am the nigger.
> Look at me.
> I am the nigger.[46]

Despite the title of the poem—*Nigger*—and the repetition of the word three times within the piece itself, Sandburg's poem is a product of deep thought and serious treatment. The first three lines evoke the stereotyped image of the "musical nigger"; but as we move on we discover that this is not the old "musical nigger." The stereotype is only a casing stuffed with the experience of the black American—from Africa to America—and rehabilitated. Thanks to a careful choice of bright and dark sentiments effectively juxtaposed, the poem presents a man of joy and sorrows. He is soft; he is hard. His "breaking crash of laughter" is muted by "foam of teeth." His "lazy love of the banjo thrum" is offset by the active experience of being "sweated and driven for the harvest-wage." Unlike the Africa of the "fat black bucks" of Vachel Lindsay's poetry, the Africa in Carl Sandburg's *Nigger* is more than a flood of "basic savagery" and unbridled instincts. It is a complex, bitter, sweet heritage.

The total effect is the emergence of a toughened and stable being who, like some of Langston Hughes's speakers later, IS in the present as real as his experience WAS—a man who has seen all the many faces of life and is still undaunted. The use of the definite article "the" throughout the poem before the word "nigger" is significant. It underscores the doggedness of the speaker's survival. He was; he still is:

> I am the nigger.
> Look at me.
> I am the nigger.

Nigger and poems like it by other whites did not capitalize on the exotic Negro; they nevertheless assisted in creating a wider audience for the Negro "stuff."

RIDGELY TORRENCE

White playwrights who used Negro materials also produced the same effect. In this connection one of the first dates that comes to mind is 5 April 1917—a date which James Weldon Johnson describes as "the beginning of a new era" in "the entire history of the Negro in the American theatre."[47] It was on that date that the Coloured Players, at the Garden Theatre in Madison Square Garden, New York, gave a performance of Ridgely Torrence's one-act plays, *The Rider of Dreams, Granny Maumee,* and *Simon the Cyrenian.* James Weldon Johnson's recording of the impact of the event is enthusiastic: "the stereotyped traditions regarding the Negro's histrionic limitations were smashed."[48] The dramatic critic of the *New Republic* described the occasion as "the emergence of an artistic Cinderella into the palace where she belongs."[49] Eight years later, Alan Dale, the dramatic editor of the *New York American,* was to "recall with the greatest pleasure" Ridgely Torrence's three one-act plays, and regret the absence of other plays like them.[50]

Let us examine two of the plays.

As the curtain rises on *Granny Maumee,* we see an old black woman and her nineteen-year-old great-granddaughter, Pearl. The old woman (Granny Maumee, herself) whose only son, Sam, was unjustly lynched fifty years ago, cultivates a burning hatred for the white man as she awaits the arrival of another great-granddaughter, Sapphie, and her newly born son whom she expects to be a reincarnation of her beloved son. Sapphie arrives; but instead of bringing a black boy with pure black blood, she brings a fair-skinned baby with a good quantity of white blood in his veins—the son of her white boss who "des would have his way."[51] This betrayal apparently kills Granny Maumee.

The subject, therefore, is a combination of well-known elements of black experience in America: the lynching of the innocent, the exploitation of the black woman and, to some extent, the unenviable fate of the mulatto. The treatment is serious. Torrence's apparent effort to observe the traditional rules of the "Three Unities"—of action, of place, and of time—heightens the tragic tension.

Nevertheless, *Granny Maumee* is anything but a masterpiece. Its expository section is well done, thanks to a series of ironic situations which seem to grow out of each other. But it comes apart when it gets to its denouement which is imposed upon it rather than built out of the exposition and complication. Granny Maumee's recovery of her sight fifty years after "her eyes," in the words of Pearl, "was swiveled in w'ite man's fire before she see the w'ite man mix with her blood," is too weak a prop for the reversal of situation.[52]

The play which has started with what promised to be an organic plot degenerates into a mechanical toy of deus ex machina. Not even the author-Granny obvious manipulation of the Christian faith in the exclamation: "Ask an' we shill receive" can restore our belief. One has the impression of witnessing the type of work Horace had in mind when he warned against openings that promise more than they can deliver:

> What did this promise produce to match a wide mouth?
> The mountain will go into labor and deliver a silly mouse![53]

This is also true of the portrayal of Granny Maumee as a person. The working of her mind has a solid foundation and is understandable. As far as the white man is concerned, she is a true (even if stereotyped) daughter of what Claude McKay, in *The White Fiends,* calls "black land where black deeds are done."[54] As a matter of fact, Pearl makes the point: "Sometimes when her mine runs on 'bout the burnin' she begins to work back'ards. . . . You know what I means. Away from the love of Gawd, back to that Affykin devil stuff."[55]

However, her eleventh-hour forgiveness of the white man, far from being consistent with her character, reveals what looks like a playwright's inability to resist the temptation of introducing a pinch of "the problem." Thus Granny dies, like several other blacks in literature, suffering yet virtuous.

Nathan Irvin Huggins has suggested that Torrence's plays, like those of other playwrights of that period, only tried to do "what the more pedestrian novels had been doing for some time, treating the Negro as a serious subject although in stereotyped ways."[56] Perhaps, it would be more accurate to say that Ridgely Torrence tried to treat the stereotyped Negro in a fresh and serious way. The object of imitation was essentially the same. What was new and serious was the manner of imitation.

This fact is more evident in *The Rider of Dreams.* Madison Sparrow, the central character of the comedy, is hardly a more serious subject than the stereotyped music-loving, dancing "niggers" of the minstrel stage—the type of 'merrymakers, aflame with the rhythm of their [black] blood and the joy of [uninhibited] freedom," we find in *Danse Calinda,* another play by Torrence.[57] Indeed, the source of the comic in his character—a comicodramatic element which borders on tragedy—is his naive struggle to dream and to live his music in a world that measures success by hard work and the dollars and cents that accrue therefrom. He complains: "I don't understan' dis worl'. If I want to make music why cain't folks lemme alone to make music? If I dream a fine dream why is it I always wake's up? Looks to me like somebody's always trying to crowd me out an' git me in a tight place."[58]

What is new is the deliberate effort to create something serious out of frivolous characters and situations. Unfortunately, however, the attempt is not uniformly effective, at least from an artistic point of view. Thus among the essentially true-to-type characters of Madison and Lucy we have the incredible "great latent power" of Uncle Williams[59] which, providing a link between the complication of the play and its resolution, converts the latter into an imposition on the play as a whole. How the old man comes to be in possession of the eight hundred dollars which Madison has stolen from his wife's savings is as miraculous as Granny Maumee's recovery of her sight after she had lost it fifty years before.

None of the three plays is a first-rate artistic creation. The importance accorded to them is based on what Matthew Arnold calls "historic estimate." Their position in the course of the development of Negro drama makes each of them "of more importance as [drama] than in itself it really is."[60] Yet their significance as an attempt to reinterpret stereotyped Negro material cannot be overemphasized. Some of the young writers of the 1920s were to do the same thing in their appropriate genres. Witness Langston Hughes's *Not Without Laughter* (1930) where Jimboy and Aunt Hager manifest relationship with the worlds of Madison and Lucy both in their dominant traits and in how those traits have been treated.

Ridgely Torrence could not completely avoid exoticism in his portrayal of the Negro. Nevertheless, he belonged to that group of white writers who, through serious treatment, went very close to extracting and rehabilitating ideas, traits, and traditions that had been tinkered into clichés.

EUGENE O'NEILL

This could also be said of Eugene O'Neill in his play *The Emperor Jones* which, like Torrence's three one-act pieces, was an epoch-making production, and therefore deserves a closer look. This is the story of a black Pullman porter who kills a fellow Negro, Jeff, at a game. Imprisoned, he kills a white prison guard who maltreats him, escapes from prison, and runs to a West Indian island where he becomes a dictator. A Cockney trader, Henry Smithers, whom he has been protecting, raises the natives against him. He flees and commits suicide with a silver bullet (he has preserved it for that purpose) to avoid the shame of being killed by the natives whom he despises.

The action, though well defined, is minimally visual; for, the first and last scenes aside, the play is essentially a monologue. The action takes place in the mind of Brutus Jones who relives his past. The atmosphere is poetic as the hero runs from the realistic present symbolized by the sound of a tom-tom into the dream-past (his past experience) and back into the present through his revolver with which he kills himself.

As a character, he is well conceived and memorably painted. He is proud, conscious, and undefeated. He cannot outgrow his past sins and guilt. Yet he is ready to commit those sins again. His creation is a courageous experiment[61]—an experiment which "marks a historic step . . . in the treatment of Negro characters in drama."[62] In spite of the spotlight on the exotic aspect of his being, the Negro, here, is not a "comic relief, or a pathetic victim; he is a man, presented as of powerful dramatic interest in his own right."[63]

The Emperor Jones is also significant in another way. It brought into focus a pattern of response that was to be strengthened by the appearance of *All God's Chillun Got Wings*[64] and that was to be adopted by the critics of the products of the Harlem Renaissance. While many whites and some blacks praised the portrayals, many blacks, especially those of the middle class, condemned them. Thus Paul Robeson was "damned all over the place"[65] for associating himself with the plays.

Admittedly, none of Eugene O'Neill's plays portrayed the Negro in the best of lights—that is, in a way most blacks of the period would like to see themselves. Yet the playwright's achievement for and interest in the Negro in the dramatic literature cannot be overemphasized. In addition to personal examples and assistance in creating a viable audience for Negro "stuff," he had some wise words for Negro artists—a piece of advice which was significant even if some of the budding artists had either thought it up themselves or received it from some other quarters:

If I have one thing to say—(and I grant that "I" is a presumption)—to Negroes who work, or have the ambition to work, in any field of artistic expression, it is this: Be yourself! Don't reach out for *our* stuff which *we* call good! Make *your stuff* and *your good!* You have within your race an opportunity—and a shining goal!—for new forms, new significance. Every white who has sense ought to envy you! *We* look around with accustomed eyes at somewhat jaded landscapes—at least too familiar—while to *you* life ought to be as green—and as deep—as the sea! There ought to be a Negro play written by a Negro that no white could ever have conceived or executed. By this I don't mean greater—because all art is equally great—but *yours, your own,* an expression of what is deep in you, is *you,* by *you*!![66]

Something was also happening in the realm of fiction. Many years before Vachel Lindsay, Ridgely Torrence, Eugene O'Neill, and several other white writers tried to give serious treatment to their Negro material in poetry and drama, some other whites had started boring into the literary mold of black stereotypes in fiction. A comprehensive survey of this trend goes as far back as the mid-nineteenth century, focusing on the portrayal of such Negroes as Jim in Mark Twain's *Huckleberry Finn* (1884) who, in spite of his black skin, and superstition, is shown as an ordinary human being endowed with ordinary human sensitiveness and love of liberty.

GERTRUDE STEIN

It is, however, at the turn of the century that we find Negro characters emphasized as speaking for themselves as artistic creations rather than for their creators as pro- or anti-Negro propagandists. Nonetheless, like their counterparts in drama and poetry, they were essentially the old stereotypes given a fresh and serious treatment. This is exemplified by one of the pioneers of the trend, Gertrude Stein's "Melanctha,"[67] a piece in which subtle human minds are planted in the bosoms of eroded stereotypes based on colors of skins.

"Melanctha" is the tragedy of a half-white girl who wants to be at peace with the world, but whom no one can understand. The heroine from whom the story gets its title is presented as complex. There is a real attempt on the part of the author to present her as a real woman—any woman with a human mind that is often difficult to analyze and to predict its caprices, even by its owner. Nevertheless, while her almost neurotic drive towards whites and near-whites is in tune with the stereotyped concept of a black girl, her portrayal as being "intelligent" because "she had been half made with real white blood"[68] hardly separates the author's mind that conceived her from Harriet B. Stowe's in *Uncle Tom's Cabin.*

This is also true of other characters, with the possible exception of Sam who, though black, is not shiftless as would be expected. James Herbert (Melanctha's father) is loaded with almost all the known hackneyed traits of a black male. He is described as "a big black virile negro [sic." [TL, p. 90] He is a "common, decent enough, colored workman, brutal and rough." [TL, pp. 90-91] He is "a powerful, loose built, hard handed, black angry negro." [TL, p. 91] He is "always a fierce, suspicious, serious negro"; he looks "very black and evil." [TL, p. 94] He knows "black curses," and how to wield "sharp razors . . . in the negro fashion." [TL, p. 94]

John, the bishop's coachman, who has a lighter skin color, is predictably a step higher than James Herbert. He is "a decent, pleasant, good natured, light brown negro," even though he also knows "how to use a razor to do bloody slashing." [TL, p. 94] He is "a decent, vigorous mulatto with a prosperous house and wife and children." [TL, p. 91] Still higher on the scale is Jane Harden, a very light-skinned woman: "She had much white blood and that made her see clear. . . . her white blood was strong in her and she had grit and endurance and vital courage." [TL, p. 104]

Rose Johnson, Melanctha's benefactress, is in a class of her own. Her portrayal is serious and deep; but it hardly redeems her from being a stereotype. Having been raised by "white folks," she owes all her good qualities to "habit" and all her bad ones to "nature." Gertrude Stein summarizes her character:

Rose Johnson was a real black, tall, well built, sullen, stupid, childlike, good looking negress. . . . Rose Johnson was a real black negress but had been brought up quite like their own child by white folks.

Rose Johnson laughed when she was happy but she had not the wide, abandoned laughter that makes the warm broad glow of negro sunshine. Rose was never joyous with the earth-born, boundless joy of negroes. Hers was just ordinary, any sort of woman laughter.

Rose Johnson was careless and was lazy, but she had been brought up by white folks and she needed decent comfort. *Her white training had only made for habits, not nature. Rose had the simple, promiscuous unmorality of the black people.* [TL, pp. 85-86. Emphasis added]

"Nature," certainly, is stronger than "habit." The author, ironically, wonders at the relationship she has established between her two creations—this "real black negress," Rose, and the "half-white girl," Melanctha:

Why did the subtle, intelligent, attractive, half white girl Melanctha Herbert love and do for and demean herself in service to this coarse, decent, sullen, ordinary, black childish Rose, and why was this unmoral, promiscuous, shiftless Rose married, and that's not so common either, to a good man of the negroes, while Melanctha with her white blood and attraction and her desire for a right position had not yet been really married. [TL, p. 86]

The only logical answer to this question points to the seriousness and complexity of the author's attitude towards her characters whose minds she has made too subtle and lifelike to be absolutely understandable and predictable by an observer, or even by the characters themselves. This attitude, however, is etiolated by the author's preconception of her subjects.

Leo Stein has revealed that "Melanctha" is a reworking of its author's first book, *Q. E. D.* (1903)—later published as *Things As They Are* in 1950—a book whose material "had nothing to do with Negroes."[69] That white characters could easily be converted into black ones and vice versa would have been very gratifying to the exponents of that concept which saw the black man as a man like any other man. Nonetheless, from a strictly artistic point of view, this transformation is more of a liability than an asset. Entailing an arbitrary coloring of skins, it is, probably, responsible for an equally arbitrary attribution of character traits. A careful look at the three outstanding women in "Melanctha" will make this clearer.

While black Rose and half-white Melanctha owe their redeeming qualities to white upbringing and white blood respectively, Jane, who is "whiter" than Melanctha, is—contrary to the principle that governs the possession of intelligence and morals in their world—more "unmoral" than Rose whose blackness is an index of her "natural" lack of morals. Unlike Melanctha, and practically all other light-skinned characters in the story, what Jane could not get through a white upbringing, she could also not derive from her "much white blood" which, incidentally, is responsible for her clear-sightedness!

Probably, not being absolutely confident of her knowledge of Negroes, Stein, in her attempt to convert her white characters and white situations into black characters and black situations, could not resist the temptation of using the existing Negro stereotypes as a frame of reference. The result is an artificial labeling which taxes the author's energy to explain, and the reader's to understand, why a trait of character that is labeled white at one place should bear a black label at another. In fact, it almost takes courses in genetics and genealogy to understand why Melanctha, the daughter of a "very black" man and a "pale yellow, colored woman" [TL, p. 90] "had been half made with real white blood." [TL, p. 86] This problem could easily have been avoided if, for her fresh minds, Stein had created fresh bodies that were entirely motivated from within rather than by the author's mind from without.

Subsequent years saw more works which also reveal attempts on the part of their authors to give serious treatment to their Negro material. Like "Melanctha," they also have, as they well might, stereotypes as their objects of imitation. But thanks to their fresh and serious manner of imitation (realism tempered, in some cases, with impressionism) they converted the old and almost contemptuous stereotypes into beings suggestive of positive values and enviable life-styles—even if they did so to satisfy the thirst for the "primitive." Witness the tilting of the balance in favor of a supposedly Negro life-style in the juxtaposition of the "white" and "black" life-styles in Waldo Frank's *Holiday:*

No red: this [white] world is ice: it is a world in which no living thing can grow; it is a world that shrivels and that stiffens; it is a world where life like fire breaks out, passionate, isolate, burning, hungry holes in the dark sheets of death. . . .[70] The nigger world is a warm world full of beating music; a music mellow: the nigger world is a music filling world from trees down to the earth.[71]

JULIA PETERKIN

Even where they operated very close to the tears-in-the-eye-and-smile-on-the-lips plantation tradition, some freshness and seriousness are noticeable. Thus we have Julia Peterkin's treatment of the Negro folk—their beliefs and ways of life—with hardly any element of condescension or mockery in her *Green Thursday.*[72] Maum Hannah, the black mammy figure, is by no means more superstitious than her "po-buckra" neighbors: she is, perhaps, a trifle more intelligent than they. In spite of her combination of Christian religion with "unchristian" superstition and behavior, Rose, another black woman, emerges as a person, as distinct from a type. So also does her husband, Killdee, the character who appears in almost all the *Green Thursday* stories. A tragic character, he bears himself proudly in his defiance of God and Nature. Killdee is always ready to accept the consequences of his action, not like the cliché of a frightened "nigger" running away from a "ghost," but like a man: "He was no woman. No. He was a man. Hadn't he promised himself he'd be like a goat? Not a sheep. Not a frightened, huddling, scary fool. No."[73]

His sense of self-reliance is no more adequately revealed than in his attitude towards religion; and this is significant when one remembers the religious stereotypes of the Uncle Tom school. For Killdee, God is in His Heaven; he, Killdee, is on earth to take care of his own trouble. We have the following from his consciousness as he walks at night and thinks of the embarrassing but mutual love between him and Missie, the little girl who has come to live with him and Rose:

People singing to God. Asking for help. How far away they seemed. As far as those faint stars in the glowing sky. As far as God. He was alone in the night.

Something in his heart answered the singers, "Joy can' las' always needer. You sing about trouble. I'm gwine take one joy whilst I kin."[74]

In a letter to Julia Peterkin, Walter White, the Assistant Executive Secretary of the NAACP, described *Green Thursday* as "admirable" and called the writing of it "a most valuable job." He added:

Mr. Mencken and I have talked a number of times and, partly at his request and partly because I so much wanted to do so, I have tried to help secure for "Green Thursday" the circulation which it so richly deserves.[75]

His and his associates' efforts to promote *Green Thursday* included the sending of a favorable review of the book "to some two hundred fifty colored newspapers. It was widely printed."[76]

Green Thursday deserved the support it received from Walter White, if for nothing else, for the serious and fresh approach to the erstwhile stereotypes. Unfortunately for Julia Peterkin, however, her great admiration for the Black Mammy, as revealed both in her portrayal of Maum

Hannah and in her contribution to *The Crisis* 1926 Symposium, "The Negro in Art: How Shall He Be Portrayed," exposed her to attacks by both blacks and whites who believed that the Black Mammy deserved neither immortalization nor gratitude from her descendants. Mary White Ovington summarized the opinion of this group in her comments on Julia Peterkin's criticism of Negroes who were against the perpetuation of the memory of the Black Mammy:

The present-day Negro is quite right in his antagonism to the Mammy complex. Not only because her praises have been sung by the Southerners *ad nauseam,* but because fundamentally there is something the matter with her. Her virtue was not the virtue that she should rightly have shown.[77]

Whatever the case, this attempt to give serious treatment to stereotypes, this dreamlike transformation of what conventions condemned as negative values into positive ones, sustained the white man's selfish quest for the "primitive" and thereby afforded receptivity to the emerging black writers of the 1920s who were essentially interested in expressing their own dark selves.

NIGGER HEAVEN AND THE INNOCENCE OF THE NEW NEGRO LITERATURE

The white audience's appetite for the Negro "stuff" was intensified by the appearance in 1926 of Carl Van Vechten's novel *Nigger Heaven.* No other work before it had been such a stimulus. (However, the novel did not possess much of the influence—good or bad—often attributed to it in the subsequent history of the development of the Harlem Renaissance fiction.)

After the publication of *Nigger Heaven* in August 1926 the authority of Carl Van Vechten had so increased in Harlem that by October non-Harlemites, who went to this largest Negro city in the world, were "said to be 'van vechtening' around."[78] In November of that year Sir Osbert Sitwell engaged in his "exploration" of New York and later wrote:

Harlem in 1926 was no hostile fortress, as it is today, but a part of New York City, where colored people welcomed the white. Whenever there was an occasion, Carl Van Vechten was always the white master of the colored revels.[79]

However, Carl Van Vechten's interest in, and association with, Afro-Americans had not begun with his fifth novel. His family had always been a friend of Afro-Americans. His ancestors had brought Negro slaves with them on their journey from Holland to the United States but had apparently freed them when they settled in Catskill County in New York.[80] His father had helped in founding a school, the Piney School, for Negro children in Mississippi; and while he himself was in Chicago he showed his interest in blacks by writing themes about them. He also met and admired black artists like Bert Williams, George Walker, and Carita Day, a young black woman whom he took to his fraternity house to sing.[81] This interest in Negro art continued when he eventually went to New York, where its singularity at that time is underscored by Mabel Dodge Luhan's description of one of Van Vechten's attempts to induct her and her smart set into the appreciation of Negro music:

While an appalling Negress danced before us in white stockings and black buttoned boots, the man strummed a banjo and sang an embarrassing song. They both leered and rolled their suggestive eyes and made me feel first hot and then cold, for I had never been so near this kind of thing before; but Carl rocked with laughter and little shrieks escaped him as he clapped his pretty hands.[82]

He went to Harlem and received Harlemites in his apartment to the amused sorrow of a paper like *Time* which, in 1925, moaned that "sullen-mouthed, silky-haired Author Van Vechten has been playing with Negroes lately, writing prefaces for their poems, having them around the house, going to Harlem."[83]

He assisted young black writers, including Langston Hughes whose first book of poems, *The Weary Blues,* he got published in 1926 and whom he introduced to the editors of *Vanity Fair* "who bought [his] first poems sold to a magazine."[84] His articles on black singers (such as the one on Ethel Waters, Bessie Smith, and Clara Smith in *Vanity Fair* of March 1926), marked the beginning of the struggle for the acceptance of the Negro folk blues as an art form. Carl Van Vechten's interest in the Negro and his art, before the publication of *Nigger Heaven* in August, 1926, cannot be overemphasized.

This, however, is not to suggest that Van Vechten's enthusiasm was completely based on genuine belief that Negroes were producing works of high quality. The belief was not entirely absent; but the enthusiasm was also based on several other factors: an innate penchant for the off-

beat; a condescending urge to encourage the Negro; a strong desire—
especially by 1924—to prepare the reading public for his own novel,
Nigger Heaven. Thus, although he thought that Walter White's novel,
Fire in the Flint (1924), was "not very good," he enthusiastically sought
for and made the acquaintance of the black writer—a move which actually
opened the doors of Harlem before him, and led him to the position he
occupied vis-à-vis the Negro metropolis.[85] He became so conversant with
it that he was, according to Ethel Waters, "credited with knowing . . .
more about Harlem than any other white man except the captain of the
Harlem police station."[86]

Carl Van Vechten's relationship with blacks and Harlem was, therefore,
not devoid of self-interest. Yet it was intimate and self-giving. It was this
paradox that accounted in part for the reception given to his novel,
Nigger Heaven, as well as the importance (much of it unmerited) accorded to its role in the development of the Harlem Renaissance fiction.

Reactions to the portrayal of the Negro in a nonuplift way, in the
1920s, had, broadly speaking, followed the color line. The hostility of
a section of the black literati and the praise of a section of white readers
were therefore expected. What was remarkable was the intensity of the
disagreement within the black camp. Unlike what had happened in the
past, the opposition did not come exclusively from a small section of
the intelligentsia. A large part of Afro-Americans, whose attitude was
represented by W. E. B. Du Bois's, saw the novel as "a blow in the face
. . . an affront to the hospitality of black folk and the intelligence of
white."[87] Another section, made up mainly of a small group of young
writers who were willing to see the Negro used in art for art's sake, stood
behind James Weldon Johnson who maintained that Van Vechten's novel
"is all life . . . all reality," and "does not stoop to burlesque or caricature."[88] There was disagreement among white readers also. D. H. Lawrence characterized the work as "a false book by an author who lingers
in nigger cabarets hoping to heaven to pick up something to write about
and make sensation—and of course, money."[89] Frances Newman, a reviewer in the *Bookman*, described it as "absurd when it is not merely
crude." She scolded Van Vechten for continuing "to insist on becoming
a novelist, although providence must have intended him for a pleasant
commentator on other people's novels and pictures and tone poems."[90]
Ellen Glasgow, on the other hand, welcomed the book as "a sincere
interpretation of life" which "attempts to prove nothing . . . [or] mas-
querade as ethnology in the fancy dress of a novel."[91] At least one white

man suspected that it might have "aroused some animosity against [Carl Van Vechten] from certain quarters as being too friendly towards the Negroes."[92] However, unlike black reaction which can be described as generally hostile, the white reception of the novel was predominantly favorable, even though *Nigger Heaven* was completely banned in Boston.

Van Vechten's use of real names of real Harlemites, his incorporation of the lyric of a popular song, and then of real poems of a real Harlem poet (when the use of *Shake That Thing* got him and his publisher into trouble[93]), his inclusion of "a glossary of [real if] unusual Negro words and phrases"[94] encouraged the temptation to treat his novel as a depiction of real life in a real Harlem. And it was not a mistake; for Van Vechten wanted his novel to be as real as possible. He had as early as 30 June 1925, when he was thinking of the novel, communicated this intention to Gertrude Stein:

This will not be a novel about Negroes in the South or white contacts or lynchings. It will be about NEGROES, as they live now in the new city of Harlem (which is part of New York). About 400,000 of them live there now, rich and poor, fast and slow, intelligent and ignorant. I hope it will be a good book.[95]

This intention, coupled with the possibility of the desired reality shocking his audience, accounts for the extensive spadework he did to prepare the minds of his prospective readers—spadework which started about two years before the actual appearance of the novel, as revealed by his letter to Alfred A. Knopf on 20 December 1925:

To that end [to avoid shocking his audience], as you know, I have during the past year written countless articles on Negro subjects (I have one in the Tribune today and two more are in proof chez Vanity Fair) and I have seen to it that so many outoftowners as possible saw enough of the life themselves so that they would carry some news of it back to where they come from.[96]

Van Vechten's desire for verisimilitude accounts for his having James Weldon Johnson, Walter White, and Rudolph Fisher read *Nigger Heaven* and evaluate its authenticity before it was printed for the general reading public.[97] It also explains why at one point in the history of the book, he and his publisher, Alfred A. Knopf, commissioned Aaron Douglas to intensify its Negroness by illustrating it with his drawings which used

primitive African masks and statues as a motif.[98] Finally, it accounts for
the author's craftsmanship.

The framework of the novel, however, is not new. It is the old love
triangle only slightly complicated by the imposition of two other love
triangles worked into one: Byron, who loves and is loved by Mary, also
loves Lasca, who loves his body and the money of Pettijohn, who loves
Mary's education and Ruby, who loves and is loved by Anatole Longfellow, alias the Scarlet Creeper. The result is a tragic tension which
destroys or damages the sides of the original triangle: Mary, Byron, and
Pettijohn.

The style is direct, and deeply impregnated with local color—lights
and vivid colors of a Harlem night, sounds of blows of women fighting
for "mah man," loud laughter and uninhibited gaiety of a Harlem cabaret
where "the music shivered and broke, cracked and smashed. Jungle land.
Hottentots and Bantus swaying under the amber moon. Love, sex, passion . . . hate." [NH, p. 281]

It contains episodes which can easily be mistaken for slices of life
fresh from the Congo. Witness the similarities between *Nigger Heaven*
and René Maran's novel about the Congo, both in characterization and
portrayal of some incidents. Like *Batouala, Nigger Heaven* is constructed
around a love triangle.[99] Like *Batouala,* it has an episode of dancing
[NH, pp. 254-56] in which "men and women with weary faces, faces
tired of passion and pleasure" participate; where a girl "entirely nude,"
like the young women ready for initiation in *Batouala,* "perform[s] her
evil rites" amid the wailing of a distant "pipe" and "a faint reverberation
of the tom-tom" reminiscent of a Banda "li'ngha." The girl herself "was
pure black, with savage African features, thick nose, thick lips, bushy
hair which hovered about her face like a lanate halo, while her eyes
rolled back so far that only the whites were visible." She has a knife, a
phallic symbol which is similar to the "enormous painted wooden
phallus" carried by Maran's Yassigui'ndja in the initiation coda.[100] Like
Batouala, Nigger Heaven contains a home-breaker, Anatole Longfellow
who, like Maran's Bissibi'ngui, thrives on women, especially married ones.
Diction apart, Ruby's promise to Anatole ("Ah sho' will show you some
lovin', daddy," [NH, p. 15]) and Yassigui'ndja's offer to Bissibi'ngui
("My most secret flesh will be happy to serve as a sheath for your
sword"[101]) can come from the lips of either of the two women.

Carl Van Vechten does not acknowledge the influence of *Batouala*
on his novel in which, incidentally, that "véritable roman nègre" is men-

tioned. [NH, p. 56] On the other hand, he recognizes James Weldon Johnson's narrative *The Autobiography of an Ex-Coloured Man* and Paul Laurence Dunbar's novel *The Sport of the Gods*[102] as the prototypes of his book. These and the general quest for the primitive in the 1920s are sufficient as sources of influence or inspiration. Besides, if Van Vechten wanted a model for his Anatole Longfellow, he did not have, as Mercer Cook rightly points out, "to get his inspiration from anybody as far away as Maran. . . . This has always been one of the stereotypes that were directed against the black man throughout much American literature. This was one of the stereotypes: he was lazy; he wouldn't work; he was immoral."[103] As a matter of fact, attempts have been made to identify models for some of Van Vechten's characters—here in the United States as distinct from the Congo of Maran's novel:

Byron: Eric Walrond / Harold Jackman[104]
Lasca: Nora Holt, "the glamour girl Carl had met during his Harlem forays"[105]
Adora: A'lelia Walker, "Carl's Harlem hostess"[106]
Mary: Regina Anderson
Russet Durwood: H. L. Mencken[107]

The similarities demonstrated above, therefore, could as much be a coincidence as subconscious echoes of René Maran's Congo novel.

What is certain is that, in its sky-blue jacket, bearing an inscription which portrayed its author as a "historian of contemporary New York life, drawing a curious picture of a fascinating group hitherto neglected by writers of fiction," *Nigger Heaven* was to many a white man an introduction to the life he had longed for but had not found: a luxuriant sucker of an uninhibited life, cut fresh from a jungle in Africa, and planted in the heart of the "waste land." *Nigger Heaven* was bought, read, and discussed. Van Vechten's well-known relationship with Harlem added to its authority. It soon became a guidebook, and visitors carried it in their pockets as they went to Harlem. Appetite grew on what it fed on; interest in Negro "stuff" became stronger. For instance, the librarian of Queen's University in Canada wrote to James F. Drake, the New York rare book dealer, "that he has become so interested in Charles W. Chesnutt, through reading *Nigger Heaven,* that he wants a complete list of his books for the Queen's Library."[108] Negro writers were encouraged to produce more works on their people and make a name and money for themselves.

Yet Afro-Americans of the 1920s who criticized *Nigger Heaven* had
strong reasons for doing so. For example, Du Bois's suggestion that Van
Vechten saw blacks as a mass and not as individuals engaged and interested in different things[109] is not without foundation. For, apart from
the fact that almost all the characters in *Nigger Heaven* are interested in
cabarets, many of the characters look alike—at least when taken in pairs.
There is not much difference, for instance, between Anatole and Byron:
both of them are creepers at one time or another. In fact, their activities
are often so identical that it is easy to attribute what one has done to the
other. We have this in the murder of Pettijohn where Byron is arrested
for Anatole's crime. We also have it when Mary thinks that people are
talking about her because she mistakes what Anatole has done the previous night for what Byron has done that very night:

Craig's. The same crowd. The same gossip, but today it seemed to have a
new and unpleasant significance. They seemed to be talking about *her*.
She caught phrases without names:

> He went to see her last night . . .
> . . . creeper . . .
> Some sheik! Ha! Ha! [NH, p. 132]

The point is that Byron "went to see [Mary] last night" just as Anatole
"went to see" another woman.

There is hardly any difference between Olive and Ruby (both of them
are governed by their instincts); Adora and Lasca (both of them are good-
time ladies); Randolph Pettijohn, a black businessman, who has "made
it" in the way several important Americans had, is a potential creeper.
He dies in the hands of creepers. Hester Albright and Dick Sill are ashamed
of their blood. Howard Allison's words have no more weight than those
of Anatole. His Tuskegean theory of financial success is undercut with
the portrayal of Pettijohn and Adora.

Besides, Van Vechten's portrayal of a black writer could not have been
attractive to the black literati of the 1920s. As a matter of fact, Claude
McKay, who is often regarded as one of the leading apostles of the so-
called "Van Vechten Vogue,"[110] expressed surprise at the portrait of a
black writer as painted by an "author [Carl Van Vechten] who is generally regarded as a discoverer and sponsor of promising young Negro
writers."[111]

Certainly the difficulty which Byron encounters in his attempt to get
published is the universal experience of new writers. In fact, the fate of

his story is like that of Van Vechten's second book, *Pastiche et Pistaches*. According to Van Vechten,[112] this book was rejected by thirteen publishers, including Alfred A. Knopf who, however, invited and advised him to write about what he knew best—music. This is exactly what Byron is told by Russett Durwood, the only editor who invites him to discuss his story with him. Nevertheless, the traits of character attributed to him do not make him attractive. These are well summarized by Olive, who tells him what he really is:

Don't think you've fooled me. I can see the wall over there straight through you. . . . I've watched you and *know* you. You're lazy and soft and conceited. You're weak and touchy and proud and obstinate and bad-tempered. You won't have anything to do with really worthwhile people like the Sumners and the Underwoods or the young literary group . . . or Howard . . . because they've got ahead in life while you're a failure. [NH, p. 268]

We may only add that Byron has come to New York, in the first place, *not* to pursue a writing career, as he claims, but to pacify a man whose wife he had seduced. [NH, pp. 173-74]

But more than all these, what made some Afro-Americans hate Van Vechten's book was its title. There is no doubt that Van Vechten knew what he was doing when he decided to call his novel *Nigger Heaven*. A letter from his father, Charles Duane Van Vechten, who died of pneumonia seven months before the publication of the novel, had warned him about that title:

Your "Nigger Heaven" is a title I don't like. I remember that it was said of some Democratic candidate for the presidency, he couldn't be elected because he spelled *negro* with two g's, and I have myself never spoken of a colored man as a "nigger." If you are trying to help the race, as I am assured you are, I think every word you write should be a respectful one towards the black.[113]

Carl Van Vechten himself had also anticipated the hostility by 20 December 1925 when he finished the first of his three drafts. Thus he had written to his publisher, recommending some spadework to reduce shock:

Ordinarily . . . books should not be advertised so long in advance, but this book is different. It is necessary to prepare the mind not only of my own public, but of the new public which this book may possibly

reach, particularly that public which lies outside New York. If they see
the title, they will ask questions, or read "The New Negro" or something,
so that the kind of life I am writing about will not come as an actual
shock.[114]

His and his publisher's awareness of Afro-Americans' attitude towards the
term "nigger" is confirmed by a footnote in which, among other things,
they said that the term's "employment by a white person is always
fiercely resented." [NH, p. 26]
    Yet, the fact remains that Van Vechten called his book *Nigger Heaven*,
and many Afro-Americans were so put off by the phrase that they condemned the book that bore it, without opening it. For instance, recall-
ing how she first met Carl Van Vechten, Ethel Waters writes in her
autobiography:

The call boy . . . told me one night that a white man named Carl Van
Vechten wanted to see me. The name meant nothing to me, though I'd
heard of his book, *Nigger Heaven,* and had condemned it because of its
obnoxious title—without reading it.[115]

The *New York News* (Colored) maintained "that anyone who would call
a book Nigger Heaven would call a Negro Nigger."[116] When the book was
still being written, without seeing it, Wallace Thurman predicted that
blacks were going to reject it because of its title.[117] His estimate in November 1926 was that "only one-tenth of the condemnators have or will
read" the novel.[118] Langston Hughes tells of how some people who read
it "put a paper cover over it and read it surreptitiously as though it were
a dirty book—to keep their friends from knowing they were reading it."[119]
Langston Hughes's suggestion in Craig's one night that critics should
"read the book before expressing their opinion" was, according to Carl
Van Vechten, "regarded as supererogatory."[120]
    However, all the reasons for grievance notwithstanding, it will be un-
fair to claim, as Du Bois does, that "Van Vechten never heard a sob in a
cabaret."[121] Equally ill-advised is Ellen Glasgow's enthusiastic defense
(cited above) which is deeply colored by her personal racial attitudes.
Firstly, except for four chapters (the prologue, chapters 3 and 6 of book
1, and chapter 5 of book 2 which are themselves heavily charged with
irony) all the chapters in the book end sadly—either in tears, or in suppressed sorrow. Secondly, there is hardly any moment of gaiety that has

no element of sorrow or pity. For example—to mention only one of those cases that can easily escape the eye—as Rumsey and Lutie engage in what is supposed to be a happy dance, Rumsey longs for "By an' by" when he is "goin' to lay down this heavy load. . . ." [NH, p. 37] It is significant that Van Vechten had, on 3 August 1925, used these words from a Negro "sorrow song" and the line "My way's cloudy" to illustrate the difference in mood between Phillis Wheatley's poetry and the poetry of some other black poets who came after her.[122] This juxtaposition of joy and sorrow underscores the irony of the title of the novel, *Nigger Heaven*, an irony which Byron clearly explains towards the end of book 1:

Nigger Heaven! Byron moaned. Nigger Heaven! That's what Harlem is. We sit in our places in the gallery of this New York theatre and watch the white world sitting down below in the good seats in the orchestra. Occasionally they turn their faces up towards us, their hard, cruel faces, to laugh or sneer, but they never beckon. It never seems to occur to them that Nigger Heaven is crowded, that there isn't another seat, that something has to be done. It doesn't seem to occur to them either, he went on fiercely, that we sit above them, that we can drop things down on them and crush them; that we can swoop down from this Nigger Heaven and take their seats. No, they have no fear of that! Harlem! The Mecca of the New Negro! My God! [NH, p. 149]

Thirdly, a careful reading of the book shows that Van Vechten uses his characters, both as mouthpieces and as guinea pigs, to reveal the problems of the black folk in America. For instance, while Adora verbally attacks racial discrimination against the black man in employment and promotion [NH, p. 30] Mary, Byron, and Howard are shown as victims of this practice. For all her diligence Mary can never hope for promotion. Byron walks from college into an elevator, not to go to his office, but to operate it. Howard, a product of Harvard and Columbia universities, cannot get any clients because of his color.

Besides, such an unimportant matter as the belief that the blacker a person was, the more depraved and instinctive he or she would be (a belief which, as we have seen, even Gertrude Stein could not resist[123]) receives a searching criticism in the portrayal of Mary and Olive. For, although Olive is seven-eighths white, her intelligence, self-control, and sense of decency are very inferior to those of Mary who is only a golden-brown. In fact, Van Vechten seems to emphasize this point intentionally when he reads Mary's mind, and says:

Mary confessed to herself, that she did not let herself go. She had an instinctive horror of promiscuity, of being handled, even touched, by a man who did not mean a good deal to her. This might, she sometimes argued with herself, have something to do with her white inheritance, but Olive, who was far whiter, was lacking in this inherent sense of prud-cry. [NH, p. 54]

With Van Vechten's characters, we are thousands of miles away from the world of *Uncle Tom's Cabin,* where the equation of intelligence and self-control with the color of one's skin is strictly executed.

Intraracial problems are not neglected. Apart from the satiric glare directed against the Albrights' and Orville's snobbish attitude towards the Negro African and African artifacts (an attitude which borders on self-debasement), intraracial discrimination and envy are sharply focused on. Witness the following discussion on the attitude of some blacks towards their fellow blacks:

Well, old man [Byron], said Howard, I wish you luck, We'll do all we can, all of *us,* but the others. . . .

Don't they want a member of the race to get on?

Say, Dick inquired, where have you been living? They *do* not. You'll have to fight your own race harder than you do the other . . . every step of the way. They're full of envy for every Negro that makes a success. They hate it. It makes 'em wild. Why, more of us get on through the ofays than through the shines. [NH, pp. 119-20]

Dick Sill has earlier discussed the fate of black professionals:

Howard here is a lawyer, but the race doesn't want colored lawyers. If they're in trouble they go to white lawyers, and they go to white banks and white insurance companies. They shop on white One hundred and twenty-fifth Street. [NH, p. 119]

But as W. E. B. Du Bois rightly points out, Van Vechten's "book has a right to be judged primarily as a work of art."[124] In this connection, the greatest weakness of the novel stems from what Van Vechten must have regarded as one of its strengths: the conscious effort to serve the interest of the Negro. The attempt to present Negroes of all levels with a view to destroying not only the idea that all blacks are alike but also the idea that skin color is equated to moral and intellectual powers has resulted in the writing of discussions that are pedantic and in the creation of characters that are only partially convincing. The naturalness of a girl like Olive is overdrawn. On the other hand, Mary is too good and too intellectual to be readily believable. She recites Wallace Steven's poem with no difficulty. [NH, pp. 100-101] She easily recalls a 463-word passage from Gertrude Stein's "Melanctha" which she has committed to memory, obviously, to always remind her that she "shouldn't try to know everybody just to run around and get excited." [NH, pp. 57-58] She speaks very good French. She has read almost all the books in the library where she works. She is a connoisseur of modern art.

Yet *Nigger Heaven* is not a complete failure artistically. In a special note for the Avon pocket-size edition in 1951, Van Vechten described the plot of his book as "one of the oldest stories in the world, the story of the Prodigal Son, without the happy end of that Biblical history." Although this claim is not entirely justifiable since Byron's story also lacks the apparent innocence of the beginning "of that Biblical history," the construction of *Nigger Heaven* reveals a careful craftsmanship.

First of all, the symmetry of the book. The work is divided into three parts: one-chapter prologue, nine-chapter book one, nine-chapter book two. It begins with Anatole's stroll towards the Black Venus and ends almost as soon as Anatole leaves the Black Venus. Although most characters behave in the same way, the presentation of Anatole and Byron as two phases of the same person is well executed: Byron does not appear in the book until Anatole disappears in the prologue, as if he wants the reader to know that he has left his life as a "creeper" behind him at home. The first time we see them together [NH, p. 213] both of them have lost their girl friends temporarily. And what is more, Byron has started to think of going back to his life of a "creeper." The next, and last, time we see them together is when both of them (Byron is now a "creeper") "join hand" to kill Pettijohn, their common enemy, who has robbed them of their women.

More interesting, still, is the unintrusively intrusive narrative technique, which makes it possible for the author to identify himself with his characters, without losing his authorial detachment. Immediately after the prologue, in which he plays the role of a well-informed guide and introduces the reader to Harlem, the narrator identifies himself with Mary, thereby leaving the reader to explore for himself the world before him.

The narration is still in the third person, and the narrator has unlimited access to Mary's mind. But as if unable to penetrate any other character's mind, he sees and hears nothing that Mary does not see and hear. He knows nothing that is unknown to Mary. Consequently, he makes other characters speak their minds and act their feelings.

But immediately he comes to the end of Mary's section, he ceases to have access to her mind. Henceforth, readers know what is going on in the heroine's mind through what she says, or at most by inferring from what they already know about her mind.

On the other hand, Byron's mind, which was closed in Mary's section, is now thrown open. The narrator sees and knows everything that is going on in it. A very good example of this is the discussion by Mary and Byron of a story that Byron wants to write. At one point Byron shouts: "God! . . . I don't get anything but discouragement out of you!" And the narrator comments: "At the same time he made a mental note that he must put the girl's father in the story." [NH, p. 205]

Another good example is the last scene at the Black Venus. There the reader is informed of what is going on by bits of phrases and broken sentences that steal into Byron's ears. Then suddenly, Anatole reappears with Ruby. Byron knows Anatole and has seen Ruby before. But she has never been introduced to him, and he does not know her name. Therefore, throughout that scene Ruby is never mentioned by name. [NH, pp. 281-84] The overall effect of this narrative technique is the creation of an atmosphere of reality in which improbabilities look probable or necessary because the reader is in direct contact with them.

The craftsmanship of *Nigger Heaven* is not as facile as it is often thought. So far it has been neglected because, in most cases, the approach to the book has been through "what it says," and not "how it says it." The book is a work of fiction based on human life. If the men and women who lead that life are essentially stereotypes, they, at least, have their brains in their skulls and not in their skins. The exaltation of the primitive in man aside, *Nigger Heaven* is a serious treatment of Negro material. Wallace Thurman, certainly, overestimates the "upliftedness" of the novel when he expects "some of our uplift organizations and neighborhood clubs [to] plan to erect a latter-day abolitionist statue to Carl Van Vechten on the corner of 135th Street and Seventh Avenue, for the author has been most fair, and most sympathetic in his treatment of a long mistreated group of subjects."[125] Nonetheless, *Nigger Heaven* deserves a better treatment than it has received so far.

It is fashionable to portray it as a perverter of young black writers of the 1920s—a charge which is often confirmed by even those authors who are believed to have subscribed to its approach to Negro material. Arna Bontemps, for instance, once told his friends that he himself had to *struggle against* Van Vechten's influence as he wrote his *God Sends Sunday* (1931). However, there are reasons to believe that the impact (good or bad) of *Nigger Heaven* on the trend of the Harlem Renaissance literature is often blown out of proportion.

Among the features of *Nigger Heaven* that shocked several black critics was the treatment given to sex among blacks. A careful study, however, reveals that Lasca's sex habits, which border on libertinism, are only a shade less "respectable" than those of some women in Toomer's *Cane.* These, like Lasca, obey their sexual instinct with little or no inhibition. Unlike Lasca, they cannot be described as callous and decadent. Yet their sex lives are such that W. E. B. Du Bois believes that "the world of black folk will some day arise and point to Jean Toomer as a writer who first dared to emancipate the colored world from the conventions of sex."[126] *Cane* was published in 1923. While Waldo Frank, Sherwood Anderson, and Gertrude Stein have been mentioned in connection with Jean Toomer's art, Carl Van Vechten has never—and rightly too—been thought of as a possible source of influence on Jean Toomer.

Commenting, in his autobiography, on the alledged influence of Van Vechten on Negro writers of the 1920s, Langston Hughes says that to claim "that Carl Van Vechten has harmed Negro creative activities is sheer poppycock. The bad Negro writers were bad long before *Nigger Heaven* appeared on the scene. And would have been bad anyway, had Mr. Van Vechten never been born."[127] Hughes's use of the adjective "bad" is from the point of view of black assimilationist middle-class critics who strongly maintained that black men and women should be painted in the best of all possible colors. This statement therefore, could be applied to Claude McKay in whose novel *Home to Harlem* Du Bois discovered "filth" which made him "feel distinctly like taking a bath."[128]

Home to Harlem has much in common with *Nigger Heaven.* It is full of sex. It has cabarets. It has its own scenes of women fighting for "mah man." Mary Love's and Ray's perceptions of love and sex are very much alike. The fact that it was published two years after the appearance of *Nigger Heaven* points to a possible influence by Carl Van Vechten's novel. Although McKay was in France when *Nigger Heaven* was published in August 1926 he had known as early as 1924 that Van Vechten was writing a novel about Harlem.[129] Even though he did not see Van Vechten's novel "until the late spring of 1927" when his agent, William Aspenwall Bradley, sent him a copy, his own novel at that time was only "nearly completed."[130] Nevertheless, there are reasons to believe that McKay could still have written a novel like *Home to Harlem* "had Mr. Van Vechten never been born." His *Harlem Shadows* (1922) anticipated the use of "low-down" Negroes—cabaret dancers, for example—as subjects for serious artistic creation. He had as early as December 1921 revealed the stance which he later adopted in *Home to Harlem* when, in a review of *Shuffle Along,* he scolded "the convention-ridden and head-ossified Negro intelligentsia, who censure colored actors for portraying the inimitable comic characteristics of Negro life, because they make white people laugh!"[131] McKay had, many months before the appearance of *Nigger Heaven,* written and submitted for the 1925 *Opportunity* literary contest a short story entitled "Home to Harlem." It is more than probable that it was this story that he expanded into the book-length novel, *Home to Harlem,* thanks to the advice of *Harper's* and his literary agent, William Aspenwall Bradley.[132]

Before the genesis of *Home to Harlem* and the appearance of *Nigger Heaven* still later, McKay had not only made statements which anticipated his novels, he had actually written one—the unpublished *Color Scheme* (1925)—which revealed no inhibition on the part of the characters. Referring to it in a letter to A. A. Schomburg, he says that he makes his "Negro characters yarn and backbite and fuck like people the world over."[133]

In view of all this, it is safe to conclude that *Home to Harlem* does not owe much to *Nigger Heaven* beyond its becoming a best-seller partly because of the atmosphere generated by *Nigger Heaven* and the controversy over it. Like Rudolph Fisher[134] and Langston Hughes,[135] Claude McKay's choice of object and manner of imitation was essentially personal. Like Fisher and Hughes, he had treated such subjects before they came under Carl Van Vechten's pen. Van Vechten did not initiate the Harlem Renaissance literary trend. He only fostered its receptivity. He was certainly one of the authors whom Charles S. Johnson had in mind when he spoke of white writers' "share in the making of that mood of receptivity among the general public for the literature of Negro life."[136]

The extent to which individual black writers owed their images of the Negro and of Africa to white writers' images of these is discussed in the appropriate chapters. In general, however, there was the temptation for black writers (convinced that their real selves could not be the standard-ized man of the white "civilization") to back up the Negro self. In this process of black affirmation these writers drew on material from the white man's self-aggrandizing concepts of them and of Africa. When that happened the white man's participation in the Negro Renaissance was a hindrance rather than a help.

NOTES

1. Paul Guillaume, "African Art at the Barnes Foundation," *Les Arts à Paris,* reprinted in *Opportunity* 2, no. 17 (May 1924): 140-41.
   2. Albert C. Barnes, "The Temple," *Opportunity* 2, no. 17 (May 1924): 139.
   3. Paul Guillaume, "The Triumph of Ancient Negro Art," *Opportunity* 4, no. 41 (May 1926): 147.
   4. Ibid., p. 146.
   5. Ibid., p. 147.
   6. Barnes, "Temple," p. 139.
   7. Ibid.
   8. Guillaume, "Triumph," p. 147.
   9. Satie, Auric, Honegger, Milhaud, Poulenc, and Tailleferre.
   10. Alain Locke, "A Note on African Art," *Opportunity* 2, no. 17 (May 1924): 137.
   11. Guillaume, "Triumph," pp. 146-47.
   12. Kelly Miller, "After Marcus Garvey—What of the Negro?" *Contemporary Review* 131 (1927): 449-50.
   13. Editorial, "Dr. Barnes," *Opportunity* 2, no. 17 (May 1924): 133.
   14. Albert C. Barnes, "Negro Art, Past and Present," *Opportunity* 4, no. 41 (May 1926): 148.
   15. *Opportunity* 5, no. 11 (November 1927): 321.
   16. Locke, "African Art," p. 134.
   17. Malcolm Cowley, *Exile's Return: A Literary Odyssey of the 1920s* (1934; reprint ed., New York: Viking Press, 1956), pp. 236-37. *See also* Alain Locke, "Beauty Instead of Ashes," *Nation* 126, no. 3276 (18 April 1928): 433.
   18. *Toronto Star Weekly,* 25 March 1922.
   19. *The Crisis* 24, no. 5 (September 1922): 218-19, 231.
   20. ("Cultural hybrid") Léopold Sédar Senghor's phrase.
   21. Carl Van Vechten, *Nigger Heaven* (1926; reprint ed., New York: Harper, Colophon, 1971), p. 89 (hereafter cited as NH).
   22. *See also* Gustavo E. Urrutia, "Our Elegant Servitude," *Opportunity* 9, no. 10 (October 1931): 310.

23. Eugene C. Holmes, "The Legacy of Alain Locke," *Harlem: A Community in Transition,* ed. John Henrik Clarke (1964; reprint ed. New York: Citadel Press, 1969), p. 52.

24. Langston Hughes, *The Big Sea: An Autobiography* (New York: Hill and Wang, 1940), p. 228.

25. Wallace Thurman, "Harlem Facets," *The World Tomorrow* 10, no. 11 (November 1927): 466. *See also* Hughes, *Big Sea,* p. 228.

26. René Maran traces the dance back to "the 'calenda' born on the shores of Guinea and originated, in all probability in the vanished kingdom of Arada." René Maran, "Contribution of the Black Race to European Art," *Phylon* 10, no. 3 (1949): 241.

27. *See* "Jazz," *Opportunity* 3, no. 29 (May 1925): 132, 133.

28. The novels are discussed in chapter 2.

29. Hughes, *Big Sea,* p. 223.

30. Ibid., p. 224.

31. Arna Bontemps, ed., *The Harlem Renaissance Remembered* (New York: Dodd, Mead & Co., 1972), p. 5.

32. For an insightful discussion of an interdependence between black and white Americans in their individual quest for identity, *see* Nathan Irvin Huggins, *Harlem Renaissance* (New York: Oxford University Press, 1971), especially the Introduction.

33. Richard Bruce, "What Price Glory in Uncle Tom's Cabin," *Harlem: A Forum of Negro Life* 1, no. 1 (November 1928): 25.

34. "A Poem on the Negro: Vachel Lindsay's Congo," *The Crisis* 10, no. 1 (May 1915): 18-19.

35. Vachel Lindsay, *Collected Poems* (1913; reprint ed., New York: Macmillan, 1973), p. 178 (hereafter cited as LCP).

36. *The Crisis* 10, no. 1 (May 1915): 18.

37. Vachel Lindsay, "Literature," *The Crisis* 12, no. 4 (August 1916): 182.

38. "Boun' fer Canaan Lan'," E. A. McIlhenny, *Befor' de War Spirituals: Words and Melodies* (Boston: Christopher Publishing House, 1933), pp. 42-43.

39. "I heard the Angels Singin'," *The Negro and His Songs: A Study of Typical Negro Songs in the South,* ed. Howard W. Odum and Guy B. Johnson (Chapel Hill: University of North Carolina Press, 1925), p. 140.

40. Lindsay to Spingarn, "A Letter and an Answer," *The Crisis* 13, no. 3 (January 1917): 114.

41. Ibid.

42. *The Crisis,* 12, 4 (August 1916), 182.

43. Joel E. Springarn, *The Crisis* 13, no. 3 (January 1917): 114.

44. Carl Sandburg, *Complete Poems* (New York: Harcourt, Brace and Co., 1950), p. 179.

45. Ibid., p. 251.

46. Ibid., pp. 23-24.

47. James Weldon Johnson, *Black Manhattan* (1930; reprint ed., New York: Arno Press; *New York Times,* 1968), p. 175.

48. Ibid.

49. Quoted in *The Crisis* 14, no. 2 (June 1917): 81.

50. Alan Dale, "The Negro Actor," *Messenger* 7, no. 7 (January 1925): 17-18.

51. Ridgely Torrence, *Granny Maumee,* in Alain Locke and Montgomery Gregory, eds., *Plays of Negro Life: A Source-Book of Native American Drama* (1927; reprint ed., Westport, Conn.: Negro Universities Press, 1970), p. 241.

52. Ibid., pp. 245-46.

53. Horace *Epistle to the Pisones,* ll. 138-40.

54. *Selected Poems of Claude McKay* (New York: Harcourt, Brace & World, 1953), p. 38.

55. Locke and Gregory, eds., *Granny Maumee,* p. 242.

56. Huggins, *Harlem Renaissance,* p. 295. Equally inaccurate is Charles S. Johnson's portrayal of Julia Peterkin, Paul Green, DuBose Heyward, and Guy Johnson as "swinging free from the old and exhausted stereotype and reading from life" with the result that "they have created human characters who are capable of living by their own charm and power." Charles S. Johnson, ed., *Ebony and Topaz: A Collectanea* (New York: National Urban League, 1927), p. 12.

57. Locke and Gregory, eds., *Danse Calinda,* p. 377.

58. Ibid., p. 49

59. Ibid., p. 39.

60. Matthew Arnold, "The Study of Poetry," *Four Essays on Life and Letters,* ed. E. H. Brown (New York: Appleton-Century, 1947), p. 65.

61. *See also* Frederick J. Hoffman, *The Twenties: American Writing in the Postwar Decade,* rev. ed. (New York: Free Press, 1949), pp. 255-57.

62. Sterling Brown, *Negro Poetry and Drama & the Negro in American Fiction* (1937; reprint ed., New York: Atheneum, 1969), 1: 125.

63. Ibid.

64. Also by Eugene O'Neill.

65. Paul Robeson, "Reflection on O'Neill's Plays," *Opportunity* 2, no. 24 (December 1924): 369.

66. "Eugene O'Neill on the Negro Actor: Opinions of America's

Greatest Playwright," *Messenger* 7, no. 1 (January 1925): 17. O'Neill's italics.

67. One of the stories that make up Gertrude Stein, *Three Lives* (1909; reprint ed., New York: Vintage Books, 1936).

68. Stein, *Three Lives*, p. 86 (hereafter cited as TL).

69. Quoted in John Malcolm Brinnin, *The Third Rose: Gertrude Stein and Her World* (Boston: Little, Brown and Co., 1959), p. 45. For a revealing comparison of "Melanctha" and *Things As They Are see* Richard Bridgman, "Melanctha," *American Literature: A Journal of Literary History, Criticism, and Bibliography* 33, no. 3 (November 1961): 350-59.

70. (New York: Boni and Liveright, 1923), pp. 90-91.

71. Ibid., p. 146.

72. Julia Peterkin, *Green Thursday: Stories* (New York: Alfred A. Knopf, 1924).

73. Ibid., p. 36.

74. Ibid., p. 188.

75. White [Walter] to Peterkin, 3 December 1924 in the Library of Congress Manuscripts Division, Washington, D.C.

76. Ibid.

77. Mary White Ovington, "The Outer Pocket," *The Crisis* 33, no. 1 (November 1926): 31.

78. Gwendolyn Bennett, "The Ebony Flute," *Opportunity* 4, no. 47 (November 1926): 357.

79. Sir Osbert Sitwell, "New York in the Twenties," *Atlantic,* February 1962, p. 41.

80. Hughes to Van Vechten, 24 June 1925. *See also* Van Vechten's remarks on the envelope, Beinecke Rare Book and Manuscript Library, Yale University, New Haven, Conn.

81. Bruce Kellner, *Carl Van Vechten and the Irreverent Decades* (Norman: University of Oklahoma Press, 1968), pp. 195-96; Edward Lueders, *Carl Van Vechten* (New York: Twayne, 1965), p. 95; Huggins, *Harlem Renaissance,* p. 99.

82. Mabel Dodge Luhan, "Movers and Shakers," *Intimate Memories* (New York: Harcourt, Brace and Co., 1936), 3: 79-80.

83. Carl Van Vechten Papers, Manuscripts and Archives Division, New York Public Library, New York, N.Y.

84. Hughes, *Big Sea,* p. 272.

85. Kellner, *Carl Van Vechten,* p. 197.

86. Ethel Waters, *His Eye Is on the Sparrow* (1950; reprint ed., New York: Pyramid Books, 1967), p. 196.

87. W. E. B. Du Bois, "Review of *Nigger Heaven,*" *The Crisis* 33 (1926): 81-82, quoted in Van Vechten, *Nigger Heaven,* p. vii.

88. James Weldon Johnson, "Romance and Tragedy in Harlem—A Review," *Opportunity* 4, no. 46 (October 1926): 316.

89. D. H. Lawrence, *Phoenix,* ed. Edward D. McDonald (New York: Viking Press, 1936), p. 361.

90. Frances Newman, "Love in Many Guises," *Bookman* 64, no. 4 (October 1926): 228.

91. Ellen Glasgow, "The Soul of Harlem," *Bookman* 64, (December 1926): 510.

92. Van Vechten to Johnson, 21 June 1930, Beinecke Rare Book and Manuscript Library, Yale University, New Haven, Conn.

93. Alfred A. Knopf, "Reminiscence of Hergesheimer, Van Vechten, and Mencken," *Yale University Library Gazette* 24, no. 4 (April 1950): 154.

94. Citations from Van Vechten are to the Colophon edition of *Nigger Heaven.*

95. Quoted in Lueders, *Carl Van Vechten,* p. 97.

96. Knopf, *Reminiscence,* p. 153.

97. Kellner, *Carl Van Vechten,* p. 211.

98. Knopf, *Reminiscence,* p. 154.

99. Batouala loves Yassigui'ndja (his wife) who loves and is loved by Bissibi'ngui (Batouala's young friend).

100. René Maran, *Batouala: An African Love Story* ed. and trans. Alexandre Mboukou (1938; reprint ed., Rockville, Md.: New Perspective, 1973), p. 86.

101. Ibid., p. 107.

102. *See* Van Vechten, "Introduction to Mr. Knopf's New Edition," *The Autobiography of an Ex-Coloured Man* (New York: Alfred A. Knopf, 1927), pp. v-x.

103. Interview with Mercer Cook, 6 August 1975, Washington, D.C.

104. Bontemps, *Harlem Renaissance Remembered,* p. 22.

105. Kellner, *Carl Van Vechten,* p. 218.

106. Ibid., p. 217.

107. Huggins, *Harlem Renaissance,* p. 25. *See also* Wallace Thurman, "A Stranger at the Gates," *Messenger* 8, no. 9 (September 1926); Edward Lueders, *Carl Van Vechten and the Twenties* (Albuquerque: University of New Mexico Press, 1955), p. 90.

108. Bennett, "Ebony Flute," p. 357.

109. Du Bois, "Review of *Nigger Heaven,*" quoted in Van Vechten, "Introduction," p. viii.

110. Hugh M. Gloster, *Negro Voices in American Fiction* (1948; reprint ed., New York: Russell & Russell, 1965), p. 157.

111. Claude McKay, *A Long Way from Home* (1937; reprint ed., New York: Harcourt, Brace & World, 1970), p. 319.

112. Carl Van Vechten, *Notes for an Autobiography,* compiled for the Colophon edition in June 1930.

113. Carl Van Vechten Papers, Manuscripts and Archives Division, New York Public Library, Astor, Lenox and Tilden Foundations, New York, N.Y.

114. Knopf, *Reminiscence,* p. 153.

115. Waters, *His Eye Is on the Sparrow,* p. 194.

116. Van Vechten to Johnson, 7 September 1926, Beinecke Rare Book and Manuscript Library, Yale University, New Haven, Conn.

117. Thurman, "A Stranger at the Gates," p. 279.

118. Wallace Thurman, "Fire Burns: A Department of Comments," *Fire: A Quarterly Devoted to the Younger Negro Artists* 1, no. 1 (November 1926): 47.

119. Hughes, *Big Sea,* p. 270.

120. Van Vechten to Johnson, 7 September 1926.

121. Du Bois, "Review of *Nigger Heaven,"* p. ix.

122. Carl Van Vechten, "Introducing Langston Hughes to the Reader" in Langston Hughes, *The Weary Blues* (New York: Alfred A. Knopf, 1926), p. 13.

123. *See* above, pp. 20-22.

124. Du Bois, "Review of *Nigger Heaven,"* p. viii.

125. Thurman, "A Stranger at the Gates," p. 279.

126. *The Crisis* 27, no. 4 (February 1924): 161.

127. Hughes, *Big Sea,* p. 272.

128. W. E. B. Du Bois, "Two Novels," *The Crisis* 25, no. 6 (June 1928): 202.

129. Wayne F. Cooper, ed., *The Passion of Claude McKay: Selected Poetry and Prose, 1912-1948* (New York: Schocken Books, 1973), p. 28.

130. McKay, *A Long Way from Home,* p. 283.

131. *Liberator* 4 (December 1921): 24, reprinted in *The Passion of Claude McKay,* p. 62.

132. McKay, *A Long Way from Home,* p. 283; *see also The Passion of Claude McKay,* p. 27.

133. McKay to Schomburg, n.d., McKay folder of the A. A. Schomburg Papers, The Schomburg Collection, New York Public Library, New York, N.Y.

134. *See* chapter 4, pp. 179-183.

135. Ibid., pp. 157-174.

136. Charles S. Johnson, *Ebony and Topaz,* p. 13.

SYMPTOMS OF A PHENOMENON

2

After the dinner given by *Opportunity* in honor of the prizewinners in its 1925 literary contest, the *New York Herald-Tribune* spoke of the occasion as "only a somewhat more conclusive indication of a phenomenon of which there have been many symptoms."[1] It christened that phenomenon "Negro renaissance," and enumerated the symptoms: the appearance of Negro actors "in serious dramas, like 'The Emperor Jones' and 'All God's Chillun Got Wings,' " the performance of a Negro tenor, the pull of Harlem cabarets on Greenwich Villagers, the special issue of the *Survey Graphic* which was devoted to the "new Negro metropolis, described as the Mecca of the 'new Negro,' " and Countée Cullen's "poems in white magazines."

These signs, as well as the "coming-out party" organized by *Opportunity* the year before, were valid "symptoms—of the fact that the American Negro is finding his artistic voice." Nevertheless, the real story of the renaissance, as James Weldon Johnson stresses in his *Black Manhattan,* "as of almost every experience relating to the Negro in America, goes back a long way."[2] It went back to slaves' assertion of their manhood in revolts and in attempts to escape from bondage. It had its roots in the race consciousness and pride that informed several pre-Garveyite back-to-Africa movements[3] and underlay such historic gestures as the mass exodus from the inhospitable South to the North at the turn of the century, the launching of the Niagara movement as a challenge to Booker T. Washington's policy of racial harmony based on the Negro's obligation to stay in his place, and the aggressive assertion of blackness by Marcus Garvey and his followers. On a purely literary plane, it went back to the dialect poetry of Paul Laurence Dunbar and some of his contemporaries who, in parts of their works, tried to celebrate the Negro folkways at a

time when the acknowledgment of the folk Negro in literature by blacks
was an anathema, unless the intention was to make a buffoon of him for
the gratification of the white audience. Indeed, the *New York Herald-
Tribune,* probably without fully realizing it, indicated why the renaissance
looked as if it was just beginning, although it was, in reality, a continual
self-expressing development that was only reaching its flowering stage:

> The significant thing in all this . . . is not that people with more or less
> Negro blood can write—Dumas was the grandson of a Negro—but that
> these American Negroes are expressing for the most part essentially Negro
> feelings and standing squarely on their racial inheritance.[4]

When the first Africans arrived in the United States they arrived with
their folklore which comprised poetry, tales, songs, and dance. Elements
of all these cultural features were perpetuated by oral tradition. However,
with the rise of minstrelsy, some commercially minded artists appropriated
and caricatured several elements of the old Negro folklore.

> About the time John Gilbert appeared on the stage (1828) a new and
> peculiarly American form of entertainment was seen for the first time
> on our boards and soon became very popular. This was negro [sic] min-
> strelsy, which had its origin in the singing and dancing of the slaves on
> the plantations of the wealthy Southerners. When the master wanted
> amusement he sent for those among his slaves who could sing and dance.
> When he sent out invitations for a "small and early," it was the slaves
> who played the dance music. The entertaining abilities of the despised
> slave were soon recognized and the white actor began to realize he could
> make money by imitating the black man.[5]

The result of this caricaturing which, having been made popular
around 1830 by Thomas D. Rice (alias Jim Crow Rice), attracted many
white actors and then blacks who painted their black faces to portray
black characters was the creation of a situation in which it was difficult
for the more assimilated American Negro to comfortably and openly
identify not only with the debased elements but also with the folk culture as a whole. Yet the culture did not die; it endured among the less
polished, but expressive, Negroes who, as Langston Hughes puts it, "do
not particularly care whether they are like white folks or anybody else."[6]
    Thus "the significant thing," and what made the Negro renaissance a
phenomenon, was not that the "American Negroes are expressing . . .

essentially Negro feelings and standing squarely on their racial inheritance."
It was that for the first time many people—including those who formerly
could not have been expected to do so—were expressing the feelings of
the common Negro folk. For the first time many black artists were mount-
ing their Negro feelings on their racial inheritance and were asserting
them with very little or no apology.

In this connection, the formal launching of the New Negro movement
on 21 March 1924, that is, on "a date selected around the appearance of
the novel *There Is Confusion* by Jessie Fauset,"[7] is more significant than
is often realized. We shall come back to it. Meanwhile let us briefly examine the works of some older black writers which contain a few of the
earlier symptoms of the literary awakening.

CHARLES WADDELL CHESNUTT

Much of Charles Waddell Chesnutt's fiction deals with the "Negro
problem." His Negro dialect is not always authentic; it seems to have been
used for the sole purpose of provoking laughter. Yet his portrayal of the
folk in his short stories such as those in *The Conjure Woman* (1889) anticipates, in a way, the realism of the more typical New Negro writers'
treatment of such material.

Certainly, *The Conjure Woman,* like *Uncle Tom's Cabin* and many
other works before it, equates skin color and hair texture to intelligence.
Julius McAdoo's "shrewdness" for instance, "was not altogether African,"
for "he was not entirely black, and this fact, together with the quality
of his hair, which was about six inches long and very bushy . . . suggested
a slight strain of other than negro blood."[8] Julius, nonetheless, is an
individual as distinct from a stereotype; or, better still, he is a stereotype
whom the author's "firm sense of art"—to borrow Benjamin Brawley's
phrase[9]—has individualized. Thanks to the full participation of the white
frame narrator in his tales, a third dimension is added to his character.
He is furnished with a mind; the motivation of his actions and, probably,
of his tale in "The Goophered Grapevine," for example, is adequately
established when the frame narrator concludes the story with the remark:

I found, when I bought the vineyard, that Uncle Julius had occupied a
cabin on the place for many years, and derived a respectable revenue from
the product of the neglected grapevines. This, doubtless, accounted for
his advice to me not to buy the vineyard, though whether it inspired the
goopher story I am unable to state. [CW, pp. 34-35]

This addition of a third dimension to individualize the character of an ordinary Negro often comes very close to ruining the effectiveness of the tales as in "Po' Sandy" where the art-motivated revelation of the narrator's inner mind weakens the effect of a story obviously intended (like many other plantation tales "poured freely into the sympathetic ear of a Northern-bred woman") to "disclose many a tragic incident of the darker side of slavery." [CW, pp. 40-41] The point is that the revelation that Uncle Julius's tale is motivated by his desire to stop John from pulling down the old schoolhouse because he, Uncle Julius, wants it for his secessionist church meetings weakens the "protest" or the demonstration of "the darker side of slavery." Readers cannot be expected to take seriously an "incident" of a story which is a "lie" or work of imagination. The author, here, however, seems unwilling to sacrifice art to its purpose.

This can also be said of his depiction of elements of folkways, such as superstition. The beliefs and practices are rendered with very little or no condescension. Julius McAdoo's tone is decidedly uncondescending. Annie's susceptibility to the old Negro's "lie" is believable; it counterbalances her husband, the frame narrator's paternalistic attitude towards Uncle Julius's narratives, and endows their contents with a measure of dignity. Witness Annie's reply to her husband's suggestion that Uncle Julius's story about Sis' Becky's pickaninny is "a very ingenious fairy tale":

Why, John! . . . the story bears the stamp of truth, if ever a story did. . . . those [the most unbelievable elements of the story] are mere ornamental details and not at all essential. The story is true to nature, and might have happened half a hundred times, and no doubt did happen, in those horrid days before the war. [CW, p. 159]

This type of uncondescending treatment of folkways anticipated the use of the same material in the New Negro writings—especially those of Zora Neale Hurston and Langston Hughes.

JAMES EDWIN CAMPBELL

James Edwin Campbell's dedicatory wish that "the joy and pathos" of the "song" of a man he describes as "the Negro of the old regime, confiding, loyal, picturesque," may "be a rich inheritance among men" is an index of his intention in the dialect section of his *Echoes From The*

Cabin and Elsewhere (1895). Like Jean Toomer later, he saw the Negro folk "soul" being eroded gradually by the irresistible waves of white Anglo-Saxon culture and felt called upon to eternalize elements of that "soul" in art before it completely disappeared. The poems are cast in the Gullah dialect, and Campbell's choice of the observant, witty, and insightful Ephraim Brown to speak most of them enables him to realistically paint various aspects of Negro folkways.

Some of the poems, certainly, are modeled on the stereotypes of the minstrel stage. For instance, *Uncle Eph–Epicure* capitalizes on the Negro's so-called gluttony.[10] The satire *De 'Sprise Pa'ty* [ECE, pp. 19-21] and its sequel *'Sciplinin' Sister Brown* [ECE, pp. 22-23] exploit the Negro's love of food, dance, and music. Even Susan, Ephraim's religious wife who has "b'en baptized in Ol' Mud Creek by Reb'ren Pa'son Snow" and is supposed to have nothing to do with secular songs and dance, cannot resist the devil's invitation to "cut pidgin wing" just as her mentor, the parson, cannot resist when he comes later to discipline her for "sinnin' much." [ECE, p. 23] *Uncle Eph Backslides* [ECE, pp. 30-32] brings together almost all the known black male's vices—drunkenness, banjo-plucking, and card-playing. *The Church Rally* [ECE, pp. 37-39] capitalizes on the Negro's gluttony. Nonetheless James Edwin Campbell's dialect poetry represents an honest attempt to capture the Negro folk spirit.

The satire *Ol' Doc' Hyar* [ECE, pp. 13-14] employs the folktale format, complete with refrain which insures audience participation. By transforming the class-conscious doctor, who wants his patients' money more than he cares about their recovery, into a hare the poet achieves what his models—the folk storyteller and folksinger—achieve: the establishment of an aesthetic distance between the subject matter and the audience in order to more painlessly castigate and instruct the entertained audience. At first sight, *Linkum* [ECE, pp. 24-26] looks like an exploitation of the plantation literary theme of the Negro, faithful to the grave. In reality, however, it is only a dramatization of the folk selflessness. A ten-year-old boy yields his own life to save that of a helpless infant left in his care. There is nothing in the poem to show that Linkum could have reacted differently if the skin of his charge were not white. *Song of the Corn* [ECE, pp. 27-29] —a poem which could have been written by the Claude McKay of *Songs of Jamaica* (1912)—demonstrates the production of corn from the time it is dropped into the soil to the moment it is baked and eaten as corn pone. It captures the communality of folk life. Men, women, boys, and girls work together for the good of all. *Negro Lullaby* [ECE, p. 33] puts a child to sleep while *The Courting of Miss Lady-Bug* [ECE, pp. 34-35] —a folk story—entertains an infant on Uncle Eph's knee. *Mobile-Buck* [ECE, p. 36], according to the author's footnote, "is an attempt to catch the shuffling, jerky rhythm of the famous negro dance, the Mobile-Buck." It thus anticipates such attempts by Harlem Renaissance writers to capture Negro dance rhythms as Langston Hughes's *Charleston*. [11] *De Cunjah Man* (ECE, pp. 41-42] is about a popular feature of the Negro folklore—conjuration. *When Ol' Sis' Judy Pray* [ECE, pp. 44-45] is a celebration of the effectiveness of the folk way of saying prayers.

Even in poems where the attempt to emulate the minstrel stage is most obvious, some features of the folk are celebrated. Thus we have the following description of hunting in *Uncle Eph—Epicure:*

> Sta't him [possum] out'n pawpaw thicket, chase him up er 'simmon tree,
> W'ile de music ob dat houn' pack sets de woods er-ring wid glee.
> Roun' de hill an' troo de bottom, up de holler by de spring,
> Ow! ow! ow! des a whoopin'! how dat ol' lead-houn' do sing!
> An' you hurry troo de briahs an' you tumble ober logs,
> Nebber knowin', nebber cyarin' ez you chyuh dem blessed dogs.
> An' w'en dey all see you comin', how dem dogs sing wid new grace,
> Fum de young houn's sweet, cla'r tenah ter de ol' houn's mighty bass.
> An' dar on ur lim' er grinnin' wid his tail quoiled mighty tight,
> Hangs my fren', ol' Mistah 'Possum—how dem dogs howl wid delight.
> An' you crawl out furder, furder, twel you hyuh dat ol' lim' crack,
> An' you shake er loose his tail holt, an' you put him in yo' sack.
> Den you tote him home an' feed him twel he fat des ez you please,
> Den you kill him an' hang him out er frosty night ter freeze.
>   [ECE, pp. 15-16]

De 'Sprise Pa'ty and *'Sciplinin' Sister Brown*, like Claude McKay's *Banana Bottom* (1933), dramatize the triumph of folkways over a borrowed life-style. Neither the Christian sister, Susan Brown, nor her guide, Parson Snow, can resist the urge to participate in an un-Christian folk dance. *Uncle Eph Backslides* demonstrates the folk way of brewing liquor.

PAUL LAURENCE DUNBAR

Paul Laurence Dunbar's complaints about being compelled to write dialect poems are well known.[12] So also is the lament of his autobiographical poem *The Poet* about the world closing its eyes on the good things he has written only "to praise / A jingle in a broken tongue."[13] The frequency with which he employed either literary English or a language that is nonliterary only in appearance, his rejection of the Whitman of *Leaves of Grass* (1855)[14] and adoption of conventional poetic formats even in dialect pieces, his treatment of some of his Negro folk material à la Irwin Russell, James Whitcomb Riley, and Thomas Nelson Page all show his great desire to be numbered among the mainstream American writers of his age. Yet it will be wrong either to interpret his apparent reluctance to be remembered mainly by his dialect poetry as his disapproval of that part of his work or to regard the pieces themselves as a bunch of insincerity. The legitimacy of dialect as a medium of literary representation of folkways is not in question. What Dunbar complains about is being forced to write nothing but dialect: "I am tired, so tired of dialect, . . . I send out graceful little poems, suited for any of the magazines, but they are returned to me by editors who say, 'We would be very glad to have a dialect poem, Mr. Dunbar, but we do not care for the language composition.' "[15]

In a letter dated 13 July 1895 and addressed to his friend Henry A. Tobey he confesses how his earlier ambition to be a lawyer had "died out before the all-absorbing desire to be a worthy singer of the songs of God and nature." He wishes "to be able to interpret my own people through song and story, and to prove to the many that after all we are more human than African."[16] Most of his "people" at that time were "lowly" folk; dialect provided him with a more effective means (compared with his poetry in literary English) of demonstrating and, by extension, defending their life-style.

His speakers may be crude. They may even be stereotypes; yet from time to time they articulate basic folk truths. Thus the folk philosopher in *Foolin' wid de Seasons* [DCP, 139-40] criticizes people who, instead of living and enjoying a current season, spend their time thinking about and planning for the coming one. He says:

> We been put hyeah fu' a pu'pose,
> But de questun dat has riz

> An' made lots o' people diffah
> Is jes' whut dat pu'pose is.
> Now, accordin' to my reas'nin',
> Hyeah's de p'int whaih I's arriv,
> Sence de Lawd put life into us,
> We was put hyeah fu' to live!

This sentiment can easily be misinterpreted as the stereotypical Negro attitude towards life: living from day to day with no thought about the future. The speaker's perspicacity is, nonetheless, impeccable.

This can also be said of many other poems. The chicken-stealing speaker of *Accountability* [DCP, pp. 5-6] could have come straight from the minstrel stage. But, speaking as a folk philosopher, he manages, by the seriousness of his tone, to elevate his material from the slough of minstrelsy:

> Folks ain't got no right to censuah othah folks about dey habits;
> Him dat giv' de squir'ls de bush-tails made de bobtails fu' de rabbits.
> Him dat built de gread big mountains hollered out de little valleys,
> Him dat made de streets an' driveways wasn't shamed to make de alleys.

He justifies his action before we know what that action really is. He is, as it were, inviting whomever will to cast the first stone on him for stealing. But no one will dare condemn him. He has been taught to believe that his situation in life is determined by a divine power. He is, therefore, in no way accountable for the state which has conduced to his appropriation of one of his master's chickens. Viney and other members of his implied audience cannot fail to understand that his action is informed by that philosophy which is the theme of a popular corn song:

> Our Fader, who art in heaven
> White man owe me 'leven, pay me seven,
> Thy kingdom come, thy will be done
> And ef I hadn't tuck that, I wouldn't git none.[17]

Apparently, the speaker's thought in *How Lucy Backslid* [DCP, pp. 158-60] endorses the conceptualization of the Negro in terms of sensuality and instincts. What he says, however, is the truth. Nothing is wrong with religion, but a woman who also wants to get married should think twice before searching for religion at the expense of her quest for a husband, "Fu'de men dat want to ma'y ain't a-growin' 'roun' on trees./ An' de gal dat wants to git one sholy has to try to please." In any event, the speaker affirms, religion and not a husband is more likely to be had at any time a woman chooses.

Philosophy [DCP, pp. 212-13] disagrees with a preacher's advice to his congregation that they should wear bright faces above their miseries. The speaker makes it clear, in his "broken tongue," that he does not "believe in people allus totin' roun' a frown, / But it's easy 'nough to titter w'en de stew is smokin' hot, / But, hit's mighty ha'd to giggle w'en dey's nuffin' in de pot." Although the speaker of *De Way T'ings Come* [DCP, pp. 225-26] seems to subscribe to the concept of the happy-go-lucky Negro, he is actually ridiculing the idea of giving more to the haves while the have-nots go empty-handed.

James Weldon Johnson once defined the Negro dialect as "an instrument with but two full stops, humor and pathos."[18] With Dunbar these two emotions are not so much "stops" as coatings for homely truths. Often they encapsulate uncompromising pieces of advice. Witness *A Little Christmas Basket* [DCP, pp. 174-75] whose sparkling humor woven around the personification of the uninvited winter encases the harsh advice—good deeds and not words are the essence of true religion:

> Wha's de use o' preachin' 'ligion to a man dat's sta'ved to def,
> An' a-tellin' him de Mastah will pu'vide?
> Ef you want to tech his fellin's, save yo' sermons an' yo' bref,
> Tek a little Chrismus basket by yo' side.

The tone of *Joggin' Erlong* [DCP, pp. 165-66] is sad; but at the heart of the pathos is a well-thought-out exhortation to the implied audience to persevere for "De mo'n is allus brightah w'en de night's been long." *Advice* [DCP, p. 250] tells the reader what to do in the face of some common everyday inconveniences: "Des don' pet yo' worries, / Lay 'em on de she'f." *Limitations* [DCP, pp. 250-51] counsels modesty.

As a result of their keen observation and interaction with their implied audiences, the speakers portray all aspects of folk life. We see them at parties; we see them by their firesides nodding; we see them in and out of love; we see them drunk; we see them sober. We see them full of hope; we see them disillusioned "when dey's nuffin' in de pot." Dunbar's knowledge of the Negro folk was stronger than that of Russell, Riley, and Page; his portrayal of their ways was, therefore, more complex and subtle.

More importantly, like the most representative Harlem Renaissance writers later, he strove to present the Negro as he really was. It was obviously this that William Dean Howells had in mind when he spoke of Dunbar's objective analysis of his race and said, "One sees how the poet exults in his material as the artist always does; it is not for him to blink its commonness, or to be ashamed of its rudeness."[19] Dunbar saw his mission as a writer as that of interpreting his race through poetry and prose and proving to the doubtful that the black American was "more human than African." He, therefore anticipated the New Negro writers in his attempt to demonstrate and, if necessary, defend the Afro-American folkways.

The defense in some cases was direct. Witness *Ode to Ethiopia* [DCP, pp. 15-16] which boils with racial pride and awareness of a maligned people:

> No other race, or white or black,
> When bound as thou wert, to the rack,
>   So seldom stooped to grieving;
> No other race, when free again,
> Forgot the past and proved them men
>   So noble in forgiving.
>
> Go on and up! Our souls and eyes
> Shall follow thy continuous rise;
>   Our ears shall list thy story
> From bards who from thy root shall spring,
> And proudly tune their lyres to sing
>   Of Ethiopia's glory.

Ethiopia should be proud not only of her strength as revealed in her survival in spite of all odds but also of her nobleness and magnanimity. In most poems, however, the defense is subtle and consists in negating unfavorable impressions created about blackness. Thus in a typical Harlem Renaissance manner, *Dely* [DCP, pp. 148-49] projects the color black as beautiful. Dely, the subject of the poem, is extraordinarily beautiful, and the speaker almost worships her, because of her blackness:

> Dely brown ez brown kin be,
>   She ain' no mullatter;

> She pure cullud,–don' you see
> Dat's jes' whut's de mattah?
> Dat's de why I love huh so,
> D'ain't no mix about huh,
> Soon 's you see huh face you know
> D' ain't no chanst to doubt huh.

Even in his essentially romantic poems in literary English that call for lily-white girls as in his models, Tennyson and Poe, Dunbar often tries to darken the skins of the girls and/or furnish them with negroid features, thus showing that negroness also deserves a song. Accordingly, *Song* [DCP, p. 13] is addressed to "my African maid," while the subject of *To a Lady Playing the Harpe* [DCP, p. 116] is described as "dusk sorceress of the dusky eyes / And soft dark hair." Similarly Dinah, with her "brown arms" and "eyes of jet and teeth of pearl, / Hair, some say, too tight a-curl," is, for the speaker, "very near perfection's dream." [DCP, pp. 188-89]

In some cases still, it is behavioral traits attributed to blacks that are defended or, at least, portrayed in a positive way. For instance, such a poem as *Angelina* [DCP, pp. 138-39] anticipates Claude McKay's and Langston Hughes's treatment of cabaret dancers. Dancing, the speaker implies, cannot be incompatible with godliness, for "dey's somep'n downright holy in de way our faces shine, / When Angelina Johnson comes a-swingin' down de line."

The mainstay of Dunbar's dialect poetry, however, is the muted illustration of Negro folkways. We see this in *The Turning of the Babies in the Bed* [DCP, p. 170] and *The Party* [DCP, pp. 83-86] where folk beliefs and events are dramatized. We also see it in the celebration of individual folk artists. The singing of the folk artist Malindy, for example, is almost projected as the best of all possible vocal music on earth. Malindy is apparently illiterate; she has not learnt any music; yet her singing is "sweetah dan de music / Of an edicated band." [DCP, p. 83] Mockingbirds forget their art when she sings; every heart is touched. *Deacon Jones' Grievance* [DCP, pp. 39-40] and *The Ol' Tunes* [DCP, pp. 53-54], pieces which sound like poetic versions of Rudolph Fisher's *Vestiges: Harlem Sketches*[20] in their lament of the dying folkways in the face of modernity, are also celebrations of folk arts. Both the sixty-year-old Deacon Jones and the speaker of *The Ol' Tunes* recall nostalgically the folk way of singing.

Personally, Paul Laurence Dunbar was not a folk artist. His art was
both academic and self-conscious. As James Weldon Johnson puts it,
"the folk artists . . . although working in the dialect, sought only to express themselves for themselves, and to their *own group,*" while Dunbar
"wrote mainly for the delectation of audience that was an outside
group."[21] Yet a surrogate for the folk artist without an adequate means
of preserving folkways for posterity and against the onslaught of modernity, Dunbar was, in some of his more successful poems (such as *The
Haunted Oak,* and *The Turning of the Babies in the Bed*), a sort of aman-
uensis— a recorder of experiences he either observed or learned from the
people who lived them.[22] His use of the old folk material seems to be
based on the thought expressed by the old man in *The Voice of the
Banjo*: "the future cannot hurt us while we keep the past in mind."
[DCP, p. 124] Far from being a liability, the acceptance of past experience is an indispensable step in an attempt at self-definition. It was a
positive attitude towards the past which was to inform some of the
themes treated in the Harlem Renaissance writings.

Although this stance cannot palliate the apparent tastelessness and
self-debasement manifested in such poems as *Parted, Fishing, Chrismus
on the Plantation, The News, A Coquette Conquered, The Deserted
Plantation, Signs of the Times, Expectation,* and *Possum* (which either
perpetuate the old plantation image of the Negro, or capitalize on the
stereotyped Negro's love of food—especially possum), it places the poet's
seeming betrayal in a new perspective. It is a feature of his attempt to
rehabilitate the Negro self. Whatever his situation in life, the plantation
Negro contained an essential part of that self. To reject his experience—
joy, sorrow, humiliation and exaltation—was to discard an essential part
of the self. Besides, in the more successful of those poems that deal with
plantation life, or apparently capitalize on the stereotyped Negro image,
Dunbar has made some quiet attempts to modify the picture. On the surface *A Corn Song* [DCP, p. 59] irredeemably panders to the amateurs of
the plantation tradition. The white master paternally sits at his door and
listens to his slaves sing one of their secular songs (as distinct from
spirituals).[23] A careful reading, however, reveals that the singing Negroes
here are not of the type found in Thomas Nelson Page's work. By establishing two voices—the speaker's in literary English, and the slaves' in
dialect—the master is placed in an ironic position. The "tear" in his eyes
could be that of guilt. As for the slaves, their song is in no way a mark

of happiness—the joy of being blessed with a master. Their "steps" are described as "halting," "belabored, slow, and weary." They sing to keep from weeping. Although their song is superficially direct and innocent, it is pregnant with accusation:

> Oh, we hoe de co'n
> Since de ehly mo'n;
> Now de sinkin' sun
> Says de day is done.

As Sterling Brown rightly points out, "the seculars [corn-songs] were more favored by the masters and overseers who preferred their gay light-heartedness to the brooding of the spirituals."[24] But that was because they helped the masters to set their conscience at rest by consciously and conscientiously getting themselves to believe that their slaves enjoyed their state of servitude even though in reality they knew that that was not true. In Dunbar's *Corn Song*, however, the mask of gaiety is flimsy. It is too weak a material to anesthetize the master's conscience. It is no wonder, therefore, that he should feel a pang of grief as he sits at the door of his "big house" and listens. This, of course, is not the effect sought for and achieved on the minstrel stage, or even in Russell's and Page's works.

This can also be said of *A Banjo Song*. [DCP, pp. 20-21] The subject—the banjo-plucking Negro—is a popular minstrel material. But the poet has retrieved it from the stereotyped mold by revamping the tone. The image of the speaker we visualize is not the grinning prancing nigger, but that of a meditator with tears in his eyes and a "lump" of suppressed sorrow in his larynx. Although he plucks his banjo in earnest, he does not belong with the happy-go-lucky niggers of the minstrel stage whose quest for joy is almost a vocation. He plays his banjo to escape for a moment from the sad realities of his situation of which he is fully conscious. Under the joy he derives from his "ol' banjo" is a current of excruciating sorrow:

> An' somehow my th'oat gits choky,
> An' a lump keeps tryin' to rise
> Lak it wan'ed to ketch de water
> Dat was flowin' to my eyes;

> An' I feel dat I could sorter
>   Knock de socks clean off o' sin
> Ez I hyeah my po' ol' granny
>   Wif huh tremblin' voice jine in.

The seemingly happy-go-lucky banjo-plucking speaker could have agreed with the speakers of the more direct statement *We Wear the Mask* [DCP, p. 71] and Langston Hughes's *Minstrel Man.* [25]

Paul Laurence Dunbar died in 1906, almost two decades before the formal launching of the New Negro literary movement. His poetry has several attributes of the Old Negro writing. The voices of his folk speakers are often infirm of purpose their racial awareness and self-pride often evanescent. Yet his poetry contains the rudiments of some of the motifs of the Harlem Renaissance literature.

This can also be said of his work in prose. While three of his four novels[26] and most of his short stories are of the Old Negro school of writing (and in some cases of the plantation tradition), his last novel, *The Sport of the Gods,* (1902) is a bridge between the Old and the New Negro literatures. An elaboration of a theme he had originally articulated in some of his earlier poems such as *To the Eastern Shore* [DCP, pp. 202-3], its plot belongs to the plantation tradition. A black family moves from the south to the north only to discover that its best friend is the south. What remains of it predictably decides to return to the south.[27] Nonetheless, *The Sport of the Gods,* with its treatment of the Negro migration from the south to the north, its van-vechtenite black-white night life in New York, provides a student of the Harlem Renaissance literature with some knowledge of the sociological background. But for its tone which trembles with the lesson the narrator is anxious to get across, it could easily be placed among representative New Negro novels. Some of its characters and incidents are similar to those in the Harlem Renaissance fiction. For instance, although the place where its action takes place in New York is not called Harlem, the goings-on in the "Banner Club" could have taken place in a club in the Harlem of Van Vechten's *Nigger Heaven* (1926) and McKay's *Home to Harlem* (1928). Dunbar's Hattie Sterling is not as callous and decadent as Van Vechten's Lasca Sartoris;[28] his Joe Hamilton is in no way Byron.[29] Yet their relationship resembles Lasca-Byron's in substance. It is all a story of a "green" boy, from a rural environment, who, like Byron, is dazzled by the glamor of a sophisticated New York lady who squeezes him dry and casts him out. It is not surprising that Van Vechten should acknowledge *The Sport of the Gods* as one of the sources of influence on his novel.

DANIEL WEBSTER DAVIS AND OTHER MINOR DIALECT POETS

Beside Paul Laurence Dunbar as a towering trailblazer of the writings of the Harlem Renaissance, Daniel Webster Davis is only a dwarf. For all its scope, his poetry, which ranges from Phillis Wheatleyan recognition of slavery as a blessing in disguise[30] to an assertion of the Negro's Americanness,[31] is unexceptional. Yet, realized by techniques substantially similar to Dunbar's and Campbell's, parts of it constitute signs of what was to happen in the 1920s. Davis, like all his contemporaries discussed here, is therefore important, from a historical—if not a literary—standpoint, in a study of the early "symptoms" of the Harlem Renaissance writing.

As in Dunbar's and Campbell's works, some of the poems capitalize on the stereotyped traits of the Negro. The obsession of some of his speakers with food—especially watermelon—is almost pathological. Rastus, who figures in many of the poems, saves a train and its passengers (in *Why He Saved the Engine*) only because he does not "want dat ingine tumblin' in my wadermillum patch." [WDS, p. 26] The speaker of *When de Sun Shines Hot* [WDS, pp. 34-36] prefers summer to winter only because the sunny season promises watermelons. In *Is dar Wadermilluns on High* [WDS, pp. 116-17] the speaker implies that he may not want to go to heaven unless there is a guarantee that he is going to eat watermelons up there. The speaker of *Bakin' an' Greens* [WDS, pp. 10-11] would accept every insult and hardship as long as he is furnished with his favorite dish: "bakin', wid plenty ub greens." His counterpart in *Hog Meat* [WDS, pp. 16-18] "could jes' be happy, 'doubt money, cloze or house, / wid plenty yurz an' pig feet made in ol'-fashun 'souse.' " *Ol' Virginny Reel* [WDS, pp. 75-78] laments the glorious past and capitalizes on the Negro's love of dance. *When You Gits a Rabbit Foot* [WDS, pp. 83-84] stresses the superstitious Negro. In *Miss Liza's Banjer* [WDS, pp. 103-105] Uncle Joe plays the banjo-plucking nigger.

Some of the poems also highlight the image of the Negro of the plantation tradition. In the title poem, *Wey Down Souf* [WDS, pp. 7-9] a speaker, who is currently in the north, longs to return to the south beside which the north is a hell. *Ol' Mistis* [WDS, pp. 112-15] paints an angel of a mistress who "had lin'ments fur de body, / An' de Bible fur de soul" of each of her slaves. The speaker of *Night on de Ol' Plantashun* [WDS, pp. 122-24] almost longs to return to slavery with its nights on the plantation and gives an insightful explanation of why he and his fellow slaves must have enjoyed them.

Yet the image of the Negro in Davis's poetry is not completely negative. Even in the otherwise self-debasing poems are elements of self-pride and racial awareness. *Bakin' an' Greens* describes and thus preserves for posterity the folk way of preparing "bakin an' greens." The speaker of *Ol' Virginny Reel,* like that of *Ol' Mistis,* is not unaware of the slaves' "cares an' sorrows" [WDS, p. 78]; he only celebrates a moment of relaxation and furnishes us with descriptions of folk dances which are fast disappearing before the onslaught of "waltzes, polkas, dances toe an' heel."

More importantly, in spite of their weaknesses, some of the poems are capsules of Negro folk spirit. *Signs* [WDS, pp. 43-45] dramatizes a folk practice as well as the permanence of folk spitit. Sarah Ann, having been to school, despises folk signs yet she cannot resist making some of them. *De Linin' ub de Hymns* [WDS, pp. 54-56] defends the old folk practice of lining out hymns, against the young people's determination to do away with the folk way of singing. *Stickin' to de Hoe* [WDS, pp. 57-59] is a protest against overeducation at the expense of manual labor. The folk preacher in *Skeetin' on de Ice* [WDS, pp. 72-74] may not know the geography of Egypt; he nevertheless exhibits imagination—that trait associated with Negro folk preachers—when he tells his audience that the children of Israel were able to cross the Red Sea only because " 'twuz in de winter . . . / An' de norf win' wuz a-blowin' string ernuf to raise de dead." [WDS, pp. 73-74] *Cookin' by de Ol-Time Fire-Place* [WDS, pp. 118-19] seeks to protect the old way of cooking against the modern methods of appliances and recipes. *Keep Inchin' Along* [WDS, pp. 12-13] and *De Biggis' Piece ub Pie* [WDS, pp. 14-15] are all homely pieces of advice.

In the introduction[32] to Daniel Webster Davis's first volume of poems, *Idle Moments,* John H. Smythe described the author's dialect poems as "tradition and history in dialect or patois," and maintained that "they show the power, continuity and tenacity of race under circumstances the most adverse and the most untoward, as to its preservation of type and

language, the outgrowth of a condition the race was powerless to relieve
itself from, and which unconsciously stamped itself upon the people over
thousands of miles of territory of a race foreign to the Negro race."[33]
A product of a deliberate mutilation of English syntax and a crude
attempt at phonetic transcription of the language of the folk Negro,
Davis's dialect does not always sound authentic. As "history," the poems
themselves are hardly reliable—not, however, because they recall a moment in history which many blacks and their friends would like to forget,
but because of exaggeration of sentiments whose raison d'être could only
be to gratify an outside group's ego at the expense of the black race.
Fishin' Hook an' Worms [WDS, pp. 19-21], for example, records a favorite folk hobby before and after emancipation. The whole record, however,
is almost destroyed by the speaker's overenthusiasm, which borders on
buffoonery, when he tells his audience that he prefers fishing to civil
rights. John H. Smythe obviously attaches more importance to the poetry
qua poetry than it really deserves. Yet it will be difficult to deny Davis
a place among the pre-Harlem Renaissance black writers who tried to
"express . . . for the most part essentially Negro feelings . . . standing
squarely on their racial inheritance."[34]

John Wesley Holloway had a preference for religious poems, but he
could not ignore the taste of what he describes as "a humor-loving public."[35] His work, therefore, includes such dialect poems as *Discouraged*
[HFD, pp. 27-28], *Quills* [HFD, pp. 52-53], and *The Baptizing* [HFD,
pp. 83-85] which were obviously written simply for the amusement of
an audience in quest of entertainment. Deriving their humor mainly
from a distortion of English spelling and a capitalization on the stereotyped image of the Negro, Holloway's dialect poems are often artificial
in structure and insincere in tone.

This leaning towards minstrelsy notwithstanding, some of them can
rightly be accepted along with Dunbar's works, whose influence they frequently reveal, as trailblazers of the Harlem Renaissance literary attitude.

In the first poem in his volume Holloway defines his duty as a black
poet as that of capturing and preserving in art the soul of his "dying"
race:

> I AM the voice of a race of men
>   Who lie at the point of death;
> I hold mine ear to their fainting lips,

> To catch their dying breath.
> I gather up the songs they sang
> And the words they had to say,
> To hoard them till the coming time
> Brings in better day.
>   [HFD, pp. 13]

Although the reliability of the "voice" as a custodian of the black people's heritage is endangered by the poet's great desire to cater to the taste of his audience, several aspects of the folk Negro are unashamedly presented in *From the Desert. Calling the Doctor* [HFD, pp. 57-58] is a catalogue of folk remedies, provided by a folk speaker whose serious tone retrieves the material from the burnt-cork humor often associated with it. *The Corn Song* [HFD, pp. 45-46] portrays a folk romance. Reminiscent of Daniel Webster Davis's *Bakin' an' Greens, Jes' 'Taters* [HFD, p. 61] capitalizes on the Negro's presumed gluttony. But it also records various folkways of eating potatoes. *When Lindy Plays a Rag* [HFD, pp. 65-66] celebrates a folk musician. *The Sermon on the Mount* [HFD, p. 86] is a pessimistic folk attitude towards the biblical sermon and what it means to many people. *Miss Melerlee* [HFD, p. 77] sings the praise of a brown-skinned girl whom the speaker is bold to characterize—contrary to the current practice—as "de sweetes' gal Ah evah see."

John Wesley Holloway was by no means a great poet. Most of his poems in literary English—including the religious ones which he loved so much—are puerile. In some cases they are not poetry but mere doggerel verse. His dialect hardly rises above the language of the minstrel stage. Nevertheless, his unbashful treatment of folk material in some of his poems anticipates to some extent the daredevil attitude of the New Negro writers towards the folk Negro as subject matter.

Equally deserving of a place among the forerunners of the Harlem Renaissance writing is Joseph S. Cotter. The non-New Negro Washingtonian opposition to book knowledge and political agitation at the expense of manual labor colors much of his writing. He states the idea succinctly in the preface to his play, *Caleb, The Degenerate* (1903): "The Negro needs very little politics, much industrial training, and a dogged settledness as far as going to Africa is concerned."[36] It is the main message of the play itself. An "Old" Negro writer and poet of reconciliation (of blacks and whites, of the north and the south), when he is not writing

about the tragic mulatto as in the tale "Tesney, The Deceived,"[37] he is
castigating the Negro for his many vices. Witness the satire on the shiftless Negro in "The Loafing Negro"[38] and in "Lazy Sam." [CWS, p. 53]
"Negro Love Song" [CWS, p. 49] is not only a variation on the same
theme, it is also an attack on the black male for his dependence on the
black woman. "The Vicious Negro" [CWS, pp. 53-54] characterizes the
razor-wielding Negro.

This harshness notwithstanding, the seriousness of the tone of Cotter's
folk speakers in such pieces as "Rivalry" [CWS, pp. 50-51], "Honey,
Whut's You Askin'?" [CWS, pp. 51-52], "The Christmas Tree" [CWS,
pp. 58-60] and "New Year Resolutions" [CWS, pp. 60-62] coupled with
the author's collection of Negro folk stories, including at least one African
tale ("The Jackal and Lion") [CWS, p. 142] imbues his work with a measure
of self-confidence and pride in blackness and its heritage.

More important as a pacesetter of the New Negro writing is Carmichael's
From The Heart of a Folk.[39] Based on distortions of English spelling, his
dialect is sometimes arbitrary and inauthentic. His use of such words as
"twistfurcation"[40] in *The Day of Freedom* [CHF, p. 17] and "bolognial"
in *The Favorite Diet* [CHF, p. 37] capitalizes on the stereotypical Negro's
penchant for high-sounding words. As revealed in *My Little Cabin Home*
[CHF, p. 18], his speakers are not above casting a nostalgic eye on their
ex-slave lives—a popular motif of the plantation tradition.

These minstrel traits, however, are not as pervasive in Carmichael's
poetry as in the works of some of his contemporaries. In fact, the sentiments expressed in *My Little Cabin Home* are almost neutralized by the
ecstatic mood of a similar speaker on hearing about emancipation. [CHF,
p. 17]

Although some of his poems are liable to remind the reader of specific
stereotypes of the Negro, like typical writings of the Harlem Renaissance
later, they do not endorse these images but try to redefine them by
placing the Negro traits at the root of the stereotypes in their proper
contexts. Thus, although the title *Der Fiddle Is My Comfort* [CHF, p.
36] evokes the image of the happy-go-lucky musical Negro, the poem
itself does not paint the picture of the grinning, prancing nigger of the
minstrel stage. Playing the fiddle is neither the speaker's vocation nor his
second nature. He plays it to keep from weeping.

Carmichael's poetry is permeated with folk humor, but unless his people are also laughing at themselves as the speaker of *I Use ter Dres'* [CHF,

p. 29] does, we laugh with them and not at them. Even when speakers invite the reader to join them in laughing at themselves, the laughter is not gratuitous. In *I Use ter Dres'*, for instance, the hilarity arising from the speaker's description of how he used to deck himself when he went courting is capped with folk wisdom:

> You's got to many styles fur me
> An' none don' worth a cent;
> You'd better kept dat money, boy,
> To spen' for pork an' rent.

What is more, Carmichael's poetry portrays, often without as much as authorial comments, various aspects of the folk Negro life, from love affairs (as in *The Lover's Spat* [CHF, pp. 19-20]) to religion (as in *When the Different Churches Meet* [CHF, p. 28] and *The Night I Went to Church* [CHF, pp. 14-15]).

Finally, mention must be made of Raymond Garfield Dandridge whose work, like some of the writings of the Harlem Renaissance, is replete with the folk Negro's fears, desires, and values, in spite of a nervous ambivalence towards its Negro material. With his direct statement on behalf of the Negro in America as in *Facts*[41], *Brother Mine* [DP, pp. 36-37] and *My Grievance* [DP, p. 61] Dandridge is basically faithful to the unwritten code of the Old Negro school of writers. Even some of his dialect poems such as *Weddah* [DP, pp. 34-35] and *Friendship* [DP, p. 32] subscribe to the same code as far as subject matters are concerned. Consequently, only a few of his speakers can really be described as folk. They include the speakers of *A Recalled Prayer* [DP, pp. 17-20], *Censored* [DP, p. 38], *De Innah Part* [DP, p. 41], *Hahd Cidah* [DP, p. 43], *In Ole Kintucky* [DP, p. 46], *Tracin' Tales* [DP, pp. 51-52], *Purcaution* [DP, p. 60], and *Sandy* [DP, p. 64]. Looking at the real Negro, as distinct from a caricature of him, these pieces approach their folk material in a dignified manner. An amateur of the common stereotypes of the black man seeks in vain in Dandridge's *The Poet and Other Poems* for references to watermelon, chicken-stealing, and other stocks-in-trade of the minstrel stage and its reflectors in literature. The only reference to drinking occurs in *Hahd Cidah*, and what is drunk in this poem is cider.

Although this almost over-selective approach to folk material looks like an outgrowth of the Old Negro diplomatic code of putting the best

foot forward, some of Dandridge's poems portray the folk Negro life in
a manner which anticipates its treatment by the New Negro writers.
A Recalled Prayer is built around the folkloric motif of marriage for
money and beauty. The result of such a marriage is almost always dis-
illusionment and despair. Like the beautiful girl in the African folktale
"The Disobedient Daughter Who Married a Skull,"[42] Sis Hannah May
Liza discovers that the rich man she has chosen for a husband is only a
bum. *Purcaution* is the monologue of a folk speaker who, proud of his
folk heritage, stubbornly defies public opinion in his adherence to folk
beliefs and practices. [DP, p. 60] Dandridge's anticipation of the mood
of the New Negro is also evident in such poems in literary English as
Zalka Peetruza:

> She danced, nude, to tom-tom beat,
> With swaying arms and flying feet,
> 'Mid swirling spangles, gauze and lace,
> Her all was dancing—save her face.
>
> A conscience, dumb to brooding fears,
> Companioned hearing deaf to cheers;
> A body, marshalled by the will,
> Kept dancing while a heart stood still:
>
> And eyes obsessed with vacant stare,
> Looked over heads to empty air,
> As though they sought to find therein
> Redemption for a maiden sin.
>
> 'Twas thus, amid force driven grace,
> We found the lost look on her face;
> And then, to us, did it occur
> That, though we saw—we saw not her.
>   [DP, p. 61]

Imbued with that sympathy for the underdog which was characteristic
of the Harlem Renaissance literature, the poem could have been written
by a Countée Cullen or a Claude McKay. As a matter of fact, but for the
implied awareness (on the part of the dancer) of sin and the necessity
for redemption, *Zalka Peetruza* reads like an expanded version of Claude
McKay's sonnet *The Harlem Dancer*,[43] or at least a piece inspired by the
same performer.

From Du Bois to Van Vechten

JAMES WELDON JOHNSON

In addition to lyrics and librettos for his brother, J. Rosamond's Broadway music, James Weldon Johnson's original creative works, before the launching of the Harlem Renaissance, include the novel *The Autobiography of an Ex-Coloured Man* (1912), poems (both in Standard English and dialect) most of which were collected and published in *Fifty Years and Other Poems* (1917), and the Negro sermon "The Creation" which, first published in *The Freeman* in 1920, was incorporated into *God's Trombones* in 1927. All these, in varying degrees, are impregnated with folk elements and black experience in the New World. For the purpose of the present discussion, however, we will focus mainly on *The Autobiography of an Ex-Coloured Man* and "The Creation."

Briefly stated, *The Autobiography of an Ex-Coloured Man* is the story of a man who thinks it unnecessary, as he puts it, "to go about with a label of inferiority pasted across my forehead."[44] He has been born in Georgia and has only a faint idea of his white father: "a tall man with a small, dark moustache," who wore shiny shoes or boots, a gold chain, and a great gold watch, and paid him and his mother night visits two or three times a week. [JA, p. 5] During one of these visits, this man put a ten-dollar gold coin around his neck; a few days later he and his mother moved to Connecticut, where he was brought up as "a perfect little aristocrat." [JA, pp. 6-7]

There were "some brown and black boys and girls" in the school he attended; he and his fellow white-skinned scholars enjoyed harassing them, shouting "Nigger, nigger, never die, / Black face and shiny eyes" [JA, p. 15]—which, even though it was part of a Negro folk rhyme,[45] was always regarded as an insult when addressed to a black by a nonblack. He even gave one of them the nickname "Shiny." [JA, p. 14] This identification with the white world continued until he learned, at the age of nine, that he was "coloured." After the initial shock, and inspired by Shiny's unmistakable intelligence, he resolved "to be a great man, a great coloured man, to reflect credit on the race and gain fame for myself." [JA, p. 46]

This resolve and the death of his mother pushed him into the world: to Atlanta University where he could not study because he lost his money; to Jacksonville where he went instead of revealing his misfortune to the University authorities; and to New York. Here he came in contact

with the Negro Bohemia and was discovered by a white millionaire who
took him to Europe as a personal musician. Although he was aware of
the fact that Europe was less hostile to a "coloured" man's happiness
than America, he decided to return to the United States to pursue his
ambition. He was now bent on transforming Negro folk songs into modern
and artistic music; he went to the South to collect material. There, without being recognized as a Negro, he watched the lynching of a black man.
He was, however, overwhelmed by "unbearable shame. Shame at being
identified with a people that could with impunity be treated worse than
animals." He decided never to present himself voluntarily as a black man:

> I argued that to forsake one's race to better one's condition was no less
> worthy an action than to forsake one's country for the same purpose.
> I finally made up my mind that I would neither disclaim the black race
> nor claim the white race; but that I would change my name, raise a
> moustache, and let the world take me for what it would.
>
> [JA, p. 190]

This is only the skeleton of a novel which "consists of a series of episodes which runs the gamut of Negro life in America."[46] The publishers
of the 1912 anonymous edition were absolutely right when, in their
preface, they described the work as a "vivid and startling new picture of
conditions brought about by the race question in the United States."
[JA, p. xi] They, however, exaggerated when they claimed that it
"makes no special plea for the Negro, but shows in a dispassionate, though
sympathetic, manner conditions as they actually exist between the whites
and blacks today." [JA, p. xi] It shows "conditions as they actually
exist"; but it also pleads. It is this plea that makes it a propaganda tract
without, however, weakening its position among the writings that self-
confidently expressed "essentially Negro feelings" long before the 1920s.

The narrator, as an artistic creation by the author, is a dramatization
of the implications of the Afro-American double consciousness—a dramatization as daring, in 1912, as Langston Hughes's use of the blues and
jazz as models for his poetry many years later.

Robert A. Bone is not entirely wrong when he notices traces of moral
cowardice in the narrator's behavior.[47] However, that moral cowardice
is only a subsidiary impulse. The main motivation is a conflict between
the conscious and the unconscious in the narrator's character, a struggle

between the purely Negroid and the non-Negroid aspects of his double-consciousness: the conscious effort to embrace blackness and all it stands for versus the unconscious impulse that impels him towards the white world. This accounts in part, for instance, for his withdrawal from Atlanta University, an institution that is not only essentially "coloured," but is also amid a "coloured" population. It also accounts for his earlier action at elementary school. He admires and almost identifies with "Shiny," yet he harasses and pelts boys and girls like "Shiny" with stones. Even though he believes that he has "had no particular like or dislike for these black and brown boys and girls," when he learns that he has some Negro blood in his veins, he feels "a very strong aversion to being classed with them." [JA, p. 23] The nearest he goes towards getting rid of the conflict is when he returns from Europe to America to work on Negro folk music. But like the doomed Orestes, all his efforts are in vain. He himself is unable to vouch for the genuineness of the loyalty on which his motives are based. He confesses:

I began to analyse my own motives, and found that they, too, were very largely mixed with selfishness. Was it more a desire to help those I considered my people, or more a desire to distinguish myself, which was leading me back to the United States? That is a question I have never definitely answered.

[JA, p. 147]

Taking all these into consideration, his excuse for crossing over to the white side is acceptable. It is part of the Afro-American experience. He summarizes the root cause of his "passing": "It was not discouragement or fear or search for a larger field of action and opportunity that was driving me out of the Negro race. . . . It was shame, unbearable shame." [JA, pp. 190-91] It cannot be "search for a larger field of action and opportunity" that makes him "pass," since he is aware of the fact that he "should have greater chances of attracting attention as a coloured composer than as a white one." [JA, p. 147] It is "shame" that drives him "out of the Negro race." He has, all the time, unconsciously been ashamed of the black race; not, however, because he believes that something is inherently wrong in being black but because of the inconvenience it entails. He will definitely accept blackness without its inconvenience. Thomas W. Talley comments on this absence of desire on the part of the

black man, even "during the days of his enslavement," to be white just
because of the color. He bases his conclusion on his study of Negro folk
rhymes:

One would naturally expect the Negro under hard, trying, bitter slave
conditions, to long to be white. There is a remarkable Negro Folk Rhyme
which shows that this was not the case. This rhyme is: "I'd Rather Be a
Negro Than a Poor White Man." We must bear in mind that a Folk Rhyme
from its very nature carries in it the crystallized thought of the masses.
This rhyme . . . leaves the unquestioned conclusion that, though the Negro
masses may have wished for the exalted station of the rich Southern
white man and possibly would have willingly had a white color as a pass-
port to position, there never was a time when the Negro masses desired
to be white for the sake of being white.[48]

It is true that some of the narrator's utterances in *Autobiography*
reveal elements of contempt for black people. His reaction to the black
population of Atlanta is a case in point. "The unkempt appearance, the
shambling, slouching gait and loud talk and laughter of these people
aroused in me a feeling of almost repulsion." [JA, pp. 55-56] Yet it must
be remembered that he has been brought up as "a perfect little aristocrat."
He could have reacted in the same way to a white population of the
same class. In other words, the repulsion he feels stems more from class
consciousness than from an awareness of the color of his skin.

His motivation and experience are so lifelike that when the novel first
appeared in 1912, many people believed that it was a true story.[49] Even
as late as 1932 Arthur Ficke apparently still identified James Weldon
Johnson with his narrator.[50] This attempt to present a Negro element as
he really is, without any falsification to please or hurt anyone, is, as already indicated, a feature of the Harlem Renaissance literature.

The pride implicit in it, and in the treatment which folkways receive
in the novel is another tribute to the growing self-confidence from which
black literature of the 1920s would derive its daredevil self-assertiveness.
Notice, for instance, the self-confident pride implicit in the narrator's
projection of Uncle Remus stories, the jubilee songs, the ragtime music,
and the cakewalk as some of the Negro's greatest gifts to America.
With particular reference to ragtime he asserts: "No one who has trav-
elled can question the world-conquering influence of rag-time, and I do
not think it would be an exaggeration to say that in Europe the United

States is popularly known by rag-time than by anything else it has produced in a generation." [JA, p. 87]

It is the same self-confidence that underlies the depiction of the Negro folk religion in the "big meeting" sequence as well as the unbashful, unapologetic portrayal of the goings-on at the "Club." The self-confidence is also evident in the discussion of the Negro dialect and folk humor, even though that discussion is tinged with condescension—a condescension which, in any case, is understandable since the narrator, who is also the main actor, is very much above the standard of living of the people with whom he is dealing.

In a way, *The Autobiography of an Ex-Coloured Man* is a celebration of the Negro folk. This can also be said of James Weldon Johnson's more serious dialect poems—such as the lilting lullaby entitled *De Little Pickaninny's Gone to Sleep,* and the folktale *Brer Rabbit, You's de Cutes' of 'em All* which dramatizes the mythical weakness of the overconfident and aggressively strong in the face of the bodily weak but mentally strong nature.[51] It is, however, in *The Creation* (1918) that the exaltation reached its apogee in Johnson's work, at least before this Negro sermon was combined with other poems like it and published in the volume *God's Trombones* (1927).

Operating from the consciousness of a folk preacher, who speaks to a group of believers whose lives, like his, are rooted in warm human relations, in the soil, the water, and other elements of nature (from which they derive all their needs including "pictures," to use Zora Neale Hurston's terms, with which to "adorn" their "expression"[52]) the poem is simple and direct. It eschews metaphysical abstractions and reflects the conception of *Obatala,* God the creator, in the Negro folklore:[53] a being more human than the Bible concedes. Thus he feels lonely and seeks company. He almost suffers from the blues. He smiles in happiness. Zora Neale Hurston, the folklorist, as distinct from the fictionist, documents this concept of a human God:

Negro folklore is not a thing of the past. . . . God and the Devil are paired, and are treated no more reverently than Rockefeller and Ford. . . . The angels and the apostles walk and talk like section hands. And through it all walks Jack, the greatest culture hero of the South; Jack beats them all—even the Devil, who is often smarter than God.

The Devil is next after Jack as a culture hero. He can outsmart everyone but Jack. God is absolutely no match for him. He is good-natured and full of humour.[54]

This image of God, who is almost like us, is also what emerges from many African folktales. Witness, for instance, "Le Boeuf de l'Araignée," a folktale of the Baoulé of the Ivory Coast. There God, like man, is capable of meanness. He is neither omnipotent nor omniscient. Thus the spider is able not only to dupe him but also to foil all his attempts to call him to order:

> Dieu, dieu, mais on peut le tromper
> Il suffit d'avoir du cran.
> Dieu, dieu, mais on peut le tromper
> Il est si vieux qu'il ne voit goutte.[55]

In another tale, "La Vache de dieu," he completely deceives God.[56] Its racial implications apart, the Ethiopian folktale "The Marriage of the Mouse" is also indicative of this humanness of God. The family of the white mouse visit God to ask him to let the white mouse marry from his family. But it turns out that God is weaker than the wind who is weaker than the mountain who is weaker than members of the mouse family.[57]

To sustain this picture of God who is Almighty and at the same time "one of us," images are drawn fresh from nature and from everyday life— vivid images which appeal directly to the senses:

> Then he stopped and looked and saw
> That the earth was hot and barren.
> So God stepped over the edge of the world
> And he spat out the seven seas—
> He batted his eyes, and the lightnings flashed—
> He clapped his hands, and the thunders rolled—
> And the waters above the earth came down,
> The cooling water came down.
> . . . .
> Up from the bed of the river
> God scooped the clay;
> And by the bank of the river
> He kneeled him down;
> . . . .

This Great God,
Like a mammy bending down over her baby,
Kneeled down in the dust
Toiling over a lump of clay
Till he shaped it in his own image.[58]

Although the poem is not written in dialect, it captures the basic sing-song rhythm of the Afro-American parlance, thanks to short simple words in short simple sentences that are often repeated either immediately or at a very short interval with only one or two words changed:

Then God walked around,
And God looked around
On all that he had made.
He looked at his sun,
And he looked at his moon,
And he looked at his little stars;
He looked on his world
With all its living things,
And God said: I'm lonely still.[59]

In his introduction to Talley's *Negro Folk Rhymes* Walter Clyde Curry refers to what he calls the Negro's histrionic ability and points out that the black man "takes delight in acting out in pantomime whatever he may be relating in song or story."[60] This is a good example of that ability at work, for one can visualize the preacher punctuating his sentences with gestures which, incidentally, George S. Schuyler, the assimilationist black satirist of the 1920s, ridiculed as "weekly gymnastics in the pulpits."[61]

In any event, the total effect is a refreshing originality unequalled by any of Johnson's nondialect poems whose recherché tone, on several occasions, engenders stilted inversions with their corollary bogged-down drag. Above all, it is a good example of the Negro's "expressing . . . essentially Negro feelings and standing squarely on [his] racial inheritance" long before the Negro renaissance became a fad among non-Negroes.[62]

This, however, is not to suggest that James Weldon Johnson was insulated from the non-Negro world and therefore absolutely beyond all non-Negro influence as he wrote *The Creation*. In fact, the poem is an objectification of a literary stand he took only after he had received encouragement from non-Negro elements, such as the advice of some white critics, like Floyd Dell who (castigating Johnson for his inability to "catch the essential rhythm of the Negro" in his *Fifty Years and Other Poems*) called upon him and other black writers to do for black literature what Synge had done for Irish literature[63] and the practical example given by the white writer, Ridgely Torrence, in his *Three Plays for a Negro Theatre* (1917).

Nonetheless, the status of *The Creation* as an expression of the Negro self is intact. It approaches its subject from within rather than from without. It captures, to use a phrase from Johnson's definition of what he was trying to do, "the movement, the abandon, the changes of tempo, and the characteristic syncopations of the primitive material."[64] Being Negro in the poem is neither a problem nor something to be pitied or cherished. It simply IS.

W. E. BURGHARDT DU BOIS

W. E. B. Du Bois's promotion of Pan-Africanism has already been noted. Although this was not literary, it was, together with the black leader's activities in sociopolitical and geo-economic arenas, a milestone in the development of the racial awareness to which the literary self-confidence of the 1920s owed much of its being. For Du Bois Africa was not a parasite on the back of the world, but the beginning of civilization, a continual source of knowledge and progress:

Always Africa is giving us something new or some metempsychosis of a world-old thing. On its black bosom arose one of the earliest, if not the earliest, of self-protecting civilizations, which grew so mightily that it still furnishes superlatives to thinking and speaking men. Out of its darker and more remote forest vastnesses came, if we may credit many recent scientists, the first welding of iron, and we know that agriculture and trade flourished there when Europe was a wilderness.[65]

Deeply committed to drawing the attention of the reading public to the plight of the black man or the "Negro problem," Du Bois's fiction and poetry belong to the Old Negro literature. Nevertheless, his endorsement of the Negro "sorrow songs" as pride-worthy and "the most beautiful expression of human experience born this side the seas,"[66] his

organization of the first major achievement of the Negro in the field of
drama: the pageant "Star of Ethiopia,"[67] his call for "a renaissance of
American Negro literature" as early as April 1920[68] were all symptoms of
the self-assertiveness which flourished in the black literature of the 1920s.
James Weldon Johnson refers to his book *The Souls of Black Folk* as "a
work, which, I think, has had a greater effect upon and within the Negro
race in America than any other single book published in this country
since *Uncle Tom's Cabin*. . . . I had been deeply moved by the book, and
was anxious to meet the author."[69] Claude McKay and Langston Hughes,
two of the most "racial" writers of the black renaissance, acknowledge
him as one of their sources of inspiration.[70] Although his attempt to
chart and direct the course of the New Negro literature failed, as we shall
see in the next chapter, his role in the development of the Negro's self-
assertive racial awareness was such that he could "say without boasting,"
as he actually did in 1940, "that in the period from 1910 to 1930 I was
a main factor in revolutionizing the attitude of the American Negro
toward caste. My stinging hammer blows made Negroes aware of themselves, confident of their possibilities and determined in self-assertion.
So much so that today common slogans among the Negro people are
taken bodily from the words of my mouth."[71]

CLAUDE MCKAY

Claude McKay's poetry, both in Jamaica and in the United States,
demonstrates the self-expressiveness of the Negro renaissance in its early
stages as well as the progressive acquisition of confidence by the Negro
artist in his expression of his Negro feelings, without bemoaning his fate
as an underdog in America, without apologizing to anyone.

In 1928 Marcus Garvey said:

Our race, within recent years, has developed a new group of writers who
have been prostituting their intelligence, under the direction of the white
man, to bring out and show up the worse traits of our people. . . . They
have been writing books, novels and poems, under the advice of white
publishers, to portray to the world the looseness, laxity and immorality
that are peculiar to our group. . . . [72]

The implication is clear: Claude McKay's treatment of his black material
was dictated by the white man's wishes. Garvey was, however, thinking

of the McKay of the period following the publication of *Nigger Heaven*, for by 1928, the New Negro writers—McKay with them—had supposedly prostituted their art for the delectation of the white man who also set its tone.

This is an exaggeration of what actually happened. It nevertheless underscores the importance of Claude McKay in any consideration of the self-expressiveness of the Harlem Renaissance. Like James Weldon Johnson, he helped not only to nurture the folk spirit which flowered, later, in the Harlem Renaissance but also to sustain the flowering. The seed of everything he wrote after 1926 was already in him and in his writing before that date. We have already indicated the relationship between *Home to Harlem* and *Nigger Heaven*. Suffice it, therefore, to consider the self-expressiveness of his poetry before the formal recognition of the gradually but steadily developing Negro self-affirmation that flourished as the Harlem Renaissance literature.

Claude McKay's first major achievement in literature was his poem on the exploits of a folk hero. George William Gordon, "one of the legendary heroes of Jamaica, that the peasants always talked about."[73] The poem was written in folk dialect, even though it was for a British Empire poetry competition which was organized by *T. P.'s Weekly* of London.[74] The extent to which it relied on and reflected the ordinary Jamaican people's feelings and sentiments can be inferred from the reception it got when it was published in Jamaica. According to McKay, "it created as much of a stir as *If We Must Die* created in the United States. It was denounced as inciting to riot by leading ministers of various denominations."[75] Like *If We Must Die* in the United States, it was a materialization of the black people's mind and, given the Negro's status of a colonized man, an object of both fear and admiration.

Equally expressive of Negro people are his two volumes of dialect poems: *Songs of Jamaica* (1912), and *Constab Ballads* (1912). Obviously a calculated attempt by a twenty-two-year-old Negro peasant to celebrate his people's life-styles, the volumes present all aspects of life and all attitudes of mind among the people of his native Jamaica: from courting a woman to scolding an innocent country girl who has turned fille de joie in the city; from killing a goat to preparing sugarcane for market; from the attitude of mind of an "assimilated" speaker who describes the conquering of "prejudice dat due / To obeah" as an urgent "tas' fe do";[76] to the superstition of the near-African[77] of *Little Jim* where a boy must not eat corn and alligator pear (*Persea gratissima*) because he is suffering from a wound.[78]

The tone of the speakers in these two volumes may sound bitter to the extent of seeming to convert the poems into futile protests against the invading oppressive and standardizing Western culture. But invariably the protest is only a format artistically designed to highlight the folksiness of the people and their ways of life. Consequently, what promises a great disaster often delivers only a non- or near-tragedy.

For example, the opening stanzas of *Quashie to Buccra* constitute a bitter indictment of white oppression.[79] But by the time we come to the middle of the third stanza the protest has lost its force; it has become so prideful a celebration of folk cultivation of potatoes that we cannot help smiling with the "buccra" at some point in the fifth stanza.[80] The last stanza is only one of the sides of the frame of protest that makes the speaker's description urgent and necessary. Even then, this side of the frame is almost completely destroyed by the last couplet which gives the impression that the farmer receives what his labor is worth:

> Yet still de hardship always melt away
> Wheneber it come roun' to reapin' day.[81]

This is also what happens in *Two-An'-Six*. In spite of the atmosphere of tragic doom that pervades it, the poem, after presenting the strenuous production of sugarcane from the plantation to the market, ends only in a nontragedy. The profit of "two-an'-six" will, apparently, keep "dem pickny belly full."[82]

The folk speaker in *King Banana*[83] (a poem which is a comment on McKay's own attachment to folkways and life-style as revealed in his unpublished "My Green Hills of Jamaica") celebrates the cultivation and the eating of bananas. His attack on the white method of cultivation only highlights his pride in the "old" way of production.

In *Pay-Day*[84] the speaker parades representatives of almost all his people whom he gathers "jes' outside de barrack gate":

> Faces of all types an' shade
> Brown an' yaller, black an' gray,
> Dey are waitin', waitin' dere,
> For it's policeman pay-day.

The problem or pretext, this time, is the nonarrival of the money for the payment of the policemen's salaries. As we wait for the solution we are offered an insight into the hopes and fears, likes and dislikes of the people. The facets are many and varied.

Through "mudder Mell," the mess-woman, the speaker reveals not only how policemen buy food on credit, but exactly what they eat. The presence of a "midnight girl" in the crowd offers the speaker the opportunity to express the typical peasant folk attitude towards prostitution:

> She has passed de bound'ry line,
>> An' her womanhood is sold;
> Wonder not then, as you gaze,
>> Dat, though young, she looks so bold.
>
> Once she roamed de country woods
>> Wid a free an' stainless soul,
> But she left for Kingston's slums,
>> Gave herself up to de wul':
> She has trod de downward course,
>> Never haltin' on de way . . .

We also see this folk attitude in *A Country Girl* where the speaker condemns Lelia's city life of prostitution as a sin.[85]

Through "de slimber ball-pan man," the "ice-cream lad," and Sue, the washerwoman, we see another aspect of the peasants' attitude towards the police—love and hate. They hate them because of their oppression; they like their payday because it promises some cash for their own pockets.

Then we have the formalities of the payment and the plight of the policemen themselves: the withholding of parts of their salaries for one reason or another, their payment of their debts, "to de miscellaneous crowd / Waitin' by de barrack-gate, / Chattin', chattin' very loud", and lastly, their spending what is left on "rum."

The protest of the apple-woman reveals not only the fact that food and sex are hawked on the streets of the city but also the oppression of the hypocritical policemen who punish their fellow criminals.[86] It must be pointed out, in passing, that the almost non-engagé yet sympathetic tone of the speaker in this poem and in *A Midnight Woman to the Bobby*,[87] anticipates Claude McKay's treatment of prostitution and of "low-down" characters in his United States writings—notably, the poems *Harlem*

Shadows and *The Harlem Dancer,* and the novels *Home to Harlem* and *Banjo.*

In any case, the total effect of this format of protest—a format in which comedy and tragedy are interwoven—is the emergence of folk who are stable in their most shaken moments, passive, yet aggressive and never giving up. Witness, for example, the aggressive stoicism of the folk speaker in *Hard Times,* [88] the sick and hungry wife in *Two-An' Six,* [89] the mother in that catalogue of folk wisdom, *Heart-Stirring* [90] as well as the indomitable spirit of the folk in *Whè Fe Do?* [91]—a spirit which has its being in the Negro's gift of laughter.

With regard to style per se, the dialect poems are essentially dramatic, thanks to the adoption, in some cases, of the call-and-response pattern. The language is authentic and, like any other black idiom, enriched with arresting metaphors, similes, and invectives. Witness, for example, the concreteness of the midnight woman's opening remark to the police officer:

> No palm me up, you dutty brute,
> You' jam mout' mash like ripe bread-fruit;
> You fas'n now, but wait lee ya,
> I'll see you grunt under de law. [92]

Or the impressive third stanza of *King Banana* where the sound of fire is likened to the chirps of a hundred thousand crickets:

> Out yonder see smoke a rise,
>   An' see de fire wicket;
> Deh go'p to heaben wid de nize
>   Of hundred t'ousan' cricket. [93]

Or still, the homespun analogy of the following stanza from *Heart-Stirring:*

> But sometime', chil', you jump from fryin'-pan
> 'Traight in a fire; an', try as you can,
> You caan' come out, but always wishin' den
> Fe get back in de fryin'-pan again. [94]

Walter Jekyll describes the language in which the dialect poems are written as "a feminine version of masculine English"—a refined, softened variant of English whose relation to Standard English is like "what Italian is to Latin."[95] It is an English dialect of ex-African: a synthesis of Standard English and some remembered phrases and words of African origin. Look at this stanza from *A Midnight Woman to the Bobby:*

> Say wha'? – 'res' me? – you go to hell!
> You t'ink Judge don't know unno well?
> You t'ink him gwin' go sentance me
> Widout a soul fe witness i'?[96]

where "unno" or "onnoo," defined in a footnote as "an African word, meaning 'you' collectively," sounds like an echo of the Igbo pronoun "unu" (the plural form of "*gi*") which also means " 'you' collectively."

Discussing the style of Claude McKay's United States poems, Eugenia Collier wonders "what kind of works McKay would have produced had he used for his models not the Western romantics but poet-musicians of Africa." She comes to the conclusion that "any question of what he might have done is merely academic."[97] In view of what we have noticed above about McKay's technique in his early poetry, that question is not as academic as it sounds. The dialect poems, both in theme and treatment, are strongly rooted in the soil of the Afro-Jamaican folk culture. They capture and transmit the moods and perceptions of the people through, to use Walter Jekyll's phrase, "the thoughts and feelings of a Jamaican of pure black blood."[98] Jean Wagner, probably, is aware of this when he affirms that the dialect poems were not written by McKay alone, "mais avec lui et à travers lui, le peuple ("but with him and through him, the people").[99]

Eugenia Collier, however, is absolutely right when she notices "the unmistakable stamp of blackness" superimposed upon the Western format of McKay's United States poems.[100] The leitmotiv of most of McKay's American poetry is the reaction of the black folk in a civilization that alienates them not only from nature, their most faithful companion, but also from the fulfillment of their real self. This accounts for the nostalgia of some of his speakers for the rural Jamaica. Witness, for example, the sentiment expressed in *After the Winter*[101] where the speaker longs for "the quiet hills" on "the summer isle" which he knows and remembers well. Despite (or probably, because of) the geographical out-of-reachness of the sunny village in the "nun-like hills,"[102] its features are so fresh in

the mind of the speaker, who has "embalmed [some of] the days, / Even
the sacred moments,"[103] he had spent in it, that anything that resembles
them, as in *The Tropics in New York,* sets him weeping.[104] And his tears,
like those of the biblical Prodigal Son, are not simply symptoms of pains
of hunger; they are also a manifestation of a subconscious feeling of
shame for the apparent error of choice.

With regard to the attitudes of McKay's speakers towards Africa, one
can only say that they are not immune from the ambivalence of the
Afro-American of the period towards the Dark Continent. Thus we have
conflicts between attitudes in separate poems as well as within single
poems. For example, in *Cudjoe Fresh from de Lecture,* we have the
following sympathetic, if crude, explanation of the black man's skin
color and his "backwardness" in spite of the fact that he and his white
brother had started their evolutionary race together from monkeys:

> No'cos say we get cuss mek fe we 'kin come so,
> But fe all t'ings come 'quare, same so it was to go;
> Seems our lan' [Africa] must ha' been berry low-do'n place,
> Mek it tek such long time in tu'ning out a race[105]

juxtaposed to the Phillis Wheatley-Jupiter Hammon perception of the
transportation of Africans in chains to America as a blessing in disguise:[106]

> I t'ink it do good, tek we from Africa
> An' lan' us in a blessed place as dis a ya.
> Talk 'bouten Africa, we would be deh till now,
> Maybe same half-naked—all day dribe buccra cow,
> An, tearin' 'rough de bush wid all de monkey dem,
> Wile an' uncibilise', an' neber comin' tame.[107]

We also have a clash of attitudes in the sonnet *Africa* where a pride-
and love-inspiring image of a mother of science, glory, and wealth, whose
passing away is lamented, in the quartrains suddenly succumbs in an unexpected clash with a shame- and hate-inspiring image of a prostitute
démodée erected in the last couplet.[108]

On the other hand, while *In Bondage* expresses, almost with no reser-
vation, a speaker's identification with what is unmistakably the image of
Africa,[109] and *Heritage* unequivocally praises the speaker's ancestry,[110]

a poem like *America*[111] eliminates all possibility of his ever belonging effectively to his mother Africa,[112] for the choice here is voluntary and conscious. The speaker is aware of the hostility of the "cultured hell" against him, and the doom awaiting the dehumanizing complex.

Nonetheless, Claude McKay's voice in the American poems, as in the dialect volumes, is expressive of black experience and of his racial self. This, however, does not mean that its beauty and firmness owe nothing to the non-Negro world. From 15 September 1889 (when he was born) to the spring of 1922 (when his *Harlem Shadows* was published) McKay, the protégé of Walter Jekyll, was not unaffected by non-Negro outside influences. McKay himself acknowledged his admiration for Byron, Shelley, Keats, Blake, Burns, Whitman, Heine, Baudelaire, Verlaine, and Rimbaud. He almost consciously tried to adopt what he thought was their manner of using their racial and social material.[113] Some of his Jamaican poems (especially *Old England*)[114] reveal what Wayne Cooper and Robert Reinders call "his thoroughly British orientation[115] — an orientation which he himself confirms when, describing the direction of his and other young Jamaicans' education as English, he confesses that "it was so successful that we really believed we were little black Britons."[116]

Walter Jekyll not only rescued him from the constabulary which he hated so much, he was also responsible for the publication of his first two volumes of poems, *Songs of Jamaica* and *Constab Ballads*. In fact, while his decision to write in dialect was not made for him by Walter Jekyll, it is doubtful whether he could have continued in that direction without the white man's encouragement. His account of his move in that direction and the encouragement that followed it is revealing. All his first poems, at least the ones he gave to Mr. Jekyll to read (after their accidental meeting) were in Standard English except for "one short one about an ass that was laden for the market, laden with native vegetables who had suddenly sat down in the middle of the road and wouldn't get up. Its owner was talking to it in the Jamaican dialect, telling it to get up." It was this that Walter Jekyll liked, and advised him to write more like it. "This is the real thing," the white English expatriate praised. "The Jamaican dialect has never been put into literary form except in my Annansy stories. Now is your chance as a native boy to put the Jamaican dialect into literary language. I am sure that your poems will sell."[117]

McKay, of course, started writing dialect poems mainly; and Mr. Jekyll called them "beautiful," apparently to the surprise of the young Jamaican poet.[118] Frank Harris later claimed that he could "trace [Jekyll's] influence" in McKay's poetry, although he did not say the type of influence those traces revealed.[119] Still later, McKay himself was to credit his "literary mentor," Walter Jekyll, with having impressed "the difference between propaganda and art . . . on my boyhood mind."[120]

As for his "primitive" temperament which he never tired of vaunting, it is possible that it would not have been as strong as it was if it had not been reinforced by Walter Jekyll's influence, just in the same way that his Bita Plant's appreciation of and identification with folk culture was strengthened by Squire Gensir in *Banana Bottom*.[121] Certainly, it is difficult to imagine the neat and well-dressed McKay appearing like his English friend who "never dressed up" and always justified his slovenliness by pointing out "that he did not leave the terror of dressing up in England to come to a tropical island like Jamaica to repeat the performance."[122] Yet the adolescent poet "was enchanted with his [Jekyll's] cottage, the wild tropical flowers that grew around it and the simple way he lived."[123] As a matter of fact, after visiting this lover of the "primitive" for the first time, he ran away from home to live in Kingston "because it was near to where Mr. Jekyll lived in the Blue Mountains."[124]

He was later to come under the influence of Frank Harris and Sinclair Lewis. In short, it is almost impossible to enumerate all the patterns of non-Negro influence on Claude McKay's works. The Jamaican poet-novelist knew and hobnobbed with too many whites!

Yet it will be very difficult to depreciate the self-expressiveness of those works because of their exposure to influences alien to the indigenous black cultural perceptions. In the first place, Claude McKay was also a part of that non-Negro world. As he points out, he was "a child" of the Western civilization, even though he "may have become so by the comparatively recent process of grafting." He was "as conscious of his new-world birthright as of [his] African origin".[125] He, too, was not immune from the new-world black man's double-consciousness, his attempt, on some occasions, to pose as a purely unstandardized man notwithstanding.[126] Secondly, he did not go into the friendships, like a calabash dipper to waterpot, empty and ready to be filled up with liquid attitudes. His association with Western culture did not mutate his basic conception of the world. There is some justification, therefore, for his coming down upon critics who failed to recognize his adult self as a continuation of his boyhood.[127]

JESSIE REDMON FAUSET

Although *There Is Confusion* (1924) marked the formal launching of
the New Negro literary movement, strictly speaking, the novel should be
classed with the writings of the "old" school of Negro authors. Jessie
Fauset believed that "many, many" whites "are keenly interested in
learning about the better class of colored people;"[128] she tried to satisfy
the need in her novel.

She is physically and emotionally an affiliate of "the better class";
she is, therefore, unable to maintain enough distance between herself
and her characters and their problems. She identifies with the members
of her class and from their side she judges the "worse class." Thus the
vices of the near-angel Joanna, who hates lazy people, speaks German,
and quotes Goethe fluently, are virtues, while the virtues of the underdog
Maggie, the daughter of a laundress, are vices.[129]

Like the objectives of most narrators of the "old" Negro fiction, the
intention of Jessie Fauset's omniscient narrator is unmistakably didactic.
She preaches, passes judgment, and gets her characters to prove verbally
that each of them is a person like every other person. Thus we have the
following claim by Joanna who "quote[s] from her extensive reading":
"Colored people . . . can do everything that anybody else can do. They've
already done it. Some one colored person somewhere in the world does
as good a job as anyone else,–perhaps a better one. They've been kings
and queens and poets and teachers and doctors and everything."[130]
Even Maggie takes the un-homme-pareil-aux-autres stances when she
claims that all "foreparents" of all Americans were "nobodies,"[131] while
Peter asserts his right to full American citizenship because his "folks
helped make her [America] what she is even if they were slaves."[132]
Above all, the "plea" thesis of the novel is hardly disguised; it comes
towards the end of the book. The speaker is Joanne: "Why, nothing in
the world is so hard to face as this problem of being colored in America.
See what it does to us. . . . Oh, it takes courage to fight against it . . . to
keep it from choking us, submerging us."[133]

Nonetheless, the much ado about heredity ("By their fruits ye shall
know them"[134]) aside, Joanna's motivation and the essence of her
success is the pervasive Negro folk motif–the "Barn" song which symbol-
izes her black identity. The weight it carries in the novel is significant
not only because it is an exaltation of the Negro folk culture, but also

because it makes the novel a fairly good example of an artistic creation
with an essentially non-Negro body and a Negro soul. It is, therefore,
a metaphor and denotes the persistent survival of the Negro folk spirit
in the synthesizing caldron of American culture. The format of the novel
is consciously, and not surprisingly, Victorian. All wrongdoers are punished: if they do not die, they are subjected to a penance. Nevertheless,
what keeps the heroine going, and the novel with her, is rooted in the
folk culture. The fame she seeks is to be built on her musical heritage.
That is her ambition, and it is well defined early in the novel:

"I'm going to be the one colored person who sings best in these days, and
I never, never, never mean to let color interfere with anything I *really*
want to do."

"I dance, too," she interrupted herself, "and I'll probably do that besides.
Not ordinary dancing, you know, but queer beautiful things that are
different from what we see round here.[135]

The "queer beautiful things" turn out to be Negro children's rhymes
accompanied with a mock fertility dance. This is an acceptance of a racial
Self. It is, certainly, ironic, given Joanna's highbrowism, but it is this
discovery (by an upper-class black woman) of herself in what she could
ordinarily have regarded as a low-down culture that justifies the joint
launching of the New Negro Literary Movement and *There is Confusion*.
    The New Negro literature, however, did not come into being on that
March night. It was not even the creation of *The Crisis* and *Opportunity*
literary contests and award dinners. It was an inevitable outgrowth of
black experience in America—the Afro-American arrival in the New
World and the attempt to clothe him in an alien self. Its development
was low-key, but unintermittent. Its emergence, apparently from
nowhere in the 1920s, was partly due to the fact that many blacks with
different degrees of talent were writing at the same time and partly due
to the perception of a convention-ridden audience which suddenly became aware of a possible safety valve.

NOTES

    1. Reprinted in *Opportunity* 3, no. 30 (June 1925): 187.
    2. James Weldon Johnson, *Black Manhattan* (1930; reprint ed.,
New York: Arno Press; *New York Times,* 1968), p. 260.

3. Such as Bishop Henry McNeal Turner's.

4. Reprinted in *Opportunity* 3, no. 30 (June 1925): 187.

5. Arthur Hornblow, *A History of the Theater in America: From Its Beginning to the Present Time* (Philadelphia: J. B. Lippincott Co., 1919), 2: 107.

6. Langston Hughes, "The Negro Artist and the Racial Mountain," *Nation* 122 (23 June 1926): 693.

7. *Opportunity* 2, no. 17 (May 1924): 143.

8. Charles Waddel Chesnutt, *The Conjure Woman* (1899; reprint ed., Ann Arbor: University of Michigan Press, 1969), pp. 9-10 (hereafter cited as CW).

9. Benjamin Brawley, *The Negro Genius* (New York: Dodd, Mead & Co., 1937), p. 148.

10. James Edwin Campbell, *Echoes From The Cabin and Elsewhere* (Chicago: Donohue & Henneberry, 1895), pp. 15-16 (hereafter cited as ECE).

11. Discussed in chapter 5, pp. 165.

12. James Weldon Johnson, *Along This Way* (1933; reprint ed., New York: Viking Press, 1968), 160-61; James Weldon Johnson, ed., *The Book of American Negro Poetry* (1931; reprint ed., New York: Harcourt, Brace & World, 1959), pp. 35-36; Lida Keck Wiggins, *The Life and Works of Paul Laurence Dunbar* (New York: Kraus Reprint, 1971), p. 109.

13. Paul Laurence Dunbar, *The Complete Poems of Paul Laurence Dunbar* (New York: Dodd, Mead & Co., 1913), p. 191 (hereafter cited as DCP).

14. Johnson, *Along This Way*, p. 161.

15. Quoted in Wiggins, *Life and Works*, p. 109.

16. Ibid., p. 47.

17. Quoted in Sterling Brown, *Negro Poetry and Drama & The Negro in American Fiction* (1937; reprint ed., New York: Atheneum, 1969), 1: 21. The songs were variously known as "fiddle-sings," "corn-songs," and "jig-tunes". See ibid.

18. Johnson, *Book of American Negro Poetry*, p. 41.

19. W. D. Howells, "Life and Letters," *Harper's Weekly* (27 June 1896): 630.

20. In *The New Negro*, Alain Locke (1925; reprint ed., New York: Atheneum, 1969).

21. Johnson, *Along This Way*, p. 159. Johnson's emphasis.

22. He learned much from his mother, who had been a slave.

23. *See* note 17.

24. Ibid., p. 22.

25. In *The New Negro*, p. 144.

26. *The Fanatics* (New York: Dodd, Mead, 1901); *The Love of Landry* (New York: Dodd, Mead, 1900); *The Uncalled* (New York: Dodd, Mead, 1898).

27. Like his characters, Dunbar was never an admirer of the city and its ways.

28. Hattie's decision to throw Joe out is more justifiable than Lasca's since Joe is an incurable drunkard.

29. Byron is a college graduate. Unlike Joe, he is not a drunkard. Joe, unlike Byron, revenges himself on Hattie Sterling by killing her.

30. See *Emancipation* where the speaker says among other things that "E'en in our slav'ry we can trace the kindly hand of God, / That took us from our sunny land and from our native sod, / Where, clad in Nature's simple garb, man roamed a savage wild, / Untamed his passions; half a man half a savage child." Daniel Webster Davis, *'Weh Down Souf and Other Poems* (Cleveland: Helman-Taylor Co., 1897), pp. 28-29 (hereafter cited as WDS).

31. *See De Nigger's Got to Go,* ibid., pp. 48-52; *Exposition Ode,* ibid., pp. 65-71.

32. Reprinted as the appendix in Davis, *'Weh Down Souf,* pp. 129-33.

33. Ibid., p. 129.

34. Reprinted in *Opportunity* 3, no. 30 (June 1925): 187.

35. *See* the author's Foreword. John Wesley Holloway, *From the Desert* (New York: Neale Publishing Co., 1919) (hereafter cited as HFD).

36. Joseph S. Cotter, *Caleb, the Degenerate: A Play in Four Acts* (Louisville: Bradley & Gilbert Co., 1903), p. 4.

37. Joseph S. Cotter, *Negro Tales* (New York: Cosmopolitan Press, 1912), pp. 35-49.

38. Joseph S. Cotter, *A White Song and a Black One* (Louisville: Bradley & Gilbert Co., 1909), p. 47 (hereafter cited as CWS).

39. Waverley Turner Carmichael, *From the Heart of a Folk: A Book of Songs* (Boston: Cornhill Co., 1918) (hereafter cited as CHF).

40. This is possibly the name of a dance.

41. Raymond Garfield Dandridge, *The Poet and Other Poems* (Cincinnati: Raymond G. Dandridge, 1920), p. 47 (hereafter cited as DP).

42. *See* Elphinstone Dayrell, *Folk Stories from Southern Nigeria, West Africa* (1910; reprint ed., New York: Negro Universities Press, 1969), pp. 38-41.

43. Claude McKay, *Selected Poems of Claude McKay* (New York: Harcourt, Brace & World, 1953), p. 61.

44. James Weldon Johnson, *The Autobiography of an Ex-Coloured Man* (1912, 1927; reprint ed., New York: Hill and Wang, 1960), p. 190 (hereafter cited as JA).

45. *See* Thomas W. Talley, *Negro Folk Rhymes: Wise and Otherwise* (New York: Macmillan, 1922), p. 11.

46. Robert A. Bone, *The Negro Novel in America,* rev. ed. (New Haven: Yale University Press, 1965), p. 46.

47. Ibid., p. 47.

48. Talley, *Negro Folk Rhymes,* pp. 248-49.

49. Carl Van Vechten, "Introduction to Mr. Knopf's New Edition" in James Weldon Johnson, *The Autobiography of an Ex-Coloured Man* (New York: Alfred A. Knopf, 1927), p. v.

50. Johnson to Van Vechten, 21 May 1932; Van Vechten to Johnson, 30 May 1932, Beinecke Rare Book and Manuscript Library, Yale University, New Haven, Conn.

51. James Weldon Johnson, *Fifty Years and Other Poems* (1917; reprint ed., Boston: Cornhill Publishing Co., 1921), p. 77.

52. Zora Neale Hurston, "Characteristics of Negro Expression" in Nathan Irvin Huggins, ed., *Voices from the Harlem Renaissance* (New York: Oxford University Press, 1976).

53. *See* Harold Courlander, *A Treasury of African Folklore* (New York: Crown Publishers, 1975), pp. 184-205; Janheinz Jahn, *Muntu: An Outline of the New African Culture* (New York: Grove Press, 1961), p. 68.

54. Hurston in *Voices from the Harlem Renaissance,* p. 229.

55. Bernard B. Dadié, *Le Pagne Noir: Contes Africains* (Paris: Présence Africaine, 1955), p. 59.

56. Ibid., pp. 107-15.

57. Harold Courlander and Wolf Leslau, *The Fire on the Mountain and Other Ethiopian Stories* (New York: Holt, Rinehart and Winston, 1950), pp. 89-92.

58. James Weldon Johnson, *God's Trombones* (1927; reprint ed., New York: Viking Press, 1969), pp. 18, 20.

59. Ibid., p. 19.

60. Talley, *Negro Folk Rhymes,* p. ix.

61. George S. Schuyler, "Note on Negro Art," *Messenger* 8, no. 4 (April 1926): 113.

62. Reprinted in *Opportunity* 3, no. 30 (June 1925), 187.

63. *The Liberator* 1 (1918): 33, cited in Eugene Levy, *James Weldon Johnson: Black Leader Black Voice* (Chicago: University of Chicago Press, 1973), p. 304.

64. Johnson, *Along This Way,* p. 336.

65. W. E. B. Du Bois, *Darkwater: Voices from Within the Veil* (1920; reprint ed. New York: Schocken Books, 1969), p. 56.

66. Du Bois, "Of the Sorrow Songs," *The Souls of Black Folk* (1903;

reprint ed., New York: Washington Square Press, 1970), p. 206.

67. Produced in New York in 1913, Washington 1915, Philadelphia 1916, Hollywood Bowl 1925. *See* W. E. B. Du Bois, *Dusk of Dawn: An Essay Toward an Autobiography of a Race Concept* (1940; reprint ed., New York: Schocken Books, 1968), pp. 272-74.

68. *The Crisis* 19, no. 6 (April 1920): 299.

69. Johnson, *Along This Way*, p. 203.

70. Claude McKay, *A Long Way from Home* (1937; reprint ed., New York: Harcourt, Brace & World, 1970), p. 110; Langston Hughes, *The Big Sea: An Autobiography* (New York: Hill and Wang, 1940), p. 93. For Du Bois's promotion of the New Negro movement through *The Crisis* see chapter 3 of this study.

71. Du Bois, *Dusk of Dawn*, p. 303.

72. Marcus Garvey, "*Home to Harlem:* An Insult to Race," *Negro World*, 29 September 1928.

73. Claude McKay, "My Green Hills of Jamaica," typescript, dated 1946, Claude McKay Papers, Schomburg Collection, New York Public Library, New York p. 3.

74. Ibid.

75. Ibid.

76. Claude McKay, *Whè Fe Do? Songs of Jamaica* (Kingston, Jamaica: Aston W. Gardner, 1912), p. 28.

77. Talley has suggested that "the superstitions of the Negro Rhymes are possibly only fossils left in one way or another by ancient native African worship." Talley, *Negro Folk Rhymes*, p. 324.

78. McKay, *Little Jim, Songs of Jamaica*, p. 23.

79. *Quashie to Buccra*, ibid., p. 13.

80. Ibid., p. 14.

81. Ibid.

82. Ibid., pp. 90-91.

83. Ibid., pp. 30-31.

84. In Claude McKay, *Constab Ballads* (London: Watts & Co., 1912), pp. 52-56.

85. *Songs of Jamaica*, pp. 119-21.

86. *The Apple-Woman's Complaint, Constab Ballads*, pp. 57-58.

87. *Songs of Jamaica*, pp. 74-76.

88. Ibid., p. 54.

89. Ibid., p. 90.

90. Ibid., p. 71.

91. Ibid., p. 29.

92. *A Midnight Woman to the Bobby*, ibid., p. 74.

93. *King Banana*, ibid., p. 30.

94. Ibid., p. 70.

95. In the preface, ibid., p. 5.

96. Ibid., p. 76.

97. Eugenia Collier, *The Four-Way Dilemma of Claude McKay*, CAAS Occasional Paper no. 6, Atlanta University, Atlanta, Ga. p. 12, n.d.

98. Preface, *Songs of Jamaica*, p. 9.

99. Jean Wagner, *Les Poétes noirs des Etats-Unis* (Paris: Nouveaux Horizons, 1965), p. 129.

100. Collier, *Four-Way Dilemma*, p. 3.

101. In Claude McKay, *Harlem Shadows* (New York: Harcourt, Brace and Co., 1922), p. 20.

102. Ibid., p. 8.

103. Ibid., p. 10.

104. Ibid., p. 8.

105. *Songs of Jamaica*, p. 56.

106. Phillis Wheatley, "To the University of Cambridge, in New England" in Benjamin Brawley, ed., *Early Negro American Writers* (1935; reprint ed. New York: Dover Publications, 1970), p. 36. Like Phyllis Wheatley (1753-1784), Jupiter Hammon, a Negro slave versifier (c. 1730-1800) saw slavery as a blessing in disguise.

107. *Songs of Jamaica*, p. 57.

108. *Harlem Shadows*, p. 35.

109. Ibid., p. 28.

110. Ibid., p. 30.

111. Ibid., p. 6.

112. *To the White Fiends, Selected Poems of Claude McKay* (New York: Harcourt, Brace & World, 1953), p. 38.

113. McKay, *A Long Way from Home*, p. 28.

114. *Songs of Jamaica*, pp. 63-65.

115. Wayne Cooper and Robert C. Reinders, "Claude McKay in England, 1920," *New Beacon Reviews* (Collection One), ed. John LaRose (London: New Beacon Books, 1968), p. 3.

116. Wayne F. Cooper, ed., *The Passion of Claude McKay* (New York: Schocken Books, 1973), p. 3.

117. McKay, "My Green Hills of Jamaica," p. 64.

118. Ibid., p. 67.

119. McKay, *A Long Way from Home*, p. 18.

120. Cooper, *The Passion of Claude McKay*, p. 95.

121. Claude McKay, *Banana Bottom* (New York: Harper & Bros., 1933).

122. McKay, "My Green Hills of Jamaica," p. 66.

123. Ibid., p. 65.

124. Ibid., p. 66.

125. Cooper, *The Passion of Claude McKay,* p. 137.

126. See, for example, McKay's preface to *Constab Ballads,* p. 7 and his discussion of housing and transportation in Jamaica, "My Green Hills of Jamaica," p. 15. *See also* his letter to Walter White from Morocco, in which he spoke of having fled from Montparnasse because of "its artificial life" and with regard to his attachment to his negritude said: ". . . although I am very free and advanced in ideas and deeds there are certain racial facts that I cannot and do not want to get away from. I may have and respect 'white' friends and wellwishers, some of them even closer to me than some 'colored' friends, but many of these 'whites' respect and admire me for what I stand for in principle and I know that my social world in frame and outlook is different from the 'white' man's." McKay to White, 1 September 1931, Beinecke Rare Book and Manuscript Library, Yale University, New Haven, Conn.

127. Cooper, *The Passion of Claude McKay,* p. 135.

128. Jessie Fauset's contribution to the symposium "The Negro in Art: How Shall He Be Portrayed," *The Crisis* 32, no. 2 (June 1926): 72.

129. Jessie Redmon Fauset, *There Is Confusion* (1924; reprint ed., New York: AMS Press, 1974), pp. 21, 55, 166.

130. Ibid., p. 45.

131. Ibid., pp. 212-13.

132. Ibid., p. 207.

133. Ibid., p. 283.

134. Ibid., p. 24. The emphasis on heredity is, probably, inevitable. The novel is set in Philadelphia whose blacks were very ancestry-conscious. Witness Alain Locke's remarks on the obsession: "Philadelphia is the shrine of the Old Negro. More even than in Charleston or New Orleans, Baltimore or Boston, what there is of the tradition of breeding and respectability in the race lingers in the old Negro families of the city that was Tory before it was Quaker. Its faded daguerotypes stare stiffly down at all newcomers, including the New Negro (who we admit, is an upstart)—and ask, 'who was your grandfather?' and failing a ready answer—'who freed you?' " Alain Locke, "Hail Philadelphia," *Black Opals* 1, no. 1 (Spring 1927): 3.

135. Fauset, *There Is Confusion,* p. 45.

BLACK JOURNALS AND THE
PROMOTION OF THE NEW
NEGRO LITERATURE

3

OPPORTUNITY*

The first black magazine that comes to mind when one thinks of the promotion of the New Negro movement of the 1920s is *Opportunity: Journal of Negro Life.* Founded in January 1923 by the National Urban League, it came into being at a time when there were, as Dr. Charles S. Johnson puts it, many "young Negro writers and scholars whose work was not acceptable to other established media because it could not be believed to be of standard quality despite the superior quality of much of it."[1] Thus, although the magazine was not established specifically for the propagation of black literature, it soon felt the necessity for "a revolution and a revelation sufficient in intensity to disturb the age-old customary cynicisms."[2] It intensified the campaign for the development of black literature and culture by arousing the spirit of competition in other black magazines interested in the promotion. Recognizing "a most amazing change in the public mind on the question of the Negro . . . a healthy hunger for more information—a demand for a new interpretation of characters long and admittedly misunderstood,"[3] it went beyond the "revelation" of other Negro "uplift" magazines and newspapers to aid young black writers who, according to it, "had dragged themselves out of the deadening slough of the race's historical inferiority complex, and . . . are leaving to the old school its labored lamentations and protests, read only by those who agree with them, and are writing about life."[4] For instance, its editor, Charles S. Johnson, addressed letters of encouragement to young promising writers like Zora Neale Hurston who, in her own words, "came to New York through *Opportunity,* and through

*An earlier version of the first part of this chapter appeared in *Phylon* of March 1979.

Opportunity to Barnard."[5] On 21 March 1924 Johnson arranged a "coming-out party" for the new group of writers.[6]

The list of guests present at the party reads like a miniature *Literary
Market Place:* Horace Liveright, publisher; Carl Van Doren, editor of the
Century; Paul Kellogg, editor of the *Survey;* Devere Allen, editor of *The
World Tomorrow;* Freda Kirchwey and Evans Clark of the *Nation;* Mr.
and Mrs. Frederick L. Allen of Harper Brothers; Louis Weitzenkorn of
the *New York World.* There were messages of goodwill from Oswald
Garrison Villard, editor of the *Nation;* Herbert Bayard Swope, editor of
the *New York World;* George W. Ochs Oakes, editor of *Current History.*
Also represented were established writers (both white and black) including Alain Locke who had demonstrated his interest in the new writers
when he looked for Langston Hughes in New York and France after
reading the young author's poems in *The Crisis.*[7] He was rightly "selected
to act as Master of Ceremonies and to interpret the new currents manifest in the literature of this younger school."[8]

The results of the party and the publicity given to it were immediate.
The Writers' Guild was established—at least in name. Its membership
included Countée Cullen, Eric Walrond, Langston Hughes, Jessie Fauset,
Gwendolyn Bennett, Harold Jackman, Regina Anderson, and a few
others. Frederick Allen of *Harper's* offered to publish Countée Cullen's
poems. The *Survey Graphic* which, in the words of W. E. B. Du Bois,
"has always been traditionally afraid of the Negro problem and has
usually touched it either not at all or gingerly,"[9] volunteered to bring
out a special Harlem number "which will express the progressive spirit
of contemporary Negro life in its new aspects and settings, using Harlem
as a stage."[10] To illustrate the issue, it announced "a Prize of *Fifty Dollars*
for the best original interpretation in painting, sculpture, etching, or
black and white drawings."[11] According to Charles S. Johnson, "this
fumbling idea lead [sic] to the standard volume of the period, the *New
Negro.*"[12] In November 1924 Countée Cullen saw four of his poems published simultaneously in four leading magazines: *Youth Sings a Song of
Rosebuds* in *Bookman; Fruit of the Flower* in *Harper's* ("a magazine,"
in the words of *The Crisis,* "whose relation to black folks resembles that
of the Devil to Holy Water"[13]); *Yet Do I Marvel* in *Century Magazine*
and *The Shroud of Color* in *American Mercury.* Mrs. Henry G. Leach's
"conviction of the capacity" of the Negro was heightened. She gave
Opportunity five hundred dollars for a literary contest.[14]

This last result enabled the magazine to sustain the flame of "revolution" which it had kindled. To judge the entries, which were to deal mainly with various aspects of the Negro life, it invited such important men and women of letters as John Farrar, editor of the *Bookman;* Carl Van Doren, editor of *Century Magazine;* Clement Wood, author; John Macy, author and editor; Montgomery Gregory, scholar; Robert Hobart Davis, dramatist and editor of *Munsey's;* Dorothy Scarborough, author, book reviewer and critic; Zona Gale, author; Edna Worthley Underwood, author and linguist; Blanche Colton Williams, author and editor.[15] For the awards it gave a dinner, the importance of which is best felt in the *New York Herald-Tribune's* characterization of it: A novel sight, that dinner—white critics, whom "everybody" knows, "Negro writers, whom "nobody" knew—meeting on common ground."[16]

The results, therefore, were as impressive as those of the "coming-out party." John Matheus's "Fog" (which won the first prize in the short story division) was recommended to the O. Henry Memorial Prize committee by Dr. Blanche Colton Williams.[17] Langston Hughes's poem, *The Weary Blues,* which had won the first prize in the poetry section of the contest, appeared in the August number of *Forum,*[18] accompanied by an illustration by Winold Reiss, the famous Bavarian artist. Such major journals as the *Nation* and *Vanity Fair* solicited more poems from him than Hughes could write.[19] His first book of poems came out a few months later, and he was invited from various parts of the country, by both black and white groups, to read his poetry.[20] Jazz poems poured in from all parts of the country for his comments; he could not help wondering whether he had "started a new school [of writing] or something."[21] Above all, Casper Holstein, a New York Negro merchant, "bursting with joy and appreciation for what [the editor of *Opportunity* had] so nobly and unselfishly undertaken," gave Charles S. Johnson a check for five hundred dollars to enable him to conduct another literary prize contest which he was sure would "prove just as productive of desirous results as this one has undoubtedly proven to be."[22] He later doubled his original gift, while the Federation of Colored Women's Clubs offered prizes for constructive journalism.[23] Thus, the revolutionary promotion continued. The awards were increased, and the departments extended to include musical composition, constructive journalism, and the Alexander Pushkin Poetry Prize. After the contest, Edward J. O'Brien chose Eugene Gordon's "Rootbound" (which had won a prize of fifteen dollars in the contest) for his

Best Short Stories of 1927. "This means," as Gwendolyn Bennett quickly and proudly pointed out, "that 'Rootbound,' winner of the fourth prize in the short story division . . . has been designated . . . as one of the stories printed in 1926 which . . . may fairly claim a position in American literature." Blanche Colton Williams also picked "Rootbound," along with Zora Neale Hurston's "Muttsy" and Dorothy West's "Typewriter" (two stories which had won the second prize in the contest) in her *O. Henry Memorial Award Volume of Short Stories for 1926.* [24] Casper Holstein once again volunteered to sponsor the 1927 competition which, incidentally, was to be the last of the first series of *Opportunity*'s literary contests.

Perhaps the greatest achievement of the last two contests (those of 1926 and 1927) was the launching of Arna Bontemps, poet, novelist, scholar, and one of the most authoritative chroniclers of the Harlem Renaissance. Bontemps had already been published by *The Crisis* before his association with *Opportunity*, [25] but it was his winning of the Alexander Pushkin Prize in 1926 and 1927 that rolled his popularity beyond the Negro world and its immediate white friends. His life, he acknowledged shortly before his death in 1973, "has never been the same since." [26] There are many other young black writers who could say the same thing about their association with *Opportunity*. *Opportunity* itself achieved its aim to some extent. It went in for "a revolution and a revelation sufficient in intensity to disturb the age-old customary cynicisms," and succeeded in making the work of many black writers "acceptable to other established media." [27]

Whether the tone of this achievement was worth the energy expended is still an open question. Its answer depends on one's attitude towards the whole phenomenon: Harlem Renaissance. One thing, however, is certain: it was not immune from the period's patterns of attitudes towards the black man as an artist and as a subject matter. While many white men and women of letters were loud in their praise of the work *Opportunity* was doing, Benjamin Brawley and several other articulate blacks were dissatisfied with the literature it sponsored. For instance, while Howard W. Odum found, in the literary trend, a commendable "new self-discovery on the part of the Negro," [28] Wallace Thurman, who was in fact one of the key figures of the New Negro movement, maintained that "the results of the renaissance have been sad rather than satisfactory, in that critical standards have been ignored, and the measure of achieve-

ment has been racial rather than literary."[29] While Carl Van Vechten,
in order to show his appreciation of its "editorship and at the same time
. . . encourage young writers to continue to give their best to *Opportunity,* "[30] offered a prize of two hundred dollars for the best signed contribution published in the magazine, critics like Thomas Millard Henry
challenged the award of the first prize for poetry to Langston Hughes in
the 1925 contest: "The *story* called "The Weary Blues" is *not* poetry;
it is a *little story* of action and life . . . the kind of stuff that Alexander
Pope called *prose* run mad. . . . Perhaps it is not bad to call such stuff
doggerel. It is a product of the inferiority complex."[31] Eugene F. Gordon
saw the award as a "Nordic" conspiracy "which required Negroid poetry
from Negroes,"[32] thus driving *Opportunity* to a desperate explanation of
how *The Weary Blues* had earned the prize:

The contest placed no restriction as to theme on poetry. The poems were
rated by the most accurate method known, the votes of the judges being
arranged by a mathematical formula. It so happened that the judge giving
"The Weary Blues" the highest rating was a Negro, whose record as a
poet, as well as a calm student of social affairs, and leader in a quite positive movement of race improvement is wholly beyond question.[33]

Countée Cullen, in his column "The Dark Tower," almost suggested
that Arna Bontemps's poem, *The Return,* did not merit the Alexander
Pushkin Poetry Prize which it had received[34]—possibly because of its
amateurishness as revealed in its faulty rhymes and clumsy syntax. Witness the first stanza where almost all the clauses dangle; and it is not clear
what the word "leaves" is supposed to rhyme with:

Once more, listening to the wind and rain,
Once more, you and I, and above the hurting sound
Of these comes back the throbbing of remembered rain,
Treasured rain falling on dark ground.
Once more, huddling birds upon the leaves
And summer trembling on a withered vine.
And once more, returning out of pain,
The friendly ghost that was your love and mine.[35]

In any case, Cullen was at this time the assistant editor of *Opportunity,*
and his apparent dissatisfaction with the success of the magazine seems

to reflect that of the magazine itself. It had repeatedly affirmed its belief in the Negro creative genius. Many a person who could read and wield the pen had interpreted this belief as an invitation to submit anything in words and on paper. Consequently, *Opportunity*'s offices were flooded with what it described as "grotesqueries." It progressively lost its temper. It warned: "The encouragement that they [the new writers] are receiving from established writers is a gracious and valuable aid . . . but this does not mean that simply because they are Negroes they can sing spirituals or write stories and verse or even dance *instinctively.*"[36]

Its courage failed it; it suspended the literary contests to "allow for our aspiring writers a margin for experimentation with more than one manuscript, in the search for the most effective channels of expression."[37] The contests were not revived until 1931 and then *Opportunity* was alarmed. The manuscripts it received, in its own words, "show a marked inclination to follow the formalism of the English essayists of the eighteenth century or to slavishly follow the style of the literary elect of the nineteenth century. As a result the writing lacks spontaneity and vigor or what is popularly called 'punch.' "[38]

The young writers had moved from writing "instinctively" to turning out things that lacked "spontaneity." *Opportunity* had lost its hold on them; and as if that was not bad enough for the black literature which it was trying to revolutionize, it seemed to have lost its own sense of direction. In one breath it condemned the apparent triumph of the Brawley school, and in the same breath it discussed the new writing as a Benjamin Brawley would:

We do not mean that OPPORTUNITY merely wishes to stimulate the adoption of those cheap devices of the new realism which currently pass for literature, nor the bizarre technique of some of the so-called modernists.[39]

Another matter is that of the jerky, hectic, incoherent composition that some people are cultivating today, but that is nothing more than the working of the bolshevistic spirit in literature. With some people the sentence has lost its integrity altogether, and writing is nothing more than a succession of coarse suggestive phrases.[40]

Yet, on the whole, the achievement of *Opportunity* was intact. The vacillation and the apparent indecision of the journal as to what it really wanted notwithstanding, it compelled some other black publications, through its successes, to adopt its revolutionary stance.

THE CRISIS

Founded in November 1910 as an organ of the NAACP, *The Crisis: a Record of the Darker Races* was already in existence, before the establishment of *Opportunity*, as a step forward in "the weary struggle of the Negro population for status through self-improvement and recognition, aided by their friends."[41] Although its main function was not publication of creative writing, it provided an outlet for young black writers, like Langston Hughes,[42] who for one reason or another had not been published by "other established media." Thus by April 1920 it could boast that "it [had] helped to discover the poetry of Roscoe Jamison, Georgia Johnson, Fenton Johnson, Lucian Watkins, and Otto Bohanan; and the prose of Jessie Fauset and Mary Effie Lee."[43]

Although not all these readily come to mind when one thinks of the New Negro writers, each of them made valuable contributions to the literary awakening and some of them, in a way, belonged to the movement. Fenton Johnson, for instance, anticipated not only the attempt to convert the demeaning traits attributed to the Negro into positive values but also the adoption, by some New Negro writers, of the whitmanesque departure from the conventional forms of poetry. Even in tone some of his poems, like *Tired* and *The Scarlet Woman*,[44] can bear comparison with some of the representative poems of the renaissance. Although Lucian Watkins died in 1921—before the formal launching of the New Negro—at least one of his poems, *Star of Ethiopia*, belongs with the New Negro writings.[45] While her novels, poems, and short stories belong to the old school, Jessie Fauset, as literary editor of *The Crisis*, was a source of inspiration and encouragement to the budding writers.[46] Langston Hughes describes her, Charles S. Johnson, and Alain Locke as "the three people who midwifed the so-called New Negro literature into being."[47]

In any event, *The Crisis* was a major force in the black literary awakening. It endorsed its parent organization, the NAACP's, encouragement of Afro-Americans in all fields of activity (including literature) by its annual award of the Spingarn medal, as well as its occasional parties and conferences at which black writers and important white artists and publishers often met. Countée Cullen and Langston Hughes, for instance, were

introduced to Carl Van Vechten by Walter White at one of these parties.[48]
In a 1920 editorial *The Crisis* called to the attention of its black readers
the existence of enough material for "a renaissance of American Negro
literature."[49] In December 1922 it organized a short story competition
on behalf of the Delta Omega Chapter of Alpha Kappa Alpha Sorority
at Virginia Union University.[50] Above all, after the establishment of
Opportunity in 1923, it refused, so to speak, to yield to that organ of
the National Urban League in the promotion of the renaissance.

Thus, in May 1924, *Opportunity* devoted an entire issue to one aspect
of the New Negro movement: African art. In June of that same year,
The Crisis called for manuscripts for its August issue which, according
to the magazine, "will be . . . devoted this year exclusively to the products
and achievements of the younger group of Negro writers."[51] In August
1924 *Opportunity* announced its first literary contest. In September *The
Crisis* hinted at its own contest and formally announced it in October.[52]
Opportunity announced its winning contestants at a special meeting in
New York on the evening of 1 May 1925.[53] *The Crisis* contest did not
coincide with *Opportunity's* only because W. E. B. Du Bois wanted, as he
put it, "to give young authors every chance . . . so that there will be no
unnecessary rivalry and all can have full benefit of this great generosity
and foresight on the part of friends."[54] At any rate, it extended its own
field of contest to include illustration and song.[55] It invited such an international figure as René Maran, the winner of the 1921 Prix Goncourt
(whom its literary editor, Jessie Fauset, must have met personally in
Paris in October 1924[56]), to be one of its judges. Among other judges
were H. G. Wells, Sinclair Lewis, Charles Waddell Chesnutt, Mary White
Ovington, J. E. Spingarn, Benjamin Brawley, William Stanley Braithwaite,
and Winold Reiss.[57]

The Crisis increased its awards from $600 in 1925 to $2,035 in 1927.[58]
In 1928 it expanded the Charles Waddell Chesnutt honoraria which it had
established the year before, making them monthly awards: "prizes of
$50 each month, $600 for a year."[59] In the same year, and thanks to
eight colored banks and five colored insurance societies, it introduced
"economic prizes" for "short stories, essays or cartoons, which will
illustrate or study or tell the story of the economic development of the
Negro: of Negroes as laborers, as farmers, as skilled workers, as business
men, in all the different lines of business."[60] As if its supporters, too,
were determined to see that it was not beaten by *Opportunity* in their

common struggle to promote the literary movement, one of them, Mrs.
E. R. Matthews, established a yearly award of $1,000 to be known as the
Du Bois Literary Prize in honor of its famous editor.[61] It was in the same
spirit that Amy E. Spingarn had started the current round of literary
awards when she donated $300 "with the hope of assisting *The Crisis*"
to promote "the contribution of the American Negro to American art
and literature."[62]

It launched the KRIGWA,[63] a workshop by which the magazine tried
its best to help and guide young writers and artists. For instance, after
the 1925 contest, the guild undertook to assist those "who did not win
prizes this time but who may later; and also those who may never win
but who will also wish to study and help the development of beauty in
the souls of black folk."[64] It addressed letters to "the five hundred and
ninety-nine [persons] who tried and received neither word nor prize"
telling them what it thought of their "effort and what Krigwa advises
and how the advice may best be followed."[65] By June 1926 the guild
had established about six branches in different parts of the country.
Some of these offered plays, especially the Krigwa Players of New York
who, establishing a Little Negro Theatre at the 135th branch of the New
York Public Library, gave three plays in three performances in May
1926.[66] Its "four fundamental principles" further demonstrate the effort
of *The Crisis* to fix the tone of the New Negro production, and strengthen
the self-possessedness and self-expressiveness of the movement as a whole:

The plays of a real Negro theatre must be: 1. *About us.* That is, they must
have plots which reveal Negro life as it is. 2. *By us.* That is, they must be
written by Negro authors who understand from birth and continual association just what it means to be a Negro today. 3. *For us.* That is, the
theatre must be supported and sustained by their entertainment and
approval. 4. *Near us.* The theatre must be in a Negro neighborhood near
the mass of ordinary Negro people.[67]

In 1927 it formed the Krigwa Academy made up of "all persons who
have received two prizes, first and second, in any one class of entries in
Crisis contests." Members of the academy were apparently going to serve
as judges in future *Crisis* contests.[68]

Still acting in its own name, *The Crisis* instituted a symposium "The
Negro in Art: How Shall He Be Portrayed (?)" to make sure the renais-

sance was not "entirely off on the wrong foot."[69] Participants included important publishers and writers. Their responses reflect their sociopolitical attitudes and justify their individual literary practices. The following summaries and excerpts constitute an index of the bases of the patterns of reaction to the New Negro literature.[70]

Carl Van Vechten: To capture what is genuinely negroid in the Afro-American, the artist should focus on the unpolished black American.

H. L. Mencken: "The artist . . . should be free to depict things exactly as he sees them." Even exaggerations like those in Cohen's stories "always keep some sort of contact with the truth." Scientific criteria should not be applied to works of art.

DuBose Heyward: The portrayal of the Negro in art should not have propaganda as its main aim. If a moral or a lesson should be present in any work of art it should be subordinated to the artistic aim.

Mary W. Ovington: Stereotypes and propaganda in art should be condemned. "What publishers, at least the best, want today is art, not propaganda. They don't want to know what the writer thinks on the Negro question, they want to know about Negroes." Happily "white artists are beginning to see the true Negro and colored writers are beginning to drop their propaganda and are painting reality."

Langston Hughes: "You [Du Bois] write about the intelligent Negroes; Fisher about the unintelligent. Both of you are right."

J. E. Spingarn: Presently many works by Afro-Americans are published because of their indigenous cultural values as distinct from "contribution to the literature of the world." Nevertheless, "the Negro race should not sniff at the *Uncle Tom's Cabins* and the *Jungles* of its own writers, which are instruments of progress as real as the ballot-box, the school-house or a stick of dynamite."

Walter White: The idea that "the only interesting material in Negro lives is in the lives of the lower or lowest classes—that upper-class Negro life is in no wise different from white life and is therefore uninteresting" in literary creation is questionable. The truth is that "it makes no difference . . . what field a writer chooses if he has the gift of perception, of dramatic and human material and the ability to write about it."

Alfred A. Knopf: No artist, black or white, should be limited in his or her choice of subject.

John Farrar: "The Negro should be treated by himself and others who write about him with just as little self-consciousness as possible." Stories like those of Octavius Roy Cohen can be "untrue" and amusing without constituting "any very great libel on the Negro."

William Lyon Phelps: "The only obligation or limitation that an artist should recognize is the truth. He cannot be criticized unless he takes the worst [Negro characters] as typical."

Vachel Lindsay: With "truth and beauty" as guiding principles, an author "should be free to choose his characters according to his desire and purpose."

Sinclair Lewis: "There is the greatest danger" that the obsession with "economic and social problems of the colored race" will lead black authors to the writing of novels that are "fundamentally alike." A good example of this is the appeal of the subject "passing" to them. But all of them must not "go on repeating the same novel (however important, however poignant, however magnificently dramatic) about the well-bred, literate and delightful Negro intellectual finding himself or herself blocked by the groundless and infuriating manner of superiority assumed by white men frequently less white than people technically known as Negroes."

Sherwood Anderson: It is "a great mistake for Negroes to become too sensitive." They should "quit thinking of Negro art[.] If the individual creating the art happens to be a Negro and some one wants to call it Negro Art let them. . . . I have lived a good deal in my youth among common Negro laborers. I have found them about the sweetest people I know."

Jessie Fauset: While any writer should be free to choose his or her characters and situations, the development of a large black reading audience will compel publishers to "produce books, even those that depict the Negro as an angel on earth." Experience has shown that white "people are keenly interested in learning about the better class of colored people. They are quite willing to be shown." The obstacle is the publisher who in many cases has "an idée fixe" as to what is good for the public.

Benjamin Brawley: While the freedom of the artist to choose his subject must be acknowledged, it is regrettable that "many artists . . . prefer today to portray only what is vulgar. There is beauty in the world as well as ugliness, idealism as well as realism."

Robert T. Kerlin: "The duty of the black artist is to be a true artist and if he is such he will show the 'sordid,' the 'foolish,' and the 'criminal' Negro in the environment and the conditions—of white creation, of course—which have made him what he is. Let the black artist not hesitate to show what 'civilization' is doing to both races."

Haldane MacFall: (No direct answer to the questions. Only tries to prove that his portrayal of the Negro in his novel did not stem from contempt or hatred.)

Georgia Douglas Johnson: All Afro-Americans cannot "reach the high levels *en masse.*" Therefore "the work of the artist" is to portray "the few who do break thru the hell-crust of prevalent conditions to high ground." He should stop capitalizing "the frailties of the struggling or apathetic mass—and portray the best that offers."

Countée Cullen: The Negro writer should be allowed "the one inalienable right" enjoyed by "all other authors": freedom to choose his subject and treat it as he wishes. Nevertheless, unlike "all other authors" whose races have "a large enough body of sound, healthy race literature" behind them, he should not "speculate in abortions and aberrations." If, in any case, he wants to write about the unpolished Negroes let him go ahead "only let him not pander to the popular trend of seeing no cleanliness in their squalor, no nobleness in their meanness and no common sense in their ignorance."

J. Herbert Engbeck: "The obligation of the artist is not to his race but to his talent." Certainly "there is a false notion among a great number of peoples that the sordid-foolish-criminal side is all there is in the Negro. The Negro will have to fight that down as the Jew has had to fight down the same impression by proving the contrary."

Julia Peterkin: "The minute any one becomes an advocate he ceases to be an artist." The Negro should be proud of himself and of his heritage, for example, the "Black Negro Mammy." "I write about Negroes because they represent human nature obscured by so little veneer; human nature groping among its instinctive impulses and in any environment which is tragically primitive and often unutterably pathetic. But I am no propagandist for or against any race."

Otto F. Mack: (From Stuttgart, Germany) Although many thinking people no longer take the uncomplimentary image of the Negro in American literature seriously, the Negro writer should fight to correct it.

Charles W. Chesnutt: The artist should be free to choose his subject. But "a true picture of life would include the good, the bad and the indifferent." The weakness of Negro writings is that they tend to be "too subjective. The colored writer, generally speaking, has not yet passed the point of thinking of himself first as a Negro, burdened with the responsibility of defending and uplifting his race." There is no reason why "a Negro oil millionaire" should be preferred by a black writer to an ordinary Negro. "A Pullman porter who performs wonderful feats in the detection of crime has great possibilities."

Unfortunately, the symposium was overtaken by a bitter quarrel engendered by the appearance of Carl Van Vechten's *Nigger Heaven* in August of that year (1926) and so was unable to settle the question as to how the black man should be portrayed in art. Nevertheless, it achieved two main things. Firstly, it brought into sharp focus the attitudes underneath the writings and criticisms of the Harlem Renaissance—attitudes which ranged from Jessie Fauset's call for a literary exhibition of "the better class of colored people" to Carl Van Vechten's recommendation of the use of the most unpolished Negroes as subject matters; from Countée Cullen's advice that a black writer should not "speculate in abortions and aberrations" to H. L. Mencken's plea that an artist should be allowed to depend completely on his or her own perception of reality. Secondly, the fact that it was instituted, along with *Opportunity*'s suspension of its literary prizes, demonstrates the effort of black journals themselves to control the direction of the literary movement.

In this connection *The Crisis* perhaps went too far. Although the magazine was a major force in the initiation of the all-out promotion of black literature by black journals, its sensitiveness and skepticism regarding the trend of the movement often dampened the enthusiasm of the young writers to express themselves as they saw fit. Beginning with little or no control over the participants in its literary contests, it progressively held them so tightly that their desire to compete was apparently stifled.

The rules of the first contest in 1924 were few and flexible. In addition to those dealing with mechanics and the submission of the entries, the main ones were: (1) The competition was open only to "persons of Negro descent in order to encourage their aptitude for art expression." (2) "Plays must deal with some phase of Negro history or experience." (3) "Essays . . . may deal with personal experience, biography, history,

scientific research, art, criticism or any subject." (4) Poetry "may be on
any subject." (5) "Illustrations may be for covers of *The Crisis* or for
decorations of *The Crisis* page, cartoons or general illustrations."[71]

The rules for the 1926 contest were less flexible. The announcement
of the contest itself was accompanied by a restrictive statement of policy:

> We want especially to stress the fact that while we believe in Negro art
> we do not believe in any art simply for art's sake. We want the earth
> beautiful but we are primarily interested in the earth. We want Negro
> writers to produce beautiful things but we stress the things rather than
> the beauty. It is Life and Truth that are important and Beauty comes
> to make their importance visible and tolerable.[72]

The rules for the 1927 competition were still more restrictive: (1) All
entrants who "must be of Negro descent" were "urged to become sub-
scribers to THE CRISIS MAGAZINE" so that they might know what
was happening to the entries. (2) Persons who had "received two prizes,
first and second, in any class of entries in CRISIS contests" should not
compete.

The prizes themselves were divided into carefully regulated categories:
Negro Business Prizes, Prizes in Literary Art and Expression, Prizes for
Poetry, Prizes for Songs, Covers for THE CRISIS, and the Charles
Waddell Chesnutt Honorarium. More than ever the emphasis was on
utility, for the journal wanted to make sure that the youths were not
engaging in "any art simply for art's sake." The declaration of the aim
of the "Business Prizes" almost said as much: "The object of these prizes
is to stimulate general knowledge of banking and insurance in modern
life and specific knowledge of what American Negroes are doing in these
fields; and to collect facts and impressions concerning Negro workers
and their relation to Negro business."[73]

As if all these were too weak to let *The Crisis* influence the subjects
and forms of the entries, the journal assumed what amounted to an
absolute control of the competition. No judges were announced. The
November issue of the magazine carried a cover drawing which had been
entered by one Vivian Schuyler, even though the final selection of prize
winners had not been made. An announcement within the number itself
revealed that the editor—at least at that stage—was the sole judge of the
entries. It said among other things:

The entries are of a higher order of merit than in any previous contest. The editor has undertaken to read every single manuscript personally and instead of the drudgery he anticipated, the work has been a joy and inspiration. He has marked all the manuscripts on a scale as follows:

A – Excellent. Only these are considered for prizes.
B+ – Good and worth publication.
B – Good.
C – Fair.
D – Poor, but with some points to commend.
E – Impossible.

After the editor has personally chosen the A manuscripts (and he has already chosen most of them), he will call in expert outside aid to confirm or criticize his decisions.[74]

The customary award dinner was suspended; checks were mailed to prize winners[75] who, obviously by accident, happened to be almost all women. The December issue carried their names, and also confirmed the determination of *The Crisis* to have full control over the award of its prizes. No judges were mentioned. Instead the introductory paragraph attached to the list of winners only said that "the Editors of THE CRISIS, with aid and suggestion of various authors, artists and experts with whom they consulted, have decided to distribute THE CRISIS prizes. . . ."[76] Not all the awards, however, were made. The "Business Prizes" were postponed because, according to the announcement, "to our great surprise only 13 of the 375 entries were made for this competition. This, we think, is much too small a number and with the consent of the donors, therefore, we are extending the time of entry for these prizes until July 1st, 1928."[77]

The 1928 contest narrowed the field of competition to "The Charles Waddell Chesnutt Honoraria," and "the Economic Prizes"—a division which the young contestants apparently found unappealing. General rules included the use of real names instead of pen names, and the fact that "the Editors of THE CRISIS in consultation with the donors (as distinct from "authors, artists and experts" of the previous year) will decide upon the prize winners."[78]

Entries closed on 31 December 1928. When prize winners were announced in June 1929 contestants learned that the award of some of the

"Economic Prizes" had once again been postponed—this time indefinitely, for the "balance" was "to be distributed from time to time as we receive such contributions on the economic development of the American Negro as seem to merit recognition."[79] Nothing much was heard about *The Crisis*'s prizes thereafter, until the institution of "The Du Bois Literary Prize" in 1931 and the attempt in August 1932 to revive the "Literary Dinners."[80] The attempt, however, did not bear much fruit in spite of *The Crisis*'s optimistic remark, "Despite depression, the Kingdom of the Spirit still lives."[81]

Depression, certainly, contributed to the death of *The Crisis*'s contests. The principal cause, nevertheless, was the excessive control assumed by the journal over its contestants. All in all, what its editor said about himself personally while accepting "The Du Bois Literary Prize" could be applied to *The Crisis*. W. E. B. Du Bois declared:

I have been striving in recent years to induce the stream of Negro-American literature, especially of our younger writers, to return to a normal, human and truthful channel, rather than to be led astray by considerations of income and sensationalism.[82]

Having said all this, it must be affirmed that the control was well-meant and, given the innocence of Black art and literature in the Roaring Twenties, justifiable. The temptation to misplace emphasis was real. *The Crisis* wanted to make sure that the Negro self-expressiveness of the renaissance was not sacrificed to its glamour.

THE MESSENGER

The Messenger, founded in November 1917 by A. Philip Randolph and Chandler Owen, never pretended to be an enthusiastic promoter of the Harlem Renaissance writing. It was too preoccupied with socioeconomic issues to concern itself with a race-conscious literary movement per se. Indeed, its column "Shafts and Darts" ridiculed the New Negro literature as it did Marcus Garvey and W. E. B. Du Bois whenever the initiator of the Niagara Movement appeared soft, too conciliatory, or unassimilationist. Witness George S. Schuyler's *Ballad of Negro Artists* where Negro artists are portrayed as getting rich and fat at the expense of the American Negro's right to full American citizenship:

I

Now old Merlin the wizard had nothing on us,
Though he conjured a castle up out of the dust;
For with nothing but gall and a stoutness of heart,
On the public we've foisted this New Negro Art.

Chorus:

Oh! this New Negro Art;
This "peculiar" art;
On the gullible public
We've foisted our "Art."

II

If old Kinkle and "Rusty" of mendicant fame,
Grabbed off wads of cash in the panhandle game;
Cannot we alleged writers and singers and such,
Playing on "racial differences," cash in as much?

Chorus:

We *can* cash in as much—
Very *nearly* as much;
Though we know we're all hams,
We can cash in as much.

III

By stupendous logrolling and licking of boots,
And fawning around influential galoots;
We have gotten a place 'neath the calcium flare.
And paying our room rent and eating good fare.

Chorus:

Oh, we're eating good fare;
Eating mighty good fare;
Though once we went hungry,
We now eat good fare.

IV

Our pet "racial differences" theory can
Be indorsed, it is true, by the Knights of the Klan;
But we care not for trifling matters like that,
When as "racial interpreters" we can grow fat.

Chorus:

Yes, we can grow fat;
Get flabby and fat;
Eating three squares a day —
And all paid for at that![83]

The *Messenger* had no more encouraging words for the development
of jazz and the blues—two of the features of the New Negro mood—
which it believed was detrimental to the status of the black man in the
United States. "A race that hums opera will stay ahead of a race that
hums the 'blues,' " it contended editorially in March 1924.[84] It had in
July 1918 ridiculed Du Bois's interest in literature and vaunted its own
preference for "Economics and Politics". Its leading critic, Theophilus
Lewis, dissociating himself later from what he called "the current jubilee
in celebration of the 'Renaissance' of Negro culture," emphatically denied
"that the spirituals are triumphs of art."[85] For the journal, the New
Negro "spirit" which was artistically à la mode was an inaccurate reflection of the New Negro "spirit" as it saw and felt it. U. S. Poston, its reviewer of Alain Locke's volume, *The New Negro,* almost spoke for it:

Is not the spirit of Garveyism, the N.A.A.C.P. and the Labor Movement
agitations by A. Phillip Randolph, Frank Crosswaith, and Chandler Owen,
Hubert Harrison and other radicals more expressive of the spirit of the
new Negro than the Sorrow Song and the spirit of Hampton and Tuskegee?
. . . as a volume designed to express the spirit of the new Negro, this NEW
NEGRO [Alain Locke's] is wanting in many respects. That virile, in-
surgent, revolutionary spirit peculiar to the Negro is missing. The recent
gesture on the part of Roland Hayes to not sing whenever his group is
segregated, is far more expressive of the spirit of the new Negro.[86]

Yet the *Messenger* did not stand on the sidewalk and watch the bandwagon of the literary promotion roll by. It had, before the literary
awakening took any recognizable form, published short stories and poems
by black writers, including Claude McKay. These, however, seem to have
been printed because of their sociopolitical stance. But with the formal
launching of the New Negro by *Opportunity* in March 1924 it started to
print pieces that were more interested in art than in sociopolitical issues.
It offered Langston Hughes a platform to experiment in a new genre
when it bought and published his first short stories, although its manag-

ing editor, Wallace Thurman called them "very bad stories."[87] Through Theophilus Lewis's theatre column, which was inaugurated in September 1923, it provided the New Negro drama with the most searching and the most disinterested, if unscholarly, monthly commentary on plays and their production. Despite its belief in the universal and international brotherhood of man, despite its contention that "humanity is one," and that "the Negro in France, is a Frenchman, in England, an Englishmen [sic], and so on,"[88] it persistently called for "stories of Negro life."[89] It even submitted, at least for some time, to the editorship of Wallace Thurman, the editor of *Fire,* a magazine which looked for its material and characters among those whom Wallace Thurman himself described as "people who still retained some individual race qualities and who were not totally white American in every respect save color of skin."[90]

The *Messenger* had no literary contests and award dinners. It was not a happy rider on the race-conscious literary bandwagon. Nonetheless, it did its best to assist the young writers, before its demise in June 1928.

FIRE

The young authors were not idle as the competition to promote them went on. Although they were grateful to the three major black journals for publishing their works, they were not, as Wallace Thurman puts it, "satisfied to be squeezed between jeremiads or have [their] works thrown haphazardly upon a page where there was no effort to make it look beautiful as well as sound beautiful."[91] They were also unhappy with what they regarded as their elders' "shoddy and sloppy publication methods . . . patronizing attitudes . . . editorial astigmatism and . . . intolerance of new points of view."[92] Thus, beginning with *Fire,*[93] various groups of them founded little magazines such as *Black Opals* (published in Philadelphia[94]) and the *Quill* (published in Boston) which unfortunately could not in several cases go beyond the first issue.

The story of *Fire* illustrates this attempt on the part of the young writers to help promote their own works. Early in the summer of 1926 seven of them—Langston Hughes, Zora Neale Hurston, Wallace Thurman, Aaron Douglas, John P. Davis, Bruce Nugent, and Gwendolyn Bennett— got together and decided to found their own journal "to be called *Fire*— the idea being," as Langston Hughes points out, "that it would burn up a lot of old, dead conventional Negro-white ideas of the past, *épater le*

bourgeois into a realization of the existence of the younger Negro writers
and artists, and provide us with an outlet for publication not available
in the limited pages of . . . the *Crisis, Opportunity,* and the *Messenger.*"[95]
They taxed themselves fifty dollars each and elected Wallace Thurman,
John P. Davis, and Bruce Nugent as editor, business manager, and director
of distribution respectively.[96]

The magazine came out in November. Its unconventional foreword
defined its radical aims. It ended as follows:

> FIRE . . .   weaving vivid, hot designs upon an ebon bordered loom and
> satisfying pagan thirst for beauty unadorned . . . the
> flesh is sweet and real . . . the soul an inward flush
> of fire. . . . Beauty? . . . flesh on fire—on
> fire in the furnace of life blazing. . . .
> > "Fy-ah,
> > Fy-ah, Lawd,
> > Fy-ah gonna burn ma soul!"[97]

Unfortunately for the youths, however, because of difficulties in
distribution the existence of the journal was hardly noticed by white
critics. Black critics who noticed it threw, to use Hughes's phrase again,
"plenty of cold water . . . on it."[98] For instance, under the heading "Writer
Brands Fire as Effeminate Tommyrot," Rean Graves in the *Baltimore
Afro-American* informed his readers that he had "just tossed the first
issue of *Fire*—into the fire, and watched the crackling flames leap and
snarl as though they were trying to swallow some repulsive dose," and
went on to comment on the contributors in terms hardly complimentary:

> Aaron Douglas who, in spite of himself and the meaningless grotesqueness
> of his creation, has gained a reputation as an artist, is permitted to spoil
> three perfectly good pages and a cover with his pen and ink hudge pudge.
> Countee Cullen has written a beautiful poem in his "From a Dark Tower,"
> but tries his best to obscure the thought in superfluous sentences.
> Langston Hughes displays his usual ability to say nothing in many words.[99]

The result of the black critics' hostility to, and the white critics' un-
awareness of, *Fire* was the failure of the first and only issue of the magazine which was eventually consumed by real fire in a basement apartment where several hundred copies of it had been stored.[100]

Yet, in spite of flaws and weaknesses of individual contributions, *Fire* achieved its artistic aim: expression of the young writers' "individual dark-skinned selves without fear or shame."[101]

Richard Bruce's two nudes with well-defined contours, Aaron Douglas's pen-and-ink sketches of a Negro preacher, a Negro painter, and a highly sensuous "serving" lady, as well as his "Incidental Art Decorations" obviously inspired by African masks and statues, underscore the young artists' intention to use any available Negro material even if it meant gratifying or hurting the feelings of parts of their audience.

This is also true of the written contributions which fall under four headings—fiction, drama, poetry, and essay—even though, with the exception of the poems which are grouped under "Flame from the Dark Tower," they are not categorized.

The first piece is Wallace Thurman's story which seems to have been chosen leader to emphasize the fact that *Fire* did not care which foot Afro-Americans, for "diplomatic" reasons, wanted to put forward. Entitled "Cordelia the Crude," it describes the life of a sixteen-year-old black prostitute. In addition to giving details as to how and where Cordelia operates, the story teems with whore houses in Harlem, and with Negroes who are only superficially clean, Negroes with "well-modeled heads, stickily plastered hair, flaming cravats, silken or broadcloth shirts, dirty underwear...."[102] The tone is candid; but the story is bad stylistically. Besides other flaws, the point of view is wobbly; the first-person narrator speaks as if he lived with Cordelia and her parents and were omniscient.

Zora Neale Hurston's play *Color Struck* and story "Sweat," which are discussed in chapter 5, capitalized on the Negro folk culture, and are, in a way, forerunners of the folklorist's later novels.

The ten-piece "Section of Poetry" is a potpourri of poems which range from Countée Cullen's sonnet *From the Dark Tower* (with the author's usual muted "protest") to Langston Hughes's experiment with jazz rhythm in *Elevator Boy,* and *Railroad Avenue.* Other contributors in this section are Helene Johnson (*A Southern Road*), Edward Silvera (*Jungle Taste* and *Finality*), Waring Cuney (*The Death Bed*), Arna Bontemps (*Length of Moon*), and Lewis Alexander (*Little Cinderella* and *Streets*).

Gwendolyn Bennett, a talented young woman who, in addition to being in charge of *Opportunity*'s literary gossip column, "The Ebony Flute," had published poems and drawings in *The Crisis, Opportunity* and the *Messenger,* contributed a story, "Wedding Day," in which she focuses on what she calls "the Harlem of Paris" and, in a considerably detached manner, lets her black Americans react to life in a non-American environment, thereby expressing some hidden parts of their selves.

The most experimental story, as far as form is concerned, comes from Richard Bruce. Written without any paragraph indentation and punctuation marks save the many ellipses, "Smoke, Lilies and Jade"[103] operates within that basic vehicle of black cultural heritage: the oral tradition.

Arthur Huff Fauset's *Intelligentsia,* which is alone in the class of "essay," is a frontal attack on the intelligentsia as distinct from what the author calls "the true intellectuals who are accomplishing things."[104] The attack, however, is not directed against any group of persons of any particular race. While it mentions Sinclair Lewis, Theodore Dreiser, H. L. Mencken, and G. B. Shaw as examples of true intellectuals, it contents itself with delineating the characteristics of the intelligentsia. The following is only one of the many traits:

They simply give art and artists a black eye with their snobbery and stupidity; and their false interpretations and hypocritical evaluations do more to heighten suspicion against the real artist on the part of the ordinary citizen than perhaps any other single factor in the clash of art and provincialism.[105]

The magazine ends as boisterously as it started with Wallace Thurman's "Fire Burns," an "editorial comment" on the reaction of blacks to Carl Van Vechten's *Nigger Heaven*—a novel for which, Wallace Thurman contends, Afro-Americans should be grateful:

Some time ago, while reviewing Carl Van Vechten's lava-laned Nigger Heaven I made the prophecy that Harlem Negroes, once their aversion to the "nigger" in the title was forgotten, would erect a statue on the corner of 135th Street and Seventh Avenue, and dedicate it to this ultra-sophisticated Iowa New Yorker.

So far my prophecy has failed to pan out, and superficially it seems as if it never will. . . .

Yet I am loathe to retract or to temper my first prophecy. . . . I defiantly reiterate that a few years hence Mr. Van Vechten will be spoken of as a kindly gent rather than as a moral leper exploiting people who had believed him to be a sincere friend.[106]

Thus *Fire* does exactly what its foreword claims for it. It flames, burns, sears, and penetrates "far beneath the superficial items of the flesh to boil the sluggish blood." The standard of the contributions is uneven; their collective tone is discordant. But this is to be expected of a journal interested in unregulated "individual" artistic expression. *Fire* is an adequate manifestation of the daredevil attitude of some of its founders towards Art.

CONCLUSION

The role of black journals in the birth and growth of the New Negro cannot be overemphasized. Some of them (including *The Crisis* and *Opportunity*) were, however, Negro "uplift" magazines,[107] and so could not completely avoid the current Negro "uplift" literary concept: the Negro must be portrayed as *un homme pareil aux autres*[108] and at his best; or, as Countée Cullen, the assistant editor of *Opportunity,* put it:

Whether they relish the situation or not, Negroes should be concerned with making good impressions. They cannot do this by throwing wide every door of the racial entourage, to the wholesale gaze of the world at large. Decency demands that some things be kept secret; diplomacy demands it; the world loses its respect for violators of this code. . . . Let art portray things as they are, no matter who is hurt, is a blind bit of philosophy.[109]

The works of Benjamin Brawley and William Stanley Braithwaite, the main leaders of opposition to the New Negro literature, are the best examples of the adherence to this "code" in poetry. Brawley's best known poems are on Chaucer and Robert Gould Shaw.[110] Braithwaite wrote about leaves, flowers, and concepts. He advised Claude McKay "to write and send to the magazines only such poems as did not betray [his] racial identity"[111] —a piece of advice which points to another aspect of the "code" style.

In addition to regulating the choice of subject, it also determined the treatment of the subject chosen. The writer should sound as learned as possible. Beautiful, if abstract, expressions should be preferred to folksily down-to-earth, but concrete, language. Thus we have the following lines from William Stanley Braithwaite's *Exit:*

No, his exit by the gate
    Will not leave the wind ajar;[112]

and the following with its archaism "trow" from the second stanza of
Brawley's *My Hero:*

This was the gallant faith, I trow,[113]

and the beautiful sound of the second stanza of Jessie Fauset's *Dead Fires,*
that does not say much:

Is this pain's surcease? Better far the ache,
    The long-drawn dreary day, the night's white wake,
Better the choking sigh, the sobbing breath
    Than passion's death![114]

The position of the black man in America, and not an awareness of
the inauthenticity of what was being produced, was mainly at the root
of the "code" and its opposition to the new trend of Negro literature.
Because of the peculiarity of that position the black man, it was argued,
must try to make "good impressions."
    Yet through their awareness of the beauty of the black self, and their
strong belief that that self had an important role to play in the general
American culture, the black journals succeeded, to some extent, in
bringing "new Negro voices into tune with the larger world of letters—
to help them discover themselves."[115]
    It is true that they were not completely responsible for their success
since they and their prizes could hardly have thrived without a white
audience and white financial support. Up to 1927 *Opportunity,* for
instance, depended almost completely on a yearly grant of eight thousand dollars from the Carnegie Foundation to the Department of Research
and Investigation of the National Urban League. The list of "Persons
Who Acted as Patrons for the First Issue" of *Fire* contains at least one
white man.[116] The *Stylus* was supported by Howard University. The
Spingarn Medal, the Amy Spingarn Awards, the Harmon Award, the
Van Vechten Award for published contributions, the Albert and Charles
Boni Prize for Negro Novel, the Du Bois Literary Prize, all had white men
and women behind them.

However, a careful study reveals that the most effective among the contests and prizes existed more because of black men and women's support than that of white men and women. Albert and Charles Boni's prize of one thousand dollars "for the best novel of Negro life written by a man or woman of Negro descent"[117] was never awarded because, according to Gwendolyn Bennett in her column "The Ebony Flute," there was without doubt no one worthy of the prize."[118] Its greatest achievement was that it nearly brought René Maran into more direct participation in the Harlem Renaissance when Alain Locke and Charles S. Johnson, encouraged by the Bonis themselves, submitted for the competition his novel, *Roman d'un Nègre,* which had been translated for the purpose by Mrs. Underwood.[119] René Maran, however, saw the movement as too race-conscious and race-motivated. He was too French to accept such a "racial" honor; he politely declined:

Quelle que soit la valeur du prix en question,-prix Albert and Charles Boni, -il m'est très difficile d'y prendre part. Elle amoindrirait en France ma situation littéraire, qui est très forte, malgré et en raison même des oppositions qu'on ne cesse de dresser contre moi, mais aussi ma situation morale, qui jusqu'ici est irréprochable. On me reprocherait d'être racial. Et je n'aurai plus qu'à disparaître.[120]

Fire cost about one thousand dollars to produce. If the "patrons" offered it any financial assistance, that assistance does not seem to have been adequate. In any case, Langston Hughes describes how the cost was defrayed:

I think Alain Locke, among others, signed notes guaranteeing payments. But since Thurman was the only one of the seven of us with a regular job, for the next three or four years his checks were constantly being attached and his income seized to pay for *Fire.* And whenever I sold a poem, mine went there, too—to *Fire.*[121]

Wallace Thurman's later attempt to resuscitate and expand the creative stance of *Fire* started and ended with the one-issue *Harlem: A Forum of Negro Life* in November 1928—ended because of lack of money.[122] After being supported by its publishers in 1928 and 1929, *The Quill* in 1930 offered itself for sale. It never reappeared. The *Poet's Journal,* a magazine which Helene Johnson and her club, The Colored Poetic

League of the World, planned to launch did not see the light of day, perhaps because of lack of money.[123] Mrs. E. R. Matthews's "Du Bois Literary Prize" announced for the fall of 1932 never got off the ground because the nominating committee could not find any "work of first-rate importance"—work worthy of "this important prize."[124]

The Harmon Award, the Spingarn Medal, and the Carl Van Vechten Award were actually given out; but they were not, as instruments of literary promotion among the young black writers, as effective as the *Opportunity* and *The Crisis* prizes which, as demonstrated above, were almost completely taken over, and sponsored by Negro businessmen and businesswomen after they had been initiated by white well-wishers.

In conclusion, therefore, one can safely say that while the taste of a white audience helped to fix the color of the products of the literary campaign by the black journals, the choice of the basic material used in the products was controlled by the journals and the young writers. As for the young authors' wish to produce in the first place (if it owed anything to prizes), it depended more on black businessmen and businesswomen than on white philanthropists. Thus, contrary to the impression often created by some critics, the involvement of whites in the literary contests and award dinners did not detract much from the self-motivation and self-expressiveness of a literary movement which developed essentially from within.

NOTES

1. Patrick J. Gilpin, "Charles S. Johnson: Entrepreneur of the Harlem Renaissance" in Arna Bontemps, ed., *The Harlem Renaissance Remembered* (New York: Dodd, Mead & Co., 1972), p. 222.

2. Ibid.

3. *Opportunity* 2, no. 15 (March 1924): 68.

4. Ibid.

5. Zora Neale Hurston, *Dusk Tracks on a Road: An Autobiography* (1942; reprint ed., Philadelphia: J. B. Lippincott, 1971), p. 168. *See also* Langston Hughes, *The Big Sea: An Autobiography* (New York: Hill and Wang, 1940), p. 218.

6. *Opportunity* 2, no. 17 (May 1924): 143.

7. Hughes, *Big Sea,* pp. 92-94; 184-86.

8. *Opportunity* 2, no. 17 (May 1924): 143.

9. *The Crisis* 31, no. 3 (January 1926): 141.

10. *Opportunity* 2, no. 20 (August 1924): 253. For the controversy on who actually suggested the publication of the issue to Paul Kellogg, *see* Abby Arthur Johnson and Ronald Maberry Johnson, *Propaganda and Aesthetics; The Literary Politics of Afro-American Magazines in the Twentieth Century* (Amherst: University of Massachusetts Press, 1979), pp. 69-70.

11. *Opportunity* 2, no. 20 (August 1924): 253. Emphasis in the original.

12. Bontemps, *Harlem Renaissance*, p. 228.

13. *The Crisis* 29, no. 2 (December 1924): 81.

14. *Opportunity* 3, no. 25 (January 1925): 3.

15. Ibid., 2, no. 21 (September 1924): 277, 279.

16. Ibid., 3, no. 30 (June 1925): 176.

17. Ibid., 3, no. 34 (October 1925): 291.

18. Ibid., pp. 238-39.

19. *See* Hughes to Van Vechten, Monday, 18 May 1925, and Thursday, 4 June 1925, Yale University.

20. *See,* for example, Hughes to Van Vechten, 23 August 1925, and 20 January 1926, Yale University.

21. Ibid.

22. *Opportunity* 3, no. 30 (June 1925): 177.

23. Ibid., 3, no. 34 (October 1925): 292.

24. Ibid., 5, no. 7 (July 1927): 212. The growing interest in black literature is further evidenced by the fact that in October 1926 Countée Cullen was invited by Idella Purnell and Witter Bynner to edit a special issue of their magazine *Palms* which was devoted to black poets. *Carolina Magazine* (published at the University of North Carolina) also brought out Negro numbers in May 1927, May 1928, and April 1929. For a discussion of these issues and the influence of *Opportunity* literary contests on their contents, *see* Johnson and Johnson, *Propaganda and Aesthetics,* pp. 74-77.

25. Bontemps, *Harlem Renaissance,* pp. 14-15.

26. Ibid., p. 20.

27. Patrick J. Gilpin, "Charles S. Johnson: Entrepreneur of the Harlem Renaissance," in Arna Bontemps, ed. *The Harlem Renaissance Remembered,* p. 222.

28. "Welcoming the New Negro," *Opportunity* 4, no. 40 (April 1926): 113.

29. Wallace Thurman, "Nephews of Uncle Remus," *Independent* 119, no. 4034 (24 September 1927): 296.

30. *Opportunity* 5, no. 1 (January 1927): 6.

31. Thomas Millard Henry, Letter to the Editor, *Messenger* 7, no. 6

(June 1925): 239. Emphasis added. Hughes's poem, *The Weary Blues,* is discussed in chapter 5.

32. *Opportunity* 3, no. 31 (July 1925): 219.

33. Ibid.

34. Ibid., 5, no. 7 (July 1927): 210.

35. Ibid., p. 194.

36. Ibid., 4, no. 39 (March 1926): 80. *Opportunities'* italics.

37. Ibid., 5, no. 9 (September 1927): 254.

38. Ibid., 9, no. 11 (November 1931): 331.

39. Ibid.

40. Benjamin Brawley, "The Writing of Essays," *Opportunity* 4, no. 45 (September 1926): 284. He had earlier discussed some other weaknesses of the new writers.

41. Ibid., 1, no. 1 (January 1923): 3.

42. Langston Hughes's first (published) poem, *The Negro Speaks of Rivers,* appeared in *The Crisis* 22, no. 2 (June 1921): 71.

43. *The Crisis* 19, no. 6 (April 1920): 298-99. Apart from the works of the writers mentioned in this passage, *The Crisis* published several stories and poems which definitely anticipated the writing of the Harlem Renaissance. *See,* for instance, Virginia P. Jackson's poem *Africa* where the speaker hears the "voice" of Africa asking her to return home. Ibid., 17, no. 4 (February 1919): 166.

44. James Weldon Johnson, ed., *The Book of American Negro Poetry* (1922, 1931; reprint ed., New York: Harcourt, Brace & World, 1959), pp. 144, 145.

45. Ibid., p. 211. *See The Crisis* 13, no. 3 (January 1917): 118.

46. *See also* chapter 2. Jessie Fauset was literary editor of *The Crisis* from November 1919 to May 1926.

47. Hughes, *Big Sea,* p. 218.

48. Ibid., p. 202; *see also* Carl Van Vechten's "Introducing Langston Hughes to the Reader," in Langston Hughes, *The Weary Blues* (New York: Alfred A. Knopf, 1926), p. 11.

49. *The Crisis* 19, no. 6 (April 1920): 299. The interest of *The Crisis* in the development of black literature, long before the 1920s, is also evident in its editor's comments in the issues of April 1911 (p. 21), November 1915 (p. 28), and November 1918 (p. 22).

50. Ibid., 25, no. 2 (December 1922): 56.

51. Ibid., 28, no. 2 (June 1924): 82.

52. Ibid., 28, no. 5 (September 1924): 199; ibid., 28, no. 6 (October 1924): 247.

53. "Contest Awards," *Opportunity* 3, no. 29 (May 1925): 142.

54. "To Encourage Negro Art," *The Crisis* 29, no. 1 (November 1924): 11.

55. Ibid., 33, no. 4 (February 1927): 192.

56. Maran to Locke, 18 October 1924, Alain Locke Papers, Moorland-Spingarn Research Center, Howard University, Washington, D.C.

57. *The Crisis* 29, no. 2 (December 1924): 74.

58. Ibid., 33, no. 4 (February 1927): 191.

59. *The Crisis* 35, no. 3 (March 1928): 76.

60. Ibid. *The Crisis*'s precise definition of the types of material that should be submitted reflects Du Bois's attempt to control the direction of the movement.

61. Ibid., 34, no. 4 (April 1931): 117. *See also* "The Donor of the Du Bois Literary Prize: An Autobiography," *The Crisis* 40, no. 5 (May 1931): 157.

62. Ibid., 28, no. 5 (September 1924): 199.

63. This organization was originally called CRIGWA (Crisis Guild of Writers and Artists). Ibid., 28, no. 6 (October 1924): 247.

64. Ibid., 30, no. 5 (September 1925): 215.

65. Ibid., 30, no. 6 (October 1925): 278.

66. Two plays by Willis Richardson: "Compromise" (published in the *New Negro*); "The Broken Banjo" (first-prize winner in *The Crisis* contest of 1925); and Mrs. R. A. Gaines-Shelton's "The Church Fight" (second-prize winner, *The Crisis* contest of 1925), performed on 3, 10, and 17 May.

67. "Krigwa Players Little Negro Theatre: The Story of a Little Theatre Movement," *The Crisis* 32, no. 3 (July 1926): 134. *The Crisis*'s italics.

68. Ibid., 33, no. 4 (February 1927): 191.

69. This phrase is from Sinclair Lewis's contribution, ibid., 32, no. 1 (May 1926): 36.

70. The responses appeared in *The Crisis* between March and November 1926. In March Van Vechten, Mencken, Heyward (pp. 219-20); in April Hughes, Spingarn, White, Knopf, Farrar, and Phelps (pp. 278-80), in May Lindsay, Lewis, Anderson (pp. 35-36); in June Fauset, Brawley, Kerlin, and MacFall (pp. 71-73); in August Johnson, Cullen, and Engbeck (pp. 193-94); in September Peterkin, Mack (pp. 238-39), and Chesnutt (pp. 28-29).

71. "The Amy Spingarn Prizes in Literature and Art," *The Crisis* 29, no. 1 (November 1924): 24.

72. Ibid., 31, no. 3 (January 1926): 115.

73. Ibid., 33, no. 4 (February 1927): 191-93.

74. Ibid., 34, no. 9 (November 1927): 312. Emphasis added.

75. Ibid.

76. Ibid., 34, no. 10 (December 1927): 347.

77. Ibid.

78. Ibid., 35, no. 3 (March 1928): 76.

79. Ibid., 36, no. 6 (June 1929): 214.

80. Ibid., 39, no. 10 (October 1932): 331.

81. Ibid.

82. "The Donor of the Du Bois Literary Prize: An Autobiography," *The Crisis* 38, no. 5 (May 1931): 157.

83. George S. Schuyler, *Shafts & Darts: A Page of Calumny and Satire, Messenger* 8, no. 8 (August 1926): 239. Schuyler's italics.

84. Ibid., 6, no. 3 (March 1924): 71.

85. Ibid., (July 1918): 27: ibid., 8, no. 10 (October 1926): 312.

86. U. S. Poston, "Review of The New Negro," ibid., VIII, (April 1926), 118.

87. Hughes, *Big Sea,* p. 234.

88. J. A. Rogers, "The Critics: Do They Tell the Truth," *Messenger* 8, no. 2 (February 1926): 44.

89. *Messenger,* 8, no. 5 (May 1926): 131, 157.

90. Wallace Thurman, "Negro Artists and the Negro," *New Republic* 52, no. 665 (31 August 1927): 37.

91. Editorial, *Harlem: A Forum of Negro Life* 1, no. 1 (November 1928): 21.

92. Ibid.

93. Strictly speaking, *Fire* was not the first Afro-American little magazine during the period under review. *Stylus* (Washington, D.C.) and *New Era* (Boston) were founded in 1916. But while *New Era* disappeared after two issues in February and March 1916, *Stylus* was as good as dead until June 1929 when its third issue appeared. The first and second numbers had been published in June 1916 and May 1921.

94. In its first issue, *Black Opals* 1, no. 1 (Spring 1927) described itself as "the expression of an idea. . . . the result of the desire of the older New Negroes to encourage younger members of the group who demonstrate talent and ambition." Contributors to the maiden issue included such well-known New Negro writers as Langston Hughes, Arthur Huff Fauset, Lewis Alexander, and Alain Locke whom it called "the father of the New Negro Movement." Gwendolyn Bennett of *Opportunity* was guest editor of the second number (Christmas 1927) in which Jessie Fauset's "Nostalgia" appeared.

Although *Black Opals* was established to serve young residents of Philadelphia, by Christmas of 1928 it had started publishing material from all parts of the country. All in all, its literary stance was conservative. Subject matters were most of the time nonracial. When they were distinctively Negro, they often dripped with tears or tumbled from pulpits. Nonetheless, some of its contributors achieved some recognition as evidenced by the prizes they received in 1927:

Opportunity contest—Idabelle Yeiser (First Prize for Personal Experience Sketch); James H. Young (Second Prize for Essay); Allan Randall Freelon (Second Prize in Art as well as two honorable mentions); Nellie R. Bright (Third Prize for Personal Experience Sketch as well as an honorable mention).

The Crisis contest—Mae V. Cowdery (First Prize for Poetry), Allan Randall Freelon (Fourth Prize in Art).

Goal, a poem by Mae V. Cowdery, which appeared in the Spring 1927 number of the magazine was selected by William S. Braithwaite for his 1928 anthology. *See Black Opals* 1, no. 2 (Christmas 1927): 16.

95. Hughes, *Big Sea,* pp. 235-36.

96. Ibid., p. 236.

97. *Fire!! A Quarterly Devoted to the Younger Negro Artists* 1, no. 1 (November 1926).

98. Hughes, *Big Sea,* p. 237.

99. Thurman, "Negro Artists and the Negro," p. 37; Hughes, *Big Sea,* 237.

100. Hughes, *Big Sea,* p. 237.

101. Langston Hughes's phrase: "The Negro Artist and the Racial Mountain," *Nation* 122, no. 3181 (23 June 1926): 694.

102. *Fire,* p. 5.

103. For an account of how Richard Bruce wrote his story, *see* Robert E. Hemenway, *Zora Neale Hurston: A Literary Biography* (Urbana: University of Illinois Press, 1977), p. 46. Langston Hughes met (Richard) Bruce (Nugent) for the first time in the summer of 1925 in Washington, D.C. He relates how he amused himself with him and one other young man, "going downtown to white theatres 'passing' for South Americans, and walking up Fourteenth Street barefooted on warm evenings for the express purpose of shocking the natives." Hughes to Van Vechten, 24 June 1925, Yale University, New Haven, Conn.

104. *Fire,* p. 46.

105. Ibid.

106. Ibid., p. 47.

107. Wallace Thurman describes them as "pulpits for alarmed and angry Jeremiahs spouting fire and venom or else weeping and moaning

as if they were either predestined or else unable to do anything else."
In the editorial, *Harlem,* p. 21.

108. The title of an autobiographical novel by René Maran, in which
the black writer tries to show that the black man is like everyone else.

109. *Opportunity* 6, no. 3 (March 1928): 90.

110. Benjamin Brawley, *Chaucer, My Hero,* in Johnson, *The Book of
American Negro Poetry,* pp. 150-51.

111. Claude McKay, *A Long Way from Home* (1937; reprint ed., New
York: Harcourt, Brace & World, 1970), p. 27.

112. Johnson, *The Book of American Negro Poetry,* p. 101.

113. Brawley, p. 150.

114. Ibid., p. 207.

115. *Opportunity* 2, no. 24 (December 1924): 355.

116. *Fire,* n.p.

117. "A Prize for Negro Novel," *Opportunity* 4, no. 39 (March 1926):
105. *See also* ibid., 4, no. 40 (April 1926): 113; "For A Prize Novel,
$1000," *The Crisis* 31, no. 5 (March 1926): 217-18.

118. *Opportunity* 5, no. 4 (April 1927): 123.

119. Locke to Maran, 23 December 1926, Alain Locke Papers, Moorland-Spingarn Research Center, Howard University, Washington, D.C.

120. Translation: Whatever is the value of the prize in question,—Albert
and Charles Boni Prize,—it will be very difficult for me to take part in it.
It will weaken, in France, not only my literary situation, which is very
strong, in spite and even because of the continual opposition against me,
but also my moral position which until now has been irreproachable. I will
be accused of being racial. And I will only have to disappear. Maran to
Locke, 25 July 1926, Alain Locke Papers, Moorland-Spingarn Research
Center, Howard University, Washington, D.C.

121. Hughes, *Big Sea,* pp. 236-37.

122. Although *Harlem* retained Fire's interest in unregulated individual
artistic expression, it solicited material from both black and white writers
and went beyond purely literary matters to deal with political and economic questions. Thus while its essays ranged from Walter White's political
statement in "For Whom Shall the Negro Vote" (pp. 5-6) to Richard
Bruce's critique of black middle-class attitudes towards the portrayal of
the Negro in art, the list of its future contributors, whose contributions
unfortunately were never published, included blacks and whites from all
fields of activity: Claude McKay, Countée Cullen, Rudolph Fisher,
Eva Jessaye (author of *My Spirituals*), Eugene Gordon, Heywood Broun,
Clarence Darrow, William Stanley Braithwaite, Charles S. Johnson,

Frank Alvah Parsons (president, New York Schools of Fine and Applied Arts), Arthur Fauset, A. Philip Randolph, James Weldon Johnson, Jean Toomer, Jessie Fauset, Nella Larsen, H. L. Mencken, Dorothy Peterson, and Dr. R. Nathaniel Dett (a composer).

123. Johnson & Johnson, *Propaganda and Aesthetics,* p. 219, footnote 71.

124. Oliver LaFarge, trustee, "The Du Bois Literary Prize", *The Crisis* 40, no. 2 (February 1933): 45.

AFFIRMATION OF BLACK SELF:
BLACK CRACKS BETWEEN WHITE
BOARDS

4

"My poems are not Negro poems, nor are they Anglo-Saxon or white or English poems,"[1] Jean Toomer wrote James Weldon Johnson on 11 July 1930 as part of his negative response to Johnson's request that he be permitted to include some of Toomer's poems in *Cane*, in his (Johnson's) revised edition of *The Book of American Negro Poetry*. Countée Cullen spent a sizeable fraction of his short life in trying to convince critics that he wanted to be known as a poet *tout court;* he was, obviously, "One of the most promising of the young Negro poets" who, according to Langston Hughes, once said, "I want to be a poet—not a Negro poet."[2] In spite of Langston Hughes's unyielding identification with Negro masses, some critics cast doubts on the Negroness of his temperament.[3] The three poets, therefore, have this in common: they have either rejected an attempt by their readers to overemphasize the Negroness of their works, or they have seen the genuineness of their Negro inspiration deemphasized by their readers.

Nevertheless, Jean Toomer, Countée Cullen, and Langston Hughes have lots of things in their works that manifest a reinforcement of the black self. This chapter and the next examine these manifestations as well as those in the works of some of their contemporaries with a view to determining to what extent they express the black self.

JEAN TOOMER

Jean Toomer's words quoted above are related to his basic concept of Afro-Americans, especially those with some non-Negro blood in their veins. In his opinion, they cannot be classified simply as Negroes and non-Negroes. They are "the result of racial blendings here in America

which has produced a new race or stock . . . the American stock or race."[4]
Although (like James Weldon Johnson's Ex-Coloured Man's declared
intention to let the world take him for what it would) this statement
came on the eve of what looks like a flight into the white race, it is a fair
definition of Jean Toomer's stance on the race question all along. He had
eight years before made the same point in different words:

> From my own point of view I am naturally and inevitably an American.
> I have strived for a spiritual fusion analogous to the fact of racial inter-
> mingling. Without denying a single element in me, with no desire to sub-
> due one to the other, I have sought to let them function as complements.
> I have tried to let them live in harmony.[5]

It is a point of view akin to W. E. B. Du Bois's definition of the implication of the Afro-American's double-consciousness: a "longing to attain
self-conscious manhood, to merge his double self into a better and truer
self" in which "he wishes neither of the older selves to be lost."[6] As such,
Jean Toomer's claim in itself is a manifestation of an aspect of the black
experience in America.

But this point of view notwithstanding, Toomer had earlier been,
both physically and emotionally, in close contact with the less sophisticated types of Negroes when in 1921 he temporarily acted as superin-
tendent of a small black industrial and agricultural school in Sparta,
Georgia. He refers to it in the letter cited above:

> Within the last two or three years, however, my growing need for artistic
> expression has pulled me deeper and deeper into the Negro group. And
> as my powers of receptivity increased, I found myself loving it in a way
> I could never love the other. It has stimulated and fertilized whatever
> creative talent I may contain within me.[7]

The result of this entry "into the Negro group" in search of "artistic
expression" was a series of sketches, stories, and poems, which were acclaimed not only as a major contribution to American letters but also as
a fair and objective portrayal of the Negro. Collected in the volume *Cane*
(1923), they earned Jean Toomer the praise of many scholars and critics,
including William Stanley Braithwaite who recognized the author as
"a bright morning star of a new day of the race in literature."[8] They
"thrilled" Sherwood Anderson "to the toes."[9] The author of *Winesburg,
Ohio* had earlier, after reading some of them in manuscript at the office

of *Double Dealer,* hailed them as "of special significance" to him because they constituted "the first negro [sic] work I have seen that strikes
me as being really negro."[10]

Admittedly, Sherwood Anderson's praise of Toomer's work for its
Negroness, as Darwin T. Turner seems to imply, is weakened by the
critic-novelist's failure to explain "his qualification for determining the
authenticity of 'Negro work,' "[11] especially as he later intensified his
praise with the categorical "You are the only negro . . . who seems really
to have consciously the artist's impulse."[12] Yet Anderson's failure to
adequately show why his evaluation should be deemed reliable does not
detract from the quality of the work he evaluates. A firsthand reflection
of the authentic as perceived and registered by a perceptive and sensitive
poet, the Negroness of Toomer's work can hardly be questioned. *Cane*
is an *artistic* record of real people and things seen and heard. Jean Toomer
himself gives us a background knowledge on the material that went into
its making:

I heard folk-songs come from the lips of Negro peasants. I saw the rich
dusk beauty that I had heard many false accents about, and of which till
then, I was somewhat skeptical. And a deep part of my nature, a part that
I had repressed, sprang suddenly to life and responded to them.[13]

An intention to imitate an object is not a guarantee that the end
product of the imitation is a true copy of the object imitated. *Cane* may
not be a word-for-word rendition of what Toomer heard. It may not be
a flawless picture of what he saw. The important facts, however, are that
he had real "Negro peasants" as his models; and that he used them as his
models because something that had been unconscious in him pushed him
not only to identify with these lowly peasants, but also to capture and
preserve their spirit in art. He thus becomes a model for the speaker/
narrator of his poems and sketches.

More than is usually true of narrators and speakers, the speaker/nar-
rator of *Cane* moves and has his being in Jean Toomer; for *Cane* (at
least without the second part) is Toomer's spontaneous response to a
rural black life-style. In fact, although much of the middle section was
written to satisfy publishers who thought that the book in its original
form was too thin for publication,[14] all the three parts are interdependent.
Their combined structure brings to a sharp focus the meaning of the work
itself: affirmation of the black self through search and acceptance.

The volume begins with our attention focused on rural Georgia, one of the spots in America where the roots of the newly deracinated African were buried after they had been traced and dug "from the goat path in Africa." ["Carma"] [15] We find our way through cane fields and pine forests, walking on pine needles which, though "elastic to the feet of the rabbits," are painful to human flesh. ["Karintha," TC, p. 2] We breathe the air heavy with the smell of cane and the smoke of sawdust—all elements of the black man's experience in the New World. Even human beings remind us, thanks to the narrator-speakers's consciousness, of the American Negro's African past and early experience in America. The masculine woman, Carma, whose "fragrance" is "the smell of farmyards," is a reincarnation of the precolonial Africa, at least as it was generally imagined: song, forest, dance, juju men, greegree, and witch doctors. [TC, p. 10] Fern is the result of miscegenation, the type of relationship that exists between the black woman Louisa and the white man Bob Stone of "Blood-Burning Moon." She is more Jewish than black: "At first sight of her I felt as if I heard a Jewish cantor sing. As if her singing rose above the unheard chorus of a folk-song." [TC, p. 15] Yet she is labeled "black," and abandoned by both whites and blacks. She leads a lonely life, always sitting "back propped against a post, head tilted a little forward because there was a nail in the porch post just where her head came which for some reason or other she never took the trouble to pull out." [TC, p. 15] A type of Andersonian grown-up woman, she is a Christ crucified, without prejudice to her authenticity as a Negro element. To pull out the nail from the crucifixlike post would be to reject a part of her experience and background and therefore a part of her self.

The near-white Esther discovers her African and slave past in the folk preacher, King Barlo, who "assumes the outline of his visioned African." [TC, p. 21] Typical of real incidents in black American experience, her conscious drive to embrace that past and part of her self through its symbol, King Barlo—"the starting point of the only patterns that her mind was to know"—ends in a fiasco. Like Omowole in John A. William's film *The Child Returns Home* who, finding himself in his dream Africa, suddenly realizes that he can no longer relate to his ancestral roots, she is disillusioned by a physical proximity to what she has hitherto adored in imagination and from a long physical distance: "She sees a smile, ugly and repulsive to her, working upward through thick licker fumes. Barlo seems hideous. . . . She draws away, frozen. Like a somnambulist she wheels around and walks stiffly to the stairs. Down them." [TC, p. 25]

We have this kind of ambivalence in "Box Seat"; we have it in "Kabnis." It is the very pivot of the North-South-North-South movement of the speaker-narrator and of the book. As a symbol of what is implicit in *Cane,* Esther's search, therefore, is only a dramatization of a moment in a greater search—that of the speaker-narrator which will end in affirmation in "Kabnis." We shall focus on this later.

Meanwhile let us return to the black folk of rural Georgia and their relations to their roots. The readiness with which the Negro women in "Blood-Burning Moon" improvise songs against the spell of the "red nigger moon" is reminiscent of their African and Afro-American ancestors' practice. Like these women, the ancestors readily improvised songs at the appearance of anything unusual or of special significance. They improvised and used songs as a means of communication—to warn, to criticize, to show approval. Louisa is still closer to her ancestors. She improvises songs, and she is as close to nature as they must have been. She belongs with trees, earth, and other natural elements. Her voice is theirs; among them, she, like an African child in a peppermint fig tree, is hardly traceable: "Her skin was the color of oak leaves on young trees in fall. Her breasts, firm and up-pointed like ripe acorns. And her singing had the low murmur of wind in fig trees." [TC, p. 28]

Unfortunately, however, these humanizing Negroisms are doomed. The voice of the Negro in the consciousness of a girl like Fern is being drowned, in spite of herself, by its Semitic counterpart. It is becoming as passive as he who is supposed to be its protector and the protector of all other Negroisms: the African Guardian of Souls of the poem *Conversion:*

> African Guardian of Souls,
> Drunk with rum,
> Feasting on a strange cassava,
> Yielding to new words and a weak palabra
> Of a white-faced sardonic god—
> Grins, cries
> Amen,
> Shouts hosanna
>
> [TC, p. 26]

Incidentally, the drunken Guardian of Souls reminds one of Batouala's father who abdicates his duty to defend his tribal customs and traditions, yields passively to the white man, and dies drunk with the white man's rum.[16]

The Negroism of the black man in America is doomed just like that mini-encyclopedia of his experience in the New World—the beautiful face rendered ugly by age and pain and sorrow not unlike that of the biblical Rachael who weeps for her children that are no more. The face is at the point of disintegration:

> Hair—
> silver-gray,
> like streams of stars,
> Brows—
> recurved canoes
> quivered by ripples blown by pain.
> Her eyes—
> mist of tears
> condensing on the flesh below
> And her channeled muscles
> are cluster grapes of sorrow
> purple in the evening sun
> nearly ripe for worms
>   [*Face*, TC, p. 8]

This nearly-ripe-for-worms condition of the Afro-American's link with his past—his past in the present—intensifies the urgency of the speaker's tone in *Song of the Son,* as he calls for, and celebrates the immortalization of the expiring black soul of the past. Like air (which is also associated with the immortal music), song (here, art) is immortal. Entrusted to song and air, the speaker believes, the "parting soul" of the past would be not only immortal but also expansive. He has been away from the mother "soil" of which he is an offspring, and has returned just "in time" to preside over the ceremony:

> In time, for though the sun is setting on
> A song-lit race of slaves, it has not set;
> Though late, O soil, it is not too late yet
> To catch thy plaintive soul, leaving, soon gone,
> Leaving, to catch thy plaintive soul soon gone.
>   [TC, p. xxi]

As an offspring of the "soil," and "seed" of the "squeezed" "dark purple ripened plums" (exploited "Negro slaves"), he is a natural custodian of their being and experience (joy and sorrow). But, unlike them whose seed he is, he is of the present. His future, however, is not a foregone conclusion. It lies in his ability to "catch" and preserve the "plaintive soul" of the past. His stability and everlastingness depend on the intermingling in a song of his strong soul of the present with the weak expiring soul of the past. He is therefore a candidate for the type of position enjoyed by Carrie K. of "Kabnis" whose strength and the resultant canonization stem, paradoxically, from her oneness with the weak Father John.

The viability of this kind of relationship is the focus of the second part of *Cane* where it is made significant either through a graphic representation of the implication of a failure to embrace one's roots or through the establishment of a conflict between the acceptance and the nonacceptance of the rapport.

The first piece, "Seventh Street," [TC, p. 39] sets the stage. "Seventh Street is a bastard of Prohibition and the War." Essentially a result of the migration of black population from the pine forest and cane fields of the South, life on the street has its roots in the vitalizing soil of the land left behind. The street is the only source of life in Washington, whose anemia is in bold relief against the street's warm blood vessels.

"Rhobert" who "wears a house, like a monstrous diver's helmet, on his head" is a symbol of materialism without the redeeming "water" of humanity which is often associated with the Negro. He sinks "as a diver would sink in mud should the water be drawn off." [TC, pp. 40-41]

"Avey" dramatizes the conflict between middle-class "respectability" and "primitive" spontaneity, also often attributed to the Negro as in the first section of the book. In spite (or even because) of "her downright laziness. Sloppy indolence" [TC, p. 44] and the misery that results from them, Avey is much more successful and happier than the ambitious, but inhibited, narrator. She knows what she wants in life; she reaches out her hand; she gets it. The narrator is in the throes of failure: his, which is real, and what he considers Avey's failure.

The conflict between "primitive" spontaneity and middle-class "respectability" is also the motif of "Theater." John cannot rise above his awareness of what the society expects of him. Thus what his body desires his thoughts repress. He is consciously ashamed of the part of his self which he suspects of being the author of his "primitive" desire. He would even repudiate that part of his self, for although he sits in the light and his "mind coincides with the shaft of light" [TC, p. 50] , he is only a half-shadow of himself. Emasculated by his "mind," he is not a complete man. Thus he sits in front of his love-object, Dorris, "nothin doin." His repressed desire expends itself in a daydream which further emasculates him.

On the contrary, with her roots in the "soil," Dorris is full of strength and life, for "Glorious songs are the muscles of her limbs./And her singing is of canebrake loves and mangrove feasting." [TC, p. 53] She belongs with Carma whose "body is a song," and Karintha whose "running is a whir." She knows that she wants John; she goes in for him: she "tosses her head and dances for him until she feels she has him." [TC, p. 51] Unfortunately for her, however, although "John's heart beats tensely against her dancing body, walls [of respectability] press his mind within his heart." [TC, p. 53] John is completely emasculated; her happiness is frustrated.

"Box Seat" goes beyond the subtle dramatization of the devitalizing effect of the attempt to subject "primitive" traits to middle-class "respectability." It almost tells the Negro in plain terms that his only salvation is in his identification with his Afro-slave past.

The central figure in this conflict is Muriel, a schoolteacher. The other actors constitute two life-styles struggling to win Muriel's adherence. Mrs. Pribby, her landlady, who is always reading a newspaper, is the eyes, ears, and tongue of society. "Her eyes are weak. They are bluish and watery from reading newspapers. The blue is steel." [TC, p. 57] In her class are other agents of the devitalizing and regimented society: Bernice, Muriel's friend, rows of houses, iron gates, chairs, box seats, clocks, and other inanimate objects.

The second life-style is led by Dan Moore. His introduction of himself is direct, and deserves quoting: "I am Dan Moore. I was born in a canefield. The hands of Jesus touched me. I am come to a sick world to heal it." [TC, p. 56] He is an "ordained" (ordained by the Messiah himself) representative of "powerful underground races" from where "the next world-savior is coming up." His mission is to "stir the root-life of a withered people. Call them from their houses, and teach them to dream." [TC, p. 56] In other words, he has "come to a sick world [the type of world portrayed in "Seventh Street"] to heal it." On his side are the "portly Negress" [TC, p. 62] and the old slave [TC, p. 65] who are more imaginary than real and are possibly a mere externalization of the Negro firmly entrenched in him. Both of them are symbols of stability. The "portly Negress," in particular, is a living example of the viability of relating to one's roots. She is what Muriel is not; or, rather, she is what Dan Moore holds out to Muriel—stability, self-confidence.

At the outset of the struggle, Mrs. Pribby's hold on Muriel is almost incontestable. "She is the town" where the struggle takes place. She is part of the prize at issue, as Muriel herself acknowledges in a self-confession: "She *is* me, somehow." [TC, p. 58] Like her, Muriel "clicks into a high-armed seat." [TC, p. 58] Like hers, "Muriel's chair is close and stiff about her. The house, the rows of houses locked about her chair." [TC, p. 60] Muriel is so much of Mrs. Pribby that her presence in Dan's life makes the apostle to the "withered people" ambivalent towards the sickness he has come to cure. Witness, for instance, how he sings the praise of Muriel [TC, p. 63] while on the other hand he faults the "portly Negress" and the old slave. He finds the Negress's eyes focused on him unpleasant. [TC, p. 62] He ignores the old slave; when he does notice him, he becomes hostile. [TC, p. 65]

Yet Muriel is not irrecoverably lost to the life-style hawked by Dan Moore. Still alive in her is an impulse "to do something with [her-] self. Something real and beautiful . . . to make people, every one . . . happy." [TC, p. 59] But hers is an impulse that is powerful and weak at the same time. It is weak because it always yields to Mrs. Pribby's wishes, as in the sequence where the mere awareness of the presence of Mrs. Pribby drives a wedge into their (her and Dan's) spontaneous embrace. [TC, pp. 60-61] It allows itself to be repressed and even tolerates Muriel's attempt to have its counterpart in Dan Moore killed.

On the other hand, it is a powerful impulse because it is spontaneous, and, unlike Mrs. Pribby's respectability, does not require any conscious effort from Muriel to well up:

Dan looks at her, directly. Her animalism, still unconquered by zoo-restrictions and keeper-taboos, stirs him. Passion tilts upward, bringing with it the elements of an old desire. Muriel's lips become the flesh-notes of a futile, plaintive longing. Dan's impulse to direct her is its flesh life.

[TC, p. 59]

Ironically, it is at the moment of its greatest weakness that it scores its greatest victory over "respectability,"—with the assistance of "respectability" itself.

Muriel represses the unrespectable impulse "to do something with [her] self. Something real and beautiful"—something capable of making her and Dan happy. She leaves Dan, the champion of the impulse, to attend a vaudeville with her girl friend, Bernice—one of the arms of the devitalizing society. There she conforms perfectly with the concept "the world of Pribby" has of her. She represses the instinctive urge to take off her coat in order to feel more comfortable, because to do so will mar the total beauty of the locale and lay her taste open to question. [TC, p. 61] "Teachers are not supposed to have bobbed hair." She has bobbed hair; she represses the urge to take her hat off. [TC, p. 61] In her "brass box seat" she smiles and claps even though she is "bored," and does not feel like clapping and smiling. [TC, p. 63]

Then comes the fight of two dwarfs (a possible prototype of Ralph Ellison's battle royal in *Invisible Man*) obviously introduced by the narrator not only as a symbol of intraracial squabbles among blacks for the benefit of the outsider but also as a demonstration, through the reaction of the audience, of how inhuman the adherence to some of the rules of "respectability" can make people.

As the dwarfs lunge and hurt each other, Muriel and her fellow spectators laugh, and clap, and call for more action. [TC, p. 65] In the end, as if to get her to contemplate fully the ramifications of her respectable enjoyment, the winning dwarf offers her a rose stained with the "blood of his battered lips." Her first reaction is to reject it in the name of "respectability" since the dwarf is not only ugly but also beneath her. However, "Berny leans forward and whispers: 'Its all right. Go on—take it.' " Thus she is encouraged to accept, for her closer contemplation, the bloodstained white rose from the ugly dwarf whose identification with the lowly status of the underground races, represented by Dan Moore, is obvious. For instance, when Dan Moore thinks of holding "a god's face that will flash white light from ebony," the dwarf flashes a mirror in his face. [TC, pp. 65-66] Indeed, the words that "form in the eyes of the dwarf" as he offers the rose to Muriel are intensified by those that form in the mind of Dan—italicized in the text:

Do not shrink. Do not be afraid of me.
Jesus
See how my eyes look at you.
the Son of God

I too was made in His image.
was once—
I give you the rose.

. . . .
"JESUS WAS ONCE A LEPER!" [TC, p. 66]

Dan Moore's celebration of the discomfiture of Muriel's "respectability" is as unconventional as it is spontaneous. He "serenely tweaks"
a man's nose. He and the man walk out to fight. Then "The man stops.
Takes off his hat and coat. Dan, having forgotten him, keeps going on."
[TC, p. 67] People who have followed them to see more blood are thus
disappointed.

The story of Bona and Paul also demonstrates the devitalizing effect
of a nonacceptance of parts of oneself. Paul has every potential for being a male Karintha or Carma. Like these women, he is full of life and
strength. "The dance of his blue-trousered limbs thrills" Bona who
describes him as "a candle that dances in a grove swung with pale bal-
loons." [TC, p. 70] Like these women also, he is the offspring of the
soil in which his roots are still located. [TC, p. 71] Although he is light-
skinned enough to pass for white, it is the Negro part of his personality
that attracts Bona who, unfortunately for him and herself, goes into
their relationship with a preconceived idea of how "a harvest moon"
like Paul should love. Paul, who is always seeing in his mind "a Negress
chant[ing] a lullaby beneath the mate-eyes of a southern planter"
[TC, pp. 71, 76], is as conscious of the suspected Negroism in him as he
is aware of his whiteness. He is especially conscious of his Negro-traits
when he, Bona, and their friends go to the Crimson Gardens and people
look at him: "Their stares, giving him to himself, filled something long
empty within him, and were like green blades sprouting in his consciousness. There was fullness, and strength and peace about it all. He saw himself, cloudy, but real." [TC, p. 75]

He is, nonetheless, determined to stifle the pro-Negro development
in his consciousness. Since, however, it is not easy to draw, in an Afro-
American mind, a thin line between what is Negro and what is not, the
result of Paul's determined assault on the Negro part of his self is the
emasculation of his entire self, for "contrary to what he had thought he
would be like, [he] is cool like dusk, and like the dusk, detached. His
dark face is a floating shade in evening's shadow." [TC, p. 73]

Ironically, when he eventually fails, a "dark face"—symbol of the
Negro element of his double-consciousness, the element he wants to
repudiate—floats back to celebrate the frustration of his attempt to reject a part of himself: "A strange thing happens. He sees the Gardens
purple, as if he were way off. And a spot is in the purple. The spot comes
furiously towards him. Face of the black man. It leers. It smiles sweetly
like a child's." [TC, p. 78]

Although the establishment of equilibrium between Paul's warring
selves (through a handshake with the black man whose face has made him
miserable) comes too late to guarantee him the possession of Bona, he is
relieved, at least temporarily, of his fear of the dark face. Reconciled
with his blackness and all it embodies, he is able to recognize that
"petals" are "petals" no matter what their colors. [TC, p. 78] The
Negro is not a dark misshapen image of the Caucasian but a paragon of
himself, with a past, present, and future.

The reconciliation of the Afro-American with his past continues in
"Kabnis," the mini-play that constitutes the third part of *Cane*. Although
the piece symbolically returns us to rural Georgia where an intensive
search for roots of black experience in America is acted out, it can be
described as an allegorical descent of the Negro into himself with a view
to understanding and affirming the black aspect of his self.

The central figure in this quest is Kabnis, a northern Negro, who has
come to the South apparently for that purpose. As the story begins he
is "propped in his bed" in his cabin room with whitewashed hearth and
chimney. He looks secure in "the warm whiteness of his bed, [and] the
lamplight" by which he tries to read himself to sleep. [TC, p. 81] But
this outward appearance of security is false. The walls of his cabin are
made of boards, "and cracks between the boards are black. These cracks
are lips the night winds use for whispering. Night winds in Georgia are
vagrant poets, whispering. . . . The warm whiteness of his bed, the lamp-
lights, do not protect him from the weird chill of their song." [TC, p. 81]

The song of the night winds is the glow of his black self in his psyche,
the real "cabin room" of which his habitat is only a symbolic projection.
Do what he will, he cannot suppress it. It corrodes the bottom of his
apparent security and jets up like the refrain of a ballad:

> The winds, like soft-voiced vagrant poets sing:
> White-man's land.
> Niggers, sing.

> Burn, bear black children
> Till poor rivers bring
> Rest, and sweet glory
> In Camp Ground.
>
> [TC, p. 85]

It seeks to make him realize the hollowness of his sense of security. He has black blood in his veins. His outward whiteness cannot save him from the white man's lynching fire. He may as well embrace and live his blackness wholeheartedly.

But Kabnis does not; and that is the source of his weakness. His body is a battleground between the white race whom he fears and the black people whom he despises. It is this battle between his two selves that makes him unstable, separating him from Lewis, "a tall wiry copper-colored man, thirty perhaps." [TC, p. 95] He has all the potential for being as stable as Lewis who is to all intents and purposes his ideal self. [TC, p. 95] All he needs is to embrace this darker self of his, and his problem will be solved. The description of his first encounter with Lewis is revealing:

His eyes turn to Kabnis. In the instant of their shifting, a vision of the life they are to meet. Kabnis, a promise of a soil-soaked beauty; uprooted, thinning out. Suspended a few feet above the soil whose touch would resurrect him. Arm's length removed from him whose will to help . . . There is a swift intuitive interchange of consciousness. Kabnis has a sudden need to rush into the arms of this man. His eyes call, "Brother." And then a savage, cynical twist-about within mocks his impulse and strengthens him to repulse Lewis. [TC, p. 96]

The "savage, cynical twist-about" that "strengthens him to repulse Lewis" is the force responsible for his being "a dream" instead of "the real Kabnis" [TC, p. 81], for Lewis who had earlier been portrayed as seeming "to be issuing sharply from a vivid dream" [TC, p. 95] is part, if not the whole, of "the real Kabnis." The "twist-about" itself is Kabnis's white consciousness. It is too potent to accept the implication of Kabnis's rushing into the arms of Lewis: an integration of the two selves through the bridging of the gap between their two attitudes towards Kabnis's slave past. These two attitudes are well dramatized in the "hole" sequence.

Here both Kabnis (for white consciousness) and Lewis (for black consciousness) execute a symbolic descent into their selves. Both of them
find Father John, a symbol of their slave past. But while Lewis recognizes
him as "a mute John the Baptist of a new religion—or a tongue-tied
shadow of an old," and is very anxious to hear him speak, "Kabnis won't
give him [Father John] a chance." [TC, p. 104] For him, he is "Father
of hell" [TC, p. 104] —the source, he believes, of his misfortune in
America. His confinement to the cellar, which serves him and Halsey as
a place of debauchery and, therefore, of degradation, is welcome. Above
all, confronted with the penetrating eyes of Lewis—his ideal self—who
tries to force him to accept "the old man as symbol, flesh, and spirit of
the past," he rises to an absolute denial: "He aint my past. My ancestors
were Southern blue bloods—." [TC, p. 107]

Ironically, this very denial is a turning point in Kabnis's relation with
Father John and his slave past which the old man represents. As in the
case of Muriel and of Paul, who reaffirm their darker selves at the very
moment they are doing their best to repudiate them, it brings him closest
to what he has been trying to avoid. Firstly, he confesses that "aint much
difference between blue and black" bloods. [TC, p. 107] No blood is
inferior to others. Secondly, he does not react in a hostile way to Lewis's
rebuke—a rebuke which diagnoses his problem: "Cant hold them, can
you? Master; slave. Soil; and the overarching heavens. Dusk; dawn. They
fight and bastardize you. The sun tint of your cheeks, flame of the great
season's multi-colored leaves, tarnished, burned. Split, shredded: easily
burned. No use." [TC, p. 107] Thirdly, in spite of his earlier denial that
there is anything called "soul" [TC, p. 81], he tells Carrie K. whose
strength derives from her unyielding effort to sustain the breath of the
old man who is now almost at the point of death, that "th' soul of me
[Kabnis] . . . needs th risin." [TC, p. 114]

Thus the ironic denial—ironic because it is, in a way, a negation of
negation—leads to a new Kabnis with a new perception—a Kabnis who
accepts his black self in the last scene of the action.

As Kabnis falls and remains prostrate, like a sinner, in front of Father
John, Carrie K., who apostlelike has been ministering to the old man,
arrives. "She is lovely in her fresh energy of the morning, in the calm
untested confidence and nascent maternity which rise from the purpose
of her present mission. She walks to within a few paces of Kabnis."
[TC, p. 114]

"Her present mission" begins at once. She is twice symbolic. She is the symbol of a new consciousness in Kabnis (Gorham B. Munson calls her a "fresh symbol of a possible future").[17] She is symbolically pregnant. The child she is expecting is a new Kabnis. As in a Christian symbolic rebirth, Kabnis confesses his flaw: that his soul needs a "risin," and accepts the principle of the target religion: "I get my life down in this scum-hole. The old man an me—." [TC, p. 114]

Although he does not complete his statement, although he rebukes the old man for mentioning "sin," he is still in the process of rebirth. In fact, he somehow repudiates his outburst: "Ralph says things. Doesnt mean to. . . . I'm what sin is. . . . Dont look shocked, little sweetheart, you hurt me." [TC, p. 115] The ceremony continues in spite of this ambivalence until we come to the last page where the process is completed:

She [Carrie K.] turns him to her and takes his hot cheeks in her firm cool hands. Her palms draw the fever out. With its passing, Kabnis crumples. He sinks to his knees before her, ashamed, exhausted. His eyes squeeze tight. Carrie presses his face tenderly against her. The suffocation of her fresh starched dress feels good to him. Carrie is about to lift her hands in prayer, when Halsey at the head of the stairs calls down. [TC, p. 116]

The interruption of Carrie K's prayer by Halsey's call is part of the ambivalence. She says her prayer later.

In any case, the Kabnis that rises and walks up the steps is a new Kabnis, rid of his robe of debauchery. The "dead coals" he carries up with him, like dry bones to which Ezekiel preaches in the valley, are a symbol of rejuvenation and, contrary to Roberta Riley's suggestion, do not "emphasize Kabnis's failure to achieve communion with his racial past."[18] Dead coals are a potential source of energy. His carrying them up with him is an acceptance of "his racial past" towards which he has been lukewarm. Indeed, he seems to be supported or even goaded in this move by that symbol of the new consciousness, Carrie K. Witness how he takes "the bucket of dead coals," and goes upstairs with it: "Turning, he stumbles over the bucket of dead coals. He savagely jerks it from the floor. And then, seeing Carrie's eyes upon him, he swings the pail carelessly and with eyes downcast and swollen, trudges upstairs to the workshop. Carrie's gaze follows him till he is gone." [TC, p. 116] In any event, Carrie K., who has called his attention to the "robe," does not ask him to drop the pail. Instead, Kabnis out of sight, "she goes to the old man and slips to her knees before him. Her lips murmur, 'Jesus, come.' " [TC, p. 116] Light filters "through the iron-barred cellar window"; the old man who, Kabnis has said, will never see light again, is "within its soft circle" together with Carrie K.–the new consciousness.

When Gorham B. Munson described "Kabnis" as "a steep slope downward," he was thinking mainly of the structural movement of the mini-play.[19] The action begins from a hill, gradually moves down into the valley, and ends up in a basement—"the hole"—about twenty feet below the surface of the earth. Nevertheless, the significance of this downward slope lies mainly in its symbolic connotation. It is an Orphean journey of a deracinated Negro to the underground from where his seed has sprung. Coming at the end of the volume whose very forward and backward (South-North-South) movement,[20] coupled with the drama of individual characters, Muriel, Paul, and even Dan, is symbolic of its narrator/speaker's ambivalence towards the object of his search (his Negro self), Ralph Kabnis's descent into "the hole" (his self), and reconciliation with Father John (the Negro in him) through the ministerial intermediary, Carrie K. (the new consciousness, or Negro self-awareness), constitute a final demarche of self-affirmation.

In the light of the above analysis, and in view of the fact that the self-affirmation through search and acceptance reflects to some extent an experience lived by Jean Toomer himself, one can safely say that *Cane* is Negro self-expressing. The thought it embodies is deeply impregnated with Negro self-awareness. With the exception of two or three cases, its objects of imitation are Negro because, or in spite, of their colors. Indeed Montgomery Gregory discovers Negro traits in the eyes of the almost completely Semitic Fernie May Rosen.[21]

However, the uniqueness of *Cane* among the Negro writings in the 1920s lies not in the thought it incarnates, not in the objects of imitation, but in its manner of imitation. It subscribed to the literary attitude within the mainstream of American literature at that period. It revolted against the established form; it experimented with new forms. It is mainly, therefore, in its manner of imitation that extraneous influence, if any, should be found.

Two names are important in this connection: Waldo Frank and Sherwood Anderson. Like Waldo Frank's *Holiday*, *Cane* combines impressionism, imagism, and quasi realism in its presentation. Since Frank was more established than Toomer it is reasonable to suspect that it was Frank who influenced Toomer and not Toomer who influenced Frank. As a matter of fact, Sherwood Anderson at one time thought that Toomer was "going to fall under the influence of Waldo Frank and his style of writing."[22] He thought that some images in "Esther," for instance, echoed Waldo Frank; he "shivered." Nevertheless, a careful scrutiny of the relationship and correspondence between Jean Toomer and Waldo Frank before the publication of their two books in 1923 reveals that *Cane* could not have owed more to Frank than *Holiday* owes to Toomer.

Some of the pieces in *Cane* had been accepted by the *Double Dealer,* the *Liberator,* and *Broom* before Toomer showed the manuscript of his best sketches to Waldo Frank,[23] and by this time all, with the possible exception of some of the pieces in the second part of the volume, had been written.[24] By this time also, Waldo Frank had not completed his *Holiday.* Toomer accompanied him to South Carolina about three months later to feel firsthand the atmosphere he sought to capture in the novel.[25] Any influence Waldo Frank had on *Cane,* he must have exercised through other channels and/or through his earlier works and not through *Holiday.*

More noticeable in *Cane* is an apparent influence of Sherwood Anderson who, ironically, suspected as indicated above that Toomer was falling under Waldo Frank's influence. Apart from Jean Toomer's own confessed indebtedness to Sherwood Anderson's *Winesburg, Ohio* and *The Triumph of the Egg,*[26] some of the pieces in *Cane* reveal very striking similarities with some of the stories in *Winesburg, Ohio.* A few examples will illustrate this point.

The heroines of Toomer's "Esther" and of Anderson's "Adventure" have much in common. Esther's imaginary but fanatic attachment to King Barlo resembles Alice Hindman's to Ned Currie who, like King Barlo, is an absent love-object. The consummation of the Esther-Barlo imaginary love affair takes place when, at the age of sixteen, Esther dreams of a baby she has had with Barlo. [TC, p. 22] The consummation of the Alice-Ned love affair takes place when Alice is sixteen years old and "Ned Currie took her into his arms and kissed her."[27] Both girls, fanatically faithful to their love-objects, refuse to have any affair with any other men. The stories of the two girls reach a climax when, at the age of twenty-seven, each of them learns the truth of her fate.

Again, the Tom-Louisa-Bob relationship in Toomer's "Blood-Burning Moon" is like the Ed-Belle-George affair in Anderson's "An Awakening."

Belle Carpenter accepts George Willard because of his position in the town, although her mind is really with Ed Handby;[28] Louisa accepts Bob Stone because of his position in the society, although her mind is really with Tom Burwell. Like Ed, Tom is not a sophisticated lover but a man of action. Like George who is castigated by Ed, Bob is punished by Tom for intrusion.

As for Avey, almost everyone familiar with *Cane* and *Wineburg, Ohio* recognizes her affinity with Andersonian women. Although extremely sensual, she does not resemble very much the more society-conscious Helen White of "Sophistication." There is, however, a measure of similarity between her affair with the narrator and the Helen-George relationship. There is in the two stories the same youthful waiting in the dark for a love-object whose attention is temporarily engaged by a college man. There are the same solitary moments spent at a deserted public place by night. It is, however, the George-Louisa relationship in "Nobody Knows" that "Avey" resembles most among Sherwood Anderson's stories.

Like Louisa Trunnion's, Avey's reputation is frowned upon by the "respectable." The narrator-lover's ineffectiveness when he yields to Avey not only the initial step but also the more active role in their embrace resembles the ineffectiveness of George Willard who also lets Louisa take the initial step and play the more active part in what he is happy that "nobody knows."

Thematically *Cane* and *Winesburg, Ohio* also have much in common. Such characters as Muriel ("Box Seat"), John ("Theater"), and the narrator ("Avey") are, like Andersonian "grotesques," all victims of societal "truths " or conventionalism.

Finally, *Cane* and *Winesburg, Ohio* resemble each other in form. It is true that Jean Toomer's book contains poems while Sherwood Anderson's novel does not contain any poetry per se in spite of its lyricism. Yet like *Winesburg, Ohio, Cane* is made up of separate pieces more or less woven together, thanks to a consistent tone, setting, a recurring theme, and the appearance of some characters in two or more pieces. Both books also end in a sort of escape: George (Anderson's narrator) from the dehumanizing environment of Winesburg; Kabnis (who, with his alter ego Lewis, is implicitly the narrator/speaker of *Cane*) from the emasculating "wasteland" of self-doubt.

Nevertheless, despite these similarities—possible results of unconscious and unintended emulation—it will be wrong to regard *Cane* as a freehand reproduction of *Winesburg, Ohio.* As a matter of fact, the similarities should not be overstressed. The people of Winesburg, Ohio, and Toomer people are not exactly alike. Most Anderson people are moral; most Toomer people are amoral. Most of the women of Winesburg, Ohio, are packs of repressed impulses; most of the Toomer women carry their natural impulses as Karintha carries beauty, "perfect as dusk when the sun goes down." Almost every Toomer woman is endowed with what almost every Anderson woman lacks: animal spontaneity and vitality—stereotyped Negro traits, certainly, but traits which, like the author's constant use of the terms "nigger," "Negress," and "liverlips," not only assume positive values in Jean Toomer's *Cane,* but are also essentially true to type.

It is significant, in this connection, that in spite of his doubt about Toomer's knowledge of Georgia and his suspicion that black readers would not like the images of black womanhood in *Cane,* W. E. B. Du Bois conceded that "they are done with a certain splendid, careless truth."[29] Equally significant is Montgomery Gregory's recognition of Toomer as America's own counterpart of Maran and *Cane* as "the [Negro] race soul."[30] René Maran was the first black man to try to look into the "soul" of the black man in Africa. His *Batouala* is credited with being a "veritable" study of the black African psychology. Whatever may be the weakness of this analogy, Gregory recognizes the "truth" of Toomer's treatment of the black man in the South. For him, "*Cane* is not OF the South, it is not OF the Negro; it IS the South, it IS the Negro—as Jean Toomer has experienced them."[31]

Whatever must have happened later to the elements of Jean Toomer's double-consciousness, the author of *Cane* at a certain point in his life not only let his Negro consciousness rise above its white counterpart but also sought consciously to promote things Negro through his art:

I feel that in time, in its social phase, my art will aid in giving the Negro to himself. In this connection, I have thought of a magazine. A magazine American, but concentrating on the significant contributions or possible contributions of the Negro to the Western world. A magazine that would consciously hoist, and perhaps at first a trifle overemphasize a negroid ideal. A magazine that would function organically for what I feel to be the budding of the Negro's consciousness. The need is great. People within the race cannot see it. In fact, they are likely to prove to be directly hostile. But with the youth of the race, unguided or misguided as they now are, there is a tragic need. Talent dissipates itself for want of creative channels of expression, and encouragement.[32]

It is possible that he did, and intended to do, everything for the Negro not as a Negro himself but as a member of the "new stock," or simply "as an artist," as Eugene Holmes claims.[33] Yet the fact remains that *Cane* does try to "giv[e] the Negro to himself." The "souls" embodied in the stories and poems that constitute the book are authentic *Souls of Black Folk* artistically reaffirmed.

COUNTÉE CULLEN

Unlike Jean Toomer, Countée Cullen never tried to deny the Negroness of his person; but he struggled to be called a "poet" as distinct from "poet" with the qualificative "Negro" attached—"Negro poet." "As a poet," he wrote about himself in the third person, "he is a rank conservative, loving the measured line and the skilful rhyme, . . . He has said perhaps with a reiteration sickening to some of his friends, that he wishes any merit that may be in his work to flow from it solely as the expression of a poet—with no racial consideration to bolster it up. He is still of the same thought."[34] He was "still of the same thought" in 1929 when, in his poem *To Certain Critics,* he declared himself ready to stand condemned for his rejection:

> Then call me traitor if you must,
> Shout treason and default!
> Say I betray a sacred trust
> Aching beyond this vault.[35]

We shall return, later, to the why and wherefore of this resolute rejection. Meanwhile, two facts must be affirmed: in spite of himself, Countée Cullen, author of *Heritage, A Song of Praise, She of the Dancing Feet Sings,* and similar poems, was a Negro poet; in spite of the opinion of some critics[36] Countée Cullen was a New Negro poet.

As a matter of fact, he himself admitted in an interview with a *Time* reporter, early in his writing career—that is, before his ambition to be simply an artist hardened into the blatant rejection of the title "Negro Poet" by 1927—that do whatever he could, he was a New Negro poet: "In spite of myself, I find that I am actuated by a strong sense of race consciousness. Although I struggle against it, it colors my writings, I fear, in spite of everything that I can do."[37] This tendency of his work to take at least part of its color from his race consciousness "in spite of everything" he could do, is no more evident than in his poem *The Ballad of the Brown Girl,* which earned him an honorable mention in the Witter Bynner Poetry Contest of 1923 and was his first major achievement in poetry.

In its original form the old English tale on which the ballad is built has nothing to do with race. In Cullen's version, however, the story has an implicit ring of the familiar experience of black women who must be abandoned by their white lovers who want to marry fairer women. Countée Cullen obviously saw his "brown girl" as a Negro:

> Her hair was black as sin is black
> And ringed about with fire;
> Her eyes were black as night is black
> When moon and stars conspire;
> Her mouth was one red cherry clipt
> In twain, her voice a lyre.
> [CCA, p. 177]

She is as dark as the subject of another poem by Cullen—*A Song of Praise* [CCA, p. 102] —the "nut-brown maiden" whose Negroness is beyond all doubt. Witness, for instance, how the "sin-black hair" of this girl with "full lips" resembles that of the "brown girl" as described in the stanza quoted above. Beside her rival whose "skin was white as almond milk" [CCA, p. 178] she is almost darker than a mulatto girl. That she suffers because of her affiliation to the black race is more than suggested by the characteristic presentation of her rival as "lily maid,/ And pride of all the south." [CCA, p. 175] One thinks of the southern part of the United States.[38] When she dies, she is characteristically buried as a slave "at her true lord's feet." [CCA, p. 182]

The abandonment of the Brown Girl differs from that of Clotel's mother or even that of the mother of James Weldon Johnson's Ex-Coloured Man because it is essentially mental, a fact which, however, makes it worse. While, like these black women, the white girl is physically abandoned to satisfy a parent and, like them, is mentally loved and retained, the Brown Girl is mentally unloved and abandoned without being spared the physical experience of being treated as an intruder. Lord Thomas would not protect her from the insult of her fair rival and when she protects herself he strangles her and orders that she be buried at their feet.

This thoughtlessness borders on racial hatred. Our sympathy, therefore, as in Brown's and Johnson's stories, is with the darker woman. Her experience is universal. But just as the poet's presentation of it has been colored by his racial awareness, our reaction to it is colored by our awareness that the injustice to which she is subjected stems partly or wholly from racial hatred.

This is also true of our reaction to the agony of the speaker of *The Shroud of Color*. [CCA, pp. 16-23] Although the speaker's romantic death wish transcends color and race, his awareness that his longing for death stems not from his hatred of life per se but from the pain engendered by nonblack people's attitudes towards the fact of his being black, compels our sympathy for him. [CCA, p. 22] It is the same awareness that makes us commiserate with the speaker of the famous *Yet Do I Marvel*. [CCA, p. 3] In spite of his acceptance of suffering as a humanly unexplainable experience of the creatures of God who, although He is "good, well-meaning, kind," lets His creatures—all His creatures—suffer, his last couplet ("Yet do I marvel at this curious thing: / To make a poet black, and bid him sing!") encapsulates a tearful racial awareness.

Color (1925), Countée Cullen's first book of poems, is full of this arousal of pity by coloring an otherwise universal experience with racial awareness. In some poems, like *Incident,* and *To my Fairer Brethren,* the coloring is evident; in some, like *Pagan Prayer,* it is subtle. In all cases, however, Cullen's speaker's mind functions like that of the speaker in his *Uncle Jim*[39] which, in spite of the speaker's rejection of the old man's thoughts as "a platitude," cannot, even at the most unsuspected moment and place, resist the subconscious urge to "stray the Grecian urn / To muse on Uncle Jim." Countée Cullen found it difficult to escape the impulse to racialize the nonracial experiences he treated in his poetry.

He lamented his inability to do so. "Somehow or other, I find my poetry of itself treating of the Negro, of his joys and his sorrows, mostly of the latter and of the heights and depths of emotion which I feel as a Negro."[40]

His later work also shows evidence of this irresistible impulse. His blackening of Christ and his dedication of the poem that embodies Him "hopefully . . . to White America"[41] are manifestations of this same impulse. This is also true of his Africanization of the ancestry of Medea who is portrayed as a victim of a white man's racial sentiment.[42] In a way, Cullen's constant and apparently non-race-motivated identification with underdogs is only an aesthetic distortion of reality, a dream-work approach to creative writing, a technique very close to what Sigmund Freud calls "incitement premium."[43] His Black Magdalenes and Medusa are all surrogates for black victims of racial discrimination. Every pain their fate causes readers who discriminate against blacks will soothe the underdog mentality that identifies with their experience or from which they derive their being.

However, this conscious or unconscious attempt to arouse pity for the Negro is not an attribute of the New Negro writer whom Cullen's mentor, Charles S. Johnson, described as dragging himself "out of the deadening slough of the race's historical inferiority complex, and . . . leaving to the old school its labored lamentations and protests, read only by those who agree with them, and . . . writing about life."[44] Countée Cullen's New Negroness, therefore, does not lie in a desire to arouse pity. It does not even lie in his basic concept of "good poetry": "lofty thought beautifully expressed"[45]—a concept which made him wonder whether some of Langston Hughes's poems are poems in the real sense of the word.[46] It does not lie in his diplomatic "code" for black literature as established in his column, "The Dark Tower":

There are some things, some truths of Negro life and thought, of Negro inhibitions that all Negroes know, but take no pride in. To broadcast them to the world will but strengthen the bitterness of our enemies, and in some instances turn away the interest of our friends. Every phase of Negro life should not be the white man's concern. The parlor should be large enough for his entertainment and instruction. . . . *Put forward your best foot.*[47]

Above all, it does not lie in his refusal to experiment like many of his white contemporaries and a few of his black ones, notably Jean Toomer and Langston Hughes, at the expense of conventional forms, beautiful images, and elevated thoughts.

Countée Cullen's New Negroness lies in his speakers' pride in the fact of being black coupled with an awareness of Africa and of their relations with her. In other words, although his forms and conscious attitudes tend to remove his works from the New Negro literature, the black-is-beautiful theme and the pervasive African motif—two of the several features of the New Negro literature—place them among the Harlem Renaissance products. The first carries with it the acceptance of demeaning stereotyped traits which, however, are converted, as in Jean Toomer's *Cane,* into positive values. Thus the speaker of *She of the Dancing Feet Sings* projects her sensuality as something to prefer to the heavenly puritanism of "a perfect place / Where dancing would be sin, / With not a man to love my face, / Nor an arm to hold me in." [CCA, p. 39] The sensuousness of the subject of *A Song of Praise* is portrayed as an admirable trait; it is one of the sources of her superiority to her fairer sister. [CCA, p. 4] In *To A Brown Boy* the brownness of a girl is translated into cleanliness, while her otherwise ridiculed "liver lips" are positively presented as more fulfilling and more to be desired than those of a white girl which expend in words what ought to be transmitted by action.[48]

If this racial pride in Countée Cullen's work is paradoxical, more so is the presence in his poem of the African motif, or what he once, almost contemptuously, described as "nebulous atavistic yearnings toward an African inheritance"—an "inheritance" which was better forgotten in favor of "the rich background of English and American poetry."[49] As a matter of fact, if we accept the stereotyped idea which sees every black man and woman as a possessor of rhythm, we can safely say that Cullen's "yearnings toward an African inheritance" are manifest not only in his use of Africa as a subject, or part thereof, but also in his lyrical ability. He himself endorsed this claim when he asserted that his inability to sing well was offset by his poetry. This, in his words, was "the way of my giving out what music is within me. Perhaps I was impelled toward the lyrical pattern, when I began to write, because a destiny took pity on my musical poverty."[50] The assumption is that he ought to be musically rich—as an Afro-American.

It is, however, in the content of some of his poems that the "ativistic yearnings" are more manifest. We feel them in *The Shroud of Color* which under the title *Spirit Birth* earned him, in 1924, another honorable mention in the Witter Bynner Poetry Contest. Here African blood is presented as a source of courage and of willingness to live on in a world that robs the Negro of his manhood not because of what he is underneath his physical appearance but because of the color of his skin which, being dark, has, even before his birth, doomed him to the status of subhuman. [CCA, p. 16] Aware of the injustice of his birth and of his experience in life, the speaker falls prostrate, determined to die, and is "lifted on a great black wing / That had no mate nor flesh-apparent trunk / To hamper it" [CCA, p. 18]—a symbol of thought blackened, deformed, and converted into a strong death wish. Roving on this "wing," he learns how everything, every man alive, struggles to live on in spite of all difficulties. [CCA, p. 20] But the "curse" is too heavy on his life to let him change his mind, and he does not do so until something deep and African in him intervenes:

> Now suddenly a strange wild music smote
> A chord long impotent in me; a note
> Of jungle, primitive and subtle, throbbed
> Against my echoing breast, and tom-toms sobbed
> In every pulse-beat of my frame. The din
> A hollow log bound with a python's skin
> Can make wrought every nerve to ecstasy,
> And I was wind and sky again, and sea,
> And all sweet things that flourish, being free
> [CCA, p. 21]

Suicide is defeatism and, as an escape from life, is regarded as cowardly, is despised and frowned upon by the society from where he has derived the "chord long impotent" in him.[51] He only needs to remember the indomitable courage and faith-in-man of the black slave ("the tree that grew / This body that I was") in the New World to reaffirm his renascent desire to live on. [CCA, p. 22]

In a way, the speaker's recognition of his ancestral roots and experience as revitalizing, at this early stage in Countée Cullen's writing career, is prophetic, for Cullen's conscious effort not to revitalize his genius from those roots and experience often results in anemic poetry—sounds and images beautiful to the eye and to the ear but hollow and light to the spirit.

Another poem which reveals Countée Cullen's "atavistic yearnings toward an African inheritance" in spite of himself, is *Atlantic City Waiter*. Here African blood and its derivatives are a source of beauty; the subject, like the dark girl of *A Song of Praise,* owes his graceful gait to his African roots. He is conscious and proud of his attractiveness; his modesty is only a flimsy "mask" above "the jungle flames" in him.

It is, however, in *Heritage,* the best-known document on the New Negro awareness of Africa, that Cullen's use of African motif reaches its apogee. In this poem a speaker who is "three centuries removed / From the scenes his fathers loved, / Spicy grove, cinnamon tree" [CCA, p. 24] tries to find out what Africa is to him. Several suggestions come into his mind. Africa is:

> Copper sun or scarlet sea
> Jungle star or jungle track,
> Strong bronzed men, or regal black
> Women from whose loins I sprang
> When the birds of Eden sang
>   [CCA, p. 24]

Africa is:

> A book one thumbs
> Listlessly, till slumber comes
>   [CCA, p. 25]

Africa and everything about her should be forgotten; they mean nothing to him.

But this claim is a lie. Unlike the Apostle Peter who denies his friend and master three time before he realizes his error, the speaker realizes the falseness of his pronouncements immediately he makes them. Thus each of his denials is followed by a reaffirmation of what is being denied. Despite the distance in time and space between him and Africa, the ancestral continent is in and around him. She is the ultimate source of the pride which he derives from his "somber flesh and skin, / With the dark blood dammed within / Like great pulsing tides of wine." [CCA, p. 25] Her impact on him is such that Christianity for him is only a surrogate for the worship of her gods of "rods, / Clay, and brittle bits of stone." His "conversion came high-priced." For him the African "outlandish heathen gods" have not been (if we may use this example), as "yielding to new words and a weak palabra / Of a white-faced sardonic god" as Jean Toomer's African Guardian of Souls in the poem *Conversion.*

[TC, p. 26] There has been a real struggle before he was converted. The struggle is still going on. He confesses his recalcitrancy:

> Jesus of the twice-turned cheek,
> Lamb of God, although I speak
> With my mouth thus, in my heart
> Do I play a double part.
> Ever at Thy glowing altar
> Must my heart grow sick and falter,
> Wishing He I serve were black, . . .
> Lord, I fashion dark gods, too,
> Daring even to give You
> Dark despairing features . . .
> [CCA, p. 27]

Even as he speaks, he knows that his confession is not accompanied by repentance. His immediate concern is to control his pride lest the old ancestral ways, whose hold on him he has underestimated because of the distance of "three centuries" that separates him from them, get out-of-hand. [CCA, p. 28]

While *Heritage* is the most effective recording of the New Negro ambivalent attitude towards Africa, it is also one of the poems in the Harlem Renaissance literature that most reveals influences extraneous to the poet himself. Certainly, Countée Cullen owes much of the details that go into his image of Africa (as inaccurate as that image is) to his imagination. Yet there are reasons to believe that his imagination was fired, if not sustained, by what he garnered from other sources: books and Tarzan-type motion pictures.[52] For instance, his speaker's portrayal of himself recalls, if it does not echo, Vachel Lindsay's poem, *The Congo*. Like Lindsay's Afro-Americans through whom the river Congo flows, the speaker's body is a little container of Africa:

> I . . . find no peace
> Night or day, no slight release
> From the unremittant beat
> Made by cruel padded feet
> Walking through my body's street.
> Up and down they go, and back,
> Treading out a jungle track.
> [CCA, p. 26]

The "flood" (of the old ancestral ways) in him which he fears might
drown him makes one think of Vachel Lindsay's river Congo. "CREEP-
ING THROUGH THE BLACK, CUTTING THROUGH THE FOREST
WITH A GOLDEN TRACK."[53]

There is still another possible source of influence on the poem which
up till now has never been suspected: René Maran. While it is unthinkable
to see any relationship between Cullen's adoration of the black skin and
other black features and Maran's portrayal of the African, the negative
or anti-African element of the ambivalence of Countée Cullen's *Heritage*
may have been, at least in part, a manifestation of a subconscious refusal
to identify with the Africa which the young poet had found in *Batouala*.
The cry in the speaker's "body" ("Strip! / Doff this new exuberance. /
Come and dance the Lover's Dance!") may have been an allusion to
René Maran's "dance of love."

Admittedly, Cullen could be alluding to another source: Pierre Loti's
"upa-upa,"[54] for instance. Countée Cullen spoke, read, and taught
French. It is possible he had read Loti's *Le Mariage de Loti* by the time
he wrote his *Heritage*. Nonetheless, it is safe to believe that an episode
which inspired the young poet's *The Dance of Love* (*After Reading
René Maran's Batouala*) could have left a strong impression on him. In
this poem we have the same ambivalence—in the speaker's way of
participating in the fertility dance. He is torn between the naked dance
(of Africa) and the "hidden beauty in the air" (of the approaching dawn
of Western civilization). Even though he later identifies with and accepts
the passionate, naked lover, the effect of the dawn on him is too potent
to let him continue "the dance of love."[55]

Whatever the case, Cullen and Maran were aware of each other. Maran
not only had Cullen's poems published in *Les Continents*,[56] he also
helped to popularize his (and other young black American writers') works
in France.[57] Cullen's writing career to some extent resembles Maran's.
His insistence that black Americans who write poetry should not be dis-
tinguished by the epithet "Negro" from their fellow Americans who do
the same thing, is akin to Maran's refusal to let the Negro (at least the
one from the New World) be seen as anything but "un homme pareil aux
autres." Like Maran, possibly frustrated by the recurring question of the
place of race-awareness in literature, Cullen turned to writing about
animals whose racial awareness is as strong as that of their human counterparts. Like René Maran, Countée Cullen is most remembered today
not as a writer *tout court* but as a black writer.

René Maran was a black man, but his vision of the black African was essentially that of a white Frenchman. Therefore, any influence that vision must have had on Cullen, or on any other New Negro writers, could rightly be regarded as belonging with the influence of writers like Vachel Lindsay.

This, however, is not to depreciate Countée Cullen's New Negroness— for he was a New *Negro* writer in spite of his disclaimer and his conscious imitation of Keats, Shelley, and other white poets in most of his poetry. The mistake in his rejection of the title "Negro poet" was not his fear that such a practice, if allowed, might introduce racial segregation and its limitations in art. He was right as far as that went. His mistake was the assumption that "Russian, French, or Chinese poetry" ceases to be "Russian, French, or Chinese poetry" when rendered in English and, by implication, that it is impossible for any Afro-American who is writing in English to produce anything Negro.[58]

Although he recognized the fact that a "poet writes out of his experience, whether it be personal or vicarious," and that "the double obligation of being both Negro and American is not so unified as we are often led to believe,"[59] he, like George S. Schuyler in his article "The Negro-Art Hokum,"[60] underestimated the role of the "collective unconscious" in any creative process. This "racial unconscious," however, was not ignored in his attempts to create. Like the night winds in Toomer's *Kabnis*, it whispered through the black cracks between the white boards of his Americanness. And it has a benign effect on his finished products, for Countée Cullen's best works are those in which the poet's conscious efforts were not strong enough to suppress the unconscious infiltration of his being Negro in the 1920s.

NOTES

1. Toomer to Johnson, 11 July 1930, Yale University, New Haven, Conn.

2. Langston Hughes, "The Negro Artist and the Racial Mountain," *Nation* 122 (23 June 1926): 692.

3. For example, *see* Harold R. Isaacs, "Five Writers and Their African Ancestors," *Phylon* 21, nos. 3; 4 (1960): 243-65; 317-36.

4. Toomer to Johnson, 11 July 1930, Yale University.

5. Toomer to the editor of the *Liberator,* 19 August 1922, Toomer Papers, Fisk University Library.

6. Du Bois, *The Souls of Black Folk* (1903; reprint ed., New York: Washington Square Press, 1970), p. 3.

7. Toomer to the editor of the *Liberator,* 19 August 1922.

8. William Stanley Braithwaite, "The Negro in American Literature," *The Crisis* 28, no. 5 (September 1924): 210.

9. Anderson to Toomer, 3 January 1924. Quoted in Darwin T. Turner, *In a Minor Chord: Three Afro-American Writers and Their Search for Identity* (Carbondale: Southern Illinois University Press, 1971), p. 2.

10. Anderson to Toomer, 22 December 1922. Quoted in Turner, *In a Minor Chord.*

11. Ibid.

12. Anderson to Toomer, undated, ca. 1922-1923, quoted in Turner, *In a Minor Chord,* p. 2.

13. Toomer to the editor of the *Liberator,* 19 August 1922.

14. Darwin Turner, Introduction, in Jean Toomer, *Cane* (1923; reprint ed., New York: Liveright, 1975), p. xxi.

15. Toomer, *Cane,* p. 10 (hereafter cited as TC).

16. René Maran, *Batouala: An African Love Story,* trans. Alexandre Mboukou (Rockville, Md.: New Perspective, 1973), p. 89.

17. Gorham B. Munson, "The Significance of Jean Toomer," *Opportunity* 3, no. 33 (September 1925): 262.

18. Roberta Riley, "Search for Identity and Artistry," *CLA Journal* (College Language Association) 17, no. 4 (June 1974): 484.

19. Munson, "The Significance of Jean Toomer," p. 262.

20. The narrator/speaker (Kabnis-Lewis) is originally from the North.

21. Montgomery Gregory, " 'Cane,' " *Opportunity* 1, no. 12 (December 1923): 375.

22. Anderson to Toomer, 14 January 1924. Quoted in Darwin T. Turner, "An Intersection of Paths," *Phylon* 17, no. 4 (June 1974): 463.

23. Turner, Introduction in *Cane,* p. xvi.

24. Turner, *In a Minor Chord,* p. 126, n. 42.

25. Ibid.

26. Toomer to Anderson, December 1922. Quoted in Turner, "An Intersection of Paths," pp. 457-58.

27. Sherwood Anderson, *Winesburg, Ohio* (1919; reprint ed., New York: Viking Press, 1960), p. 112.

28. Ibid., p. 180.

29. W. E. B. Du Bois and Alain Locke, "The Younger Literary Movement," *The Crisis* 27, no. 4 (February 1924): 161.

30. Gregory, " 'Cane,' " p. 374.

31. Ibid. Gregory's italics.

32. Toomer to Anderson, 29 December 1922. Quoted in Turner, "An Intersection of Paths," p. 460.

33. Eugene Holmes, "Jean Toomer—Apostle of Beauty," *Opportunity* 10, no. 8 (August 1932): 252.

34. Countée Cullen, ed., *Caroling Dusk: An Anthology of Verse by Negro Poets* (New York: Harper & Brothers, 1927), p. 180.

35. Countée Cullen, *On These I Stand: An Anthology of the Best Poems* (New York: Harper & Row, 1947), p. 100 (hereafter cited as CCA).

36. Wallace Thurman, for example, regarded Cullen simply as "the symbol of a fast disappearing generation of Negro writers"—meaning the "old Negro" writers. Wallace Thurman, "Negro Poets and Their Poetry," *Bookman* 67, no. 5 (July 1928): 559.

37. Quoted in an editorial, "A Word for the New Year," by Mary White Ovington, *The Crisis* 27, no. 3 (January 1924): 103.

38. In fact Darwin T. Turner visualizes Kentucky in the second line of the first stanza of the poem: "the land where the grass is blue." *In a Minor Chord,* p. 65.

39. Countée Cullen, *Uncle Jim* in James Weldon Johnson, ed., *The Book of American Negro Poetry* (1922; reprint ed., New York: Harcourt, Brace & World, 1959), pp. 229-30.

40. *Chicago Bee,* 24 December 1927.

41. Countée Cullen, *The Black Christ and Other Poems* (New York: Harper & Brothers, 1929), p. 67.

42. Countée Cullen. *The Medea and Some Poems* (New York: Harper & Brothers, 1935).

43. This nonracial identification appears in poems whose subjects are black only because their titles say so (*Black Magdalenes,* for example) or whose subjects, as in *Medusa,* are black neither in title nor in the body of the piece. *See* Sigmund Freud, *On Creativity and the Unconscious,* ed. Benjamin Nelson (New York: Harper & Row, 1958), p. 54.

44. *Opportunity* 2, no. 15 (March 1924): 68.

45. *St. Louis Argus,* 3 February 1928.

46. Countée Cullen, "Poet on Poet," *Opportunity* 4, no. 38 (February 1926): 73.

47. Ibid., 6, no. 3 (March 1928): 90. Cullen's italics.

48. Alain Locke, *The New Negro* (1925; reprint ed., New York: Atheneum, 1969), p. 129.

49. Cullen, *Caroling Dusk,* p. xi.

50. "Surrounded by His Books Countée Cullen Is Happy," interview with Countée Cullen, *Christian Science Monitor,* 23 October 1925, p. 6.

51. The Negro abhorence of suicide is well illustrated in Langston Hughes's account of Lincoln University students' reaction to the attempt of one of their peers to take his life: "Negroes are 'posed to cut *one another* with razors, but when they start to cuttin' themselves, they're gettin' too much like 'fay folks' is the most expressive comment of the student body on the case." Hughes to Van Vechten, 26 March 1925, Yale University, New Haven, Conn. *See also* the treatment of Okonkwo in Chinua Achebe's *Things Fall Apart* (1958). Because he takes his own life—even in a just cause—the Igbo leader does not receive the honor he deserves. He is "buried like a dog." *Things Fall Apart* (1958; reprint ed., London: Heinemann, 1976), p. 147. Many pseudoscientists have used this abhorence to prove either that the black race is inferior to its white counterpart or that its members have no sense of honor.

52. For Countée Cullen's reliance on books for his image of Africa, *see* Cullen's letters to Harold Jackman between January and July 1923, Yale University, New Haven, Conn.

53. Vachel Lindsay, *Collected Poems* (rev. ed. 1913; reprint ed., New York: Macmillan Co., 1973), p. 179.

54. Pierre Loti, *Le Mariage de Loti* (Paris: Calmann Levy, Editeur, 1888), p. 129.

55. Countée P. Cullen, *The Dance of Love (After Reading René Maran's Batouala), Opportunity* 1, no. 4 (April 1923): 30.

56. Maran to Locke, 1 September 1924, Alain Locke Papers, Moorland-Spingarn Research Center, Howard University, Washington, D.C.

57. Maran to Locke, 23 February 1928.

58. Cullen, *Caroling Dusk,* p. xi.

59. Ibid., p. xii.

60. *Nation* 122 (16 June 1926): 662-63.

AFFIRMATION OF BLACK SELF: THE TOM-TOM CRIES AND THE TOM-TOM LAUGHS

5

LANGSTON HUGHES

When Countée Cullen wondered whether some of Langston Hughes's poems were poems at all, he was not alone. Eugene F. Gordon and Thomas Millard Henry's description of *The Weary Blues* as a "doggerel" and "product of the inferiority complex" has already been noted.[1] Hughes's second volume of poetry, *Fine Clothes to the Jew* (1927), was unequivocally condemned by a section of the black press. The *Pittsburgh Courier* called "LANGSTON HUGHES' BOOK OF POEMS TRASH."[2] The *New York Amsterdam News* called Hughes himself "THE SEWER DWELLER," while the *Chicago Whip* named him "The poet lowrate of Harlem."[3] Even his friend, Wallace Thurman, almost agreed with his critics that he wrote "trash" when he suggested that Langston Hughes "needs to learn the use of the blue pencil and the waste-paper basket."[4]

Thurman, nevertheless, offers one of the reasons why most of the Negro literati could not have approved of some of Langston Hughes's subject matters: the apparently anti-assimilationist hue of his treatment. Thurman writes: "He went for inspiration and rhythms to those people who had been the least absorbed by the quagmire of American Kultur, and from them he undertook to select and preserve such autonomous racial values as were being rapidly eradicated in order to speed the Negro's assimilation."[5]

Langston Hughes's early poetry contained such pieces as *Young Prostitute* which is about a growing but already overworked harlot— the kind [that] come cheap in Harlem / So they say";[6] *To a Black Dancer in "The Little Savoy"* which focuses on a girl whose "breasts [are] / Like the pillows of all sweet dreams"; [HWB, p. 35] *The Cat and The Saxophone,* that jerky sputtering of a tipsy love-thirsty couple that knocked Countée Cullen "over completely on the side of bewilderment, and incredulity";[7] and the poem about a prostitute in a British colony—possibly in Africa—Natcha. She offers love "for ten shillings." [HWB, p. 79] All these are raw slices of life cut from Harlem and Africa with no palliative or the Freudian "incitement premium" offered. The pretty and sexy "wine-maiden" drunk with "the grapes of joy" in *To a Black Dancer in "The Little Savoy"* [HWB, p. 35] is, possibly, only a reflection (a literary transplant) of a young black woman whom the poet must have met, one night, in the cabaret—The Little Savoy.

Thus the source of Hughes's trouble with some black critics was not that he was not being Negro but that his work was too Negro self-express-ing. He threw wide, to use Countée Cullen's words, "every door of the racial entourage, to the wholesale gaze of the world at large" in defiance of the black middle-class assimilationist "code" of decency.

The last paragraph of his reply to George S. Schuyler's article "The Negro-Art Hokum" is an adequate definition of what he and many of his close associates—especially his co-founders of *Fire*—were trying to do:

We young Negro artists who create now intend to express our individual dark-skinned selves without fear or shame. If white people are pleased we are glad. If they are not, it doesn't matter. We know we are beautiful. And ugly too. The tom-tom cries and the tom-tom laughs. If colored people are pleased we are glad. If they are not, their displeasure doesn't matter either. We build our temple for tomorrow, strong as we know how, and we stand on the top of the mountain, free within ourselves.[8]

George S. Schuyler, who believed that "the Aframerican is merely a lampblacked Anglo-Saxon,"[9] had contended that there could be nothing "expressive of the Negro soul" in the work of the black American whose way of life was hardly different from that of other Americans. He is, Schuyler argued, "subject to the same economic and social forces that mold the actions and thoughts of the white Americans. He is not living in a different world as some whites and a few Negroes would have us believe. When the jangling of his Connecticut alarm clock gets him out of his Grand Rapids bed to a breakfast similar to that eaten by his white brother across the street . . . it is sheer nonsense to talk about 'racial differences' as between the American black man and the American white man."[10] Therefore any attempt on the part of the black American to aim at the production of any art distinctively Negro borders on self-deception, for "Negro art" belongs somewhere else. It "has been, is, and will be among the numerous black nations of Africa; but to suggest the possibility of any such development among the ten million colored people in this republic is self-evident foolishness."[11]

Langston Hughes's response was direct in spite of the young poet's initial faux pas when he strained logic by equating a desire "to be a poet—not a Negro poet" with a wish "to be white."[12] Without repudiating the Americanness of the Afro-American, he defined how a work of art by a black American can be Negro, the artist's Americanness notwithstanding. The basis is his choice of object and of manner of imitation. The black artist stands a good chance of capturing the Negro soul if he looks for his material not among the "self-styled 'high-class' Negro[es]," but among "the low-down folks, the so-called common elements." These, Hughes claimed, unlike the type of Negroes who have "Nordic manners, Nordic faces, Nordic hair, Nordic art (if any), and an Episcopal heaven," "furnish a wealth of colorful, distinctive material for any artist because they still hold their own individuality in the face of American standardizations." They could easily be found "on Seventh Street in Washington or State Street in Chicago and they do not particularly care whether they are like white folks or anybody else."

To construct works of art distinctively Negro with these elements, Hughes argued, all the Afro-American artist has to do is to bring to bear on them "his racial individuality, his heritage of rhythm and warmth, and his incongruous humor that so often, as in the Blues, becomes ironic laughter mixed with tears." It is this marriage between Negro material and the artist's "racial individuality," as a basis for the creative process, that makes Jean Toomer's *Cane* and Paul Robeson's singing "truly racial" or expressive of the Negro self. He concluded: the development of this type of black self-expressive art was his and his close associates' prideful aim.

The New Negroness of Langston Hughes resides, therefore, in one attitude of the mind: race-pride. It supports and is often indistinguishable from his African motif; it is at the base of his application of the Negro folk treatment to Negro folk material.

Langston Hughes and his associates were not the first Afro-Americans to apply folk treatment to Negro folk material. James Edwin Campbell, Paul Laurence Dunbar, Daniel Webster Davis, J. Mord Allen,[13] the early James Weldon Johnson, and many others had written about the "common [black] elements" in Negro dialect. Not all their works, however, anticipated the self-pride and self-expression of the Harlem Renaissance literature. Many of them belonged to the minstrel tradition.[14] In many cases, although their subject looked black and their language of creation supposedly was Negro, their end product lacked the Negro soul. Created purposely for the delectation of the white folk whose self-aggrandizement they also sought to sustain, these earlier works comprised mainly those Negro elements which experience had proved to be pleasurable to the white ego. They were, essentially, attempts to recreate the white man's concept of the black man. In other words, the Negro artists often borrowed their black material from the white man's imagination. With regard to their form, the dialect (folk) poems most often differed from their literary counterparts only in orthography. In some cases their folk treatment did not go beyond a distortion of English syntax.

Consequently, when Langston Hughes arrived on the scene the process he was to adopt was almost nonexistent, even though some critics confused it with the old minstrel tradition and feared that it might cater to the old self-aggrandizement of the white folk. Drawing his subjects straight from real (as distinct from imagined) Negro folks, he experimented with the blues and jazz forms and employed the real dialect of real Negroes, mainly of Washington, D.C., Harlem, and the South Side, Chicago. Among the results of his first experiments are *The Weary Blues, Jazzonia,* and *Negro Dancers*—poems which are important not only because they are three of his best, but also because they were the very ones that he showed to Vachel Lindsay at the Wardman Park Hotel, Washington, D.C., in December 1925. They set the tone for much of Langston Hughes's later poetry; as such they deserve a closer look.[15]

Thomas Millard Henry was not completely wrong when he applied the phrase "a little story of action and life" to *The Weary Blues*[16] which earned Hughes the forty-dollar first prize in the poetry section of *Opportunity*'s 1925 contest. An attempt to paint a folk creator of the blues in the very action of creation, the poem is essentially a process analysis, a rhetorical pattern which is very close to narrative. Its title notwithstanding, it is hardly a true imitation of the folk blues—a genre which James Weldon Johnson rightly described as a "repository of folk-poetry."[17] At least its form does not agree with the description of the blues pattern as given by Langston Hughes himself in 1927:

The Blues, unlike the *Spirituals,* have a strict poetic pattern: one long line repeated and a third line to rhyme with the first two. Sometimes the second line in repetition is slightly changed and sometimes, but very seldom, it is omitted. The mood of the *Blues* is almost always despondency, but when they are sung people laugh.[18]

Yet *The Weary Blues* is a successful poem. The monotonous, and therefore boring, sentence patterns with very little or no attention to syntax combine with the folk artist's "droning," "rocking," and swaying as well as the implication of the "old gas light," the "poor piano," and the "rickety stool" to underscore the dreariness of the player's life. We feel his blues-infected soul not only in the "sad raggy tune" squeezed out of the "poor" moaning piano, or in the "drowsy syncopated tune" and "mellow croon," but also in his helplessness vis-à-vis the song which rises in him and overflows, almost unaided, his tired voice in the semi-darkness of "an old gas light." The mood is that of "despondency." It is the mood of blues, an art form which Hughes thought was more dolorous than the spirituals because its sorrow is untempered by tears but intensified by an existentialistic laughter.

With regard to its coming too close to being an ordinary narrative, "a little story of action and life," it is even doubtful that it could have done otherwise, since the blues as a poetic expression is an exposé of an active experience physically lived through, or being contemplated mentally or internally ongoing. Witness the movement of the famous "St. Louis Blues" or the sequential approach of "Hard Times Blues."[19] Unexpected interjections of moods and sentiments may disturb the logical sequence of the action being rehearsed or being lived mentally; they hardly disrupt the basic layout of the experience. "What's stirrin', babe?" which, incidentally, is a good example of the blues in one of its earlier stages of development, will make this point clearer:

> Went up town 'bout four o'clock;
> > What's stirrin', babe; stirrin', babe?
> When I got dere, door was locked:
> > What's stirrin', babe, what's stirrin', babe?
>
> Went to de window an' den peeped in:
> > What's stirrin', babe; stirrin', babe?
> Somebody in my fallin' den—
> > What's stirrin', babe; stirrin', babe?[20]

The question "What's stirrin', babe?" is interjected in the first stanza to reactualize the past experience and underscore the speaker/singer's emotion: a combination of surprise and jealousy. Yet the basic structure of the action is not destroyed as can be seen if we relocate the interjecting question where it really belongs—after the first line of the second stanza: that is, when the speaker/singer really sees something "stirrin' " in his "fallin' den [his bed] ."

It is because the blues is an account of an experience lived, or an experience being lived, or an experience that will be lived that "it was assumed," as LeRoi Jones correctly points out, "that *anybody* could sing the blues. If someone had lived in this world into manhood, it was taken for granted that he had been given the content of his verses."[21] Langston Hughes sees the relationship between the blues and the experience of its author in his account of the singing habit of one George, a joy-seeking wretch who shipped out to Africa with him. According to Hughes "he used to make up his own Blues,—verses as absurd as Krazy Kat and as funny. But sometimes when he had to do more work than he thought necessary for a happy living, or, when broke, he couldn't make the damsels of the West Coast believe love worth more than money, he used to sing about the gypsy who couldn't find words strong enough to tell about the troubles in his hard-luck soul."[22] Janheinz Jahn is also aware of this storifying nature of the blues when he says that "the texts of the blues follow the African *narrative style almost entirely*."[23] This feature itself is not surprising since the blues is only a distant descendant of West African folk songs through the Afro-American work songs, saddened by the black man's experience in the New World.[24]

Whatever the case, *The Weary Blues* has something which can pass as the blues in its own right: one aspect is shown by the speaker's imitation (in the line "He did a lazy sway. . . . / He did a lazy sway. . . .) of the rhythm which the folksinger is trying to create; a second blues quality appears in the last stanza of the lyric that the pianist is in the process of composing. This stanza approximates the blues form to the extent that it could be extracted and sung as an independent folk song:

> "I got the Weary Blues
> And I can't be satisfied.
> Got the Weary Blues
> And can't be satisfied—
> I ain't happy no mo'
> And I wish that I had died."
>   [HWB, p. 23]

As a matter of fact, Langston Hughes confesses in his autobiography that it is a real "blues verse"—the first he "ever heard way back in Lawrence, Kansas, when [he] was a kid."[25]

It conforms with the three-point movement of a typical blues stanza: affirmation, reaffirmation, determination. Above all, it obeys the rule of repeated lines as well as the *a b a b c b* rhyme scheme which some of Hughes's later and more confident attempts follow, as evidenced by this stanza from *Bad Man:*

> I'm a bad, bad man
> Cause everybody tells me so.
> I'm a bad, bad man
> Everybody tells me so.
> I take mah meanness and ma licker
> Everywhere I go.[26]

Or by the third stanza of *Po' Boy Blues:*

> I fell in love with
> A gal I thought was kind.
> Fell in love with
> A gal I thought was kind.
> She made me lose ma money
> An' almost lose ma mind.
> [HFC, p. 23]

Or by the last stanza of *Hard Daddy:*

> I wish I had wings to
> Fly like de eagle flies.
> Wish I had wings to
> Fly like de eagle flies.
> I'd fly on ma man an'
> I'd scratch out both his eyes.
> [HFC, p. 86]

And by this stanza from *Bound No'th Blues:*

> Goin' down de road, Lawd,
> Goin' down de road.

Down de road, Lawd.
Way, way down de road.
Got to find somebody
To help me carry dis load.
                    [HFC, p. 87]

Just as "Aunt Sue's Stories" [HWB, p. 57] is a celebration of the oral tradition—that bastion of black civilization and cultural experience—and a product of the oral tradition, *The Weary Blues* is both a folk poem and a dramatization of the creation of a folk poem.

This is also true of the systematic, though disorganized, rhythm of *Jazzonia* which is modeled on jazz music whose flexible structure, like African musical habits from which it takes at least part of its roots, makes for improvisations capable of provoking a sigh or a smile or both. The speaker manipulates the rhythm and the imagery to create the gay, urgent, and often grotesque atmosphere inherent in jazz music. The refrain with its exotic dazzling tree (of life in the Garden of Eden) and river (Nile) heightens the gaiety and seeks to stabilize the tempo as well as the theme. Yet like a real piece of jazz music whose rhythm and duration are unpredictable, it comes to an abrupt end at a moment when we want more of it—not only because we want to know more about "Eve's eyes" and Cleopatra's "gown of gold" (the focus of the fourth stanza and the frame of reference of the refrain) but also because the very two lines that crash-stop the piece have started with a promise of at least two other lines to follow (since they are modeled on the first two lines of the second stanza which has four lines):

In a whirling cabaret
Six long-headed jazzers play
                    [HWB, p. 25]

The total effect is that of joy and sorrowful disappointment, two opposing moods which adequately reflect those of the dancing girl—an embodiment of Eve and Cleopatra, their initial joyous allurements and eventual sorrows combined. Like real American Negro jazz, *Jazzonia* has an undercurrent of sorrow.

Indeed this could be said of most of Langston Hughes's jazz poems before and after 1926. Witness the mournful pessimism beneath the otherwise Dionysian gaiety of *Harlem Night Club* [HFC, p. 32] and the

frustration that boils under the hilarious *Brass Spitoons.* [HFC, p. 28]
Jazz is like "that tune" in *Jazz Band in a Parisian Cabaret,* "that tune /
That laughs and cries at the same time." [HFC, p. 74] Langston Hughes
had earlier indicated this happy-sorrowful nature of jazz which he tried
to capture in most of his jazz poems:

> They say a jazz-band's gay.
> Yet as the vulgar dancers whirled
> And the wan night wore away,
> One said she heard the jazz-band sob
> When the little dawn was grey.
> [HWB, p. 29]

Negro Dancers [HWB, p. 26], the last of the poems which Hughes
showed to Vachel Lindsay, is also a folk material effectively treated in a
folk manner in spite of the jarring threat implicit in the two-line third
stanza:

> White folks, laugh!
> White folks, pray!

The rhythm this time is that of the Charleston. With a combination of
short lines made up mainly of monosyllabic words and gasping punctuation, the speaker captures the sprightful rhythm of the folk dance as
well as the urgency of the folk dancer's announcement. The second and
third stanzas, with their less-hurried tempo and the double entendre of a
pessimistic speaker, highlight the gaiety of the rhythm of the folk dance
and cast a shadow (of doubt) on the exuberance of the folk dancer. The
total effect, once again, is joy with an undercurrent of sorrow—a combined reflection of the folk dancer's apparent happiness and the pessimism of the speaker who, beneath the joy of the folk dancer's publication of "two mo' ways to do de buck," seeks to uncover what looks like
"I'm laughin' to keep from cryin'." Yet *Negro Dancers* is a successful
imitation of the Charleston—that folk dance whose roots several students
have followed beyond the Afro-American community in Charleston, S.C.,
into Africa.[27]
    When Langston Hughes wrote his poems or when he used the jazz and
the blues forms, he thought of his manner of imitation as Afro-American,
as distinct from African. Nevertheless, it could safely be assumed that he

would not be shocked by the idea that his poetry reveals faint rhythms
of African tom-toms and African musical habits, such as the call-and-
response technique. For one thing, his *POEM For the portrait of an
African boy after the manner of Gauguin* sees the rhythm of the tom-
tom as a component of the African blood:

> All the tom-toms of the jungles beat in my blood,
> And all the wild hot moons of the jungles shine in my soul.
> I am afraid of this civilization—
> > So hard,
> > > So strong,
> > > > So cold.
> > > > > > [HWB, p. 102]

The Afro-American, we learn from another poem, *Afraid* [HWB, p. 101],
also is lonely and afraid "among the skyscrapers"—symbols of the non-
African Western civilization—"as our ancestors" were lonely and afraid
"among the palms in Africa." As another blood component, Hughes often
hears a jungle timbre and feels a jungle rhythm in jazz music and jazz
dance, as in *Nude Young Dancer.* [HWB, p. 33] The young dancer, like
the "night-veiled girl" of *Danse Africaine* [HWB, p. 105], obviously
owes part of the effectiveness of her performance to her connection with
the jungle.

Unlike many other Afro-Americans who used African motifs in their
works, Hughes did not have to rely solely on secondhand exotic pictures
of Africa in books and on celluloids. He had been physically in contact
with the black continent before publishing—if not writing—most of his
poems that use Africa either as a motif or as a reinforcing image in his
black-is-beautiful theme. Even if he had written them before visiting
Africa, it is a mark of his satisfaction with the accuracy of his conception of the ancestral continent that the poems were published after he
had had the opportunity of knowing, to use his own words, "the real
thing, to be touched and seen, not merely read about in a book."[28]
The attitudes of his speakers towards Africa could, therefore, be credited
with a measure of sincerity instead of being simply discarded as another
faddish moonshine of the Jazz Age.

Admittedly, Hughes could not always resist the temptation of trying
to soothe the thirst in the 1920s for the exotic and the primitive. Some
of his autobiographical short stories reveal a sacrifice of realities on the

altar of masturbatory exoticism. "Luani of the Jungles," a story which appeared in the November 1928 issue of *Harlem* magazine, is a good example.

In this piece, Hughes's first-person narrator describes the physical milieu where the action takes place as accurately as his white interlocutor depicts the reception given to Luani when she returns from Europe:

> There a hundred or more members of the tribe were waiting to receive her,—beautiful brown-black people whose perfect bodies glistened in the sunlight, bodies that shamed me and the weakness under my European clothing. That night there was a great festival given in honor of Luani's coming,—much beating of drums and wild fantastic dancing beneath the moon,—a festival in which I could take no part for I knew none of their ceremonies, none of their dances. Nor did I understand a word of their language. I could only stand aside and look, or sit in the door of our hut and sip the palm wine they served me.[29]

The story, however, moves irrecoverably towards the exotic as the white man describes Luani's behavior in her home village in Nigeria, and portrays her as going "hunting and fishing, wandering about for days in the jungles."[30]

Firstly, it is doubtful that women among any tribe in Nigeria "went hunting and fishing . . . with members of the tribe" in the 1920s—at least not a chief's daughter who had lived in England and France. Secondly, it is doubtful that a Nigerian girl like Luani would leave her husband's bed of a night to walk about naked, making love with another man under palm trees—even if her husband were impotent. Perhaps a woman can, in 1981 Nigeria, tell her husband whom she has cheated sexually that "a woman can have two lovers and love them both."[31] A society which had not greatly evolved from what it was in the days of Chinua Achebe's Okonkwo would have fallen completely apart before being required to listen to such an outrageous claim.

Indeed it strains credulity to accept the idea of a white man's going to live with an African wife in her African "jungle" village. A more realistic picture is that which emerges from Langston Hughes's own account of the experience of the mulatto Edward and his black African mother. The mother was only a house servant of a white man who lived at a special place reserved for whites. When the white man returned to England, "the whites inside the compound naturally would have nothing

to do with them [Edward and his mother], nor would they give him
[Edward] a job, and the Negroes did not like his mother, because she had
lived for years with a white man, so Edward had no friends in the village,
and almost nobody to talk to."[32]

Nevertheless, the attitudes of Langston Hughes's speakers towards
Africa should be credited with a measure of sincerity. Unlike the narrators
of his "African" short stories (and they are too few to be significant) who
tend to subscribe to the exotic image of Africa, most of them who speak
of or allude to Africa were created by Hughes before 1926. It was during
the post-1926 period that the genuine Afro-American's attempt to express
himself and his ancestral heritage was falling into decadence as some New
Negro writers consciously sought to please their audience instead of seeking to express their dark selves. Thus, if Langston Hughes had chosen
after 1926 to repudiate the articles of his "manifesto" completely (and
he did not do so) his action could not have affected most of his poems
that deal with Africa either directly or indirectly. Besides, the inaccuracies
of his speakers notwithstanding, the picture of Africa that emerges from
those poems is more authentic than the images that emerge from the
writings of many other New Negro authors. For instance, unlike Countée
Cullen's romantic Africa where, as in *Heritage,* "cinnamon tree" grows,
Langston Hughes's Africa grows "palm trees," as in *Afraid.*

It is this considerably high degree of accuracy in the conception of
the face of Africa that separates Hughes's "African" poems from those
of his fellow New Negroes (who used the same motifs) without, however,
depriving them of the basic New Negro awareness of the Dark Continent's
presence in the Afro-American's life.

Hughes's black Americans, whose attitudes his first-person speakers
voice, have no illusions either of the remoteness of Africa both in time
and space or of their unquestionable right to full American citizenship.
They all "sing America" [HWB, p. 109]; they are all Americans, the darkness of their skins notwithstanding. Even in the poem *Dream Variation*
[HWB, p. 43]—where the speaker longs "to fling [his] arms wide / In
some place of the sun, / To whirl and to dance / Till the white day is
done. / Then rest at cool evening / Beneath a tall tree / While night comes
on gently"—it is America that is being sung. The dream is a wish fulfillment. Unable to belong effectively to his live society, the speaker wishes
for a place where he could relax. The motivation of this "dream" is the
motivation of the numerous back-to-Africa movements. The dream would

not occur if the live situation were not painful. This can also be said of
Our Land [HWB, p. 99] which the poet tellingly subtitled *Poem for a
Decorative Panel*–fine art, another channel of wish fulfillment. As a reaction to "this land where life is cold," the speaker wishes for a dream-
land which exists nowhere on this planet.

Nonetheless, Langston Hughes's Afro-Americans recognize and affirm
their relations with Africa whose heritage and experience they cherish
and revere as sources of pride-inspiring characteristics. In *The Negro
Speaks of Rivers* [HWB, 51] the characteristic is stability which, ironically,
has developed from the instability of the speaker's experience. The im-
permanence of his situation (as an enslaved African), from life on the
Euphrates of ancient history to the Mississippi of relatively modern times,
has toughened his mind and skin, making him as stable as the rivers whose
rise and fall in importance have not destroyed them: "My soul has grown
deep like the rivers." He could as well say as a mother says to a son in a
later poem:

> I'se still goin', honey,
> I'se still climbin',
> And life for me ain't been no crystal stair.
> [*Mother to Son,* HWB, p. 107]

Stability through the instability of Africa and her sons is also the point
of *Proem* [HWB, p. 19] which, in a way, resembles *The Negro Speaks of
Rivers.* The blackness of the speaker's skin relates him directly to the
blackness of night and of the depths of Africa. Just as the blackness of
night and of the depths of Africa is an unchangable fact, so also is the
speaker's blackness with all its fortitude already tested and confirmed.
He IS. His blackness, derived from Africa, has exposed him to a toughen-
ing experience. He IS now as real as his experience WAS.

In many other poems by Hughes the inherent characteristic of the
Afro-American African ancestry is beauty. We see this in *When Sue Wears
Red* [HWB, p. 66], a poem which Hughes wrote at the age of seventeen
about a seventeen-year-old "brownish girl" who had recently arrived from
the South, and sometimes "wore a red dress that was very becoming to
her."[33] Susanna Jones, beautiful in her "red dress," is portrayed as a
reincarnation of a dead African queen, possibly Cleopatra in view of her
obvious coquetry or tantalizing charm which "burns . . . a love-fire sharp

like pain" in the speaker's heart. The piece "Poem" [HWB, p. 58],
which was first published in the June 1922 number of *The Crisis,* is a
direct assertion of the beauty of the black race:

> The night is beautiful
> So the faces of my people.
>
> The stars are beautiful,
> So the eyes of my people.
>
> Beautiful, also, is the sun.
> Beautiful, also, are the souls of my people.

In most of Hughes's poems *night* is interchangeable with *blackness;* the
two words as well as *sun* often relate the subject in focus to Africa as the
foundation or the starting point of black life and experience in America.

Langston Hughes's speakers are hardly loud in their acknowledgment
of their relationship with Africa. When they try to be, as in *Afro-American
Fragment*[34] (which, though published in 1930, is a good summary of the
speakers' attitudes towards Africa), their voices tremble with an anti-
African note. The repetition of the first three lines ("So long, / So far
away / Is Africa") at the end of the first stanza (and, indeed, at the end
of the next and only other stanza) underscores the speaker's wish that
his disassociation of himself from Africa be taken seriously. Nevertheless,
beneath the disassociation is a strong undercurrent of affirmation of the
speaker's kinship with *Africa's Dark Face.*[35] It is one thing to stop the
"drums"; to muffle the sound already produced is another. While the
production of drum sounds requires a conscious and, under normal conditions, a voluntary effort, resurgence of the sound after the process that
produced it has been discontinued can take place in spite of the feeling
and preoccupation of the person in whose mind it has been registered.

Langston Hughes in the 1920s wrote poems like *Winter Moon, March
Moon, Sea Calm, Cross, The Jester,* and *The Minstrel Man.* These are
either nonracial, or extremely racial. When nonracial, they contain nothing that could be described as distinctively Negro. Splendid as it is, for
instance, the three-line *Suicide's Note* [HWB, p. 87] could have been
written by Alfred, Lord Tennyson:

> The calm,
> Cool face of the river
> Asked me for a kiss.

When extremely racial, they assume various aspects of the writings of the
Old Negro authors—from the Niagara fume of *The South* [HWB, p. 54]
which could have come from W. E. B. Du Bois's pen to the Old Negro
Christlike virtue of *The White Ones.* [HWB, p. 106]

Based on the experience of the black man in the New World though
these poems are, they did very little or nothing to affirm with pride
the Negro self. This assignment was left for the poems where Hughes
considerably exploited the Negro folk material and folk medium of creation or acknowledged, even if ambivalently, his ancestral heritage as it
related to Africa.

These were the basis of his New Negroness. He expressed the dark self
of the Afro-American without for the most part trying to please or displease the black man or his white brother. "With quiet ecstatic sense of
kinship with even the most common and lowly folk," as Alain Locke puts
it, he "discovers in them, in spite of their individual sordidness and backwardness, the epic quality of collective strength and beauty."[36] These
were also the basis of his originality which, ironically, laid him open to
attacks, especially from black scholars and critics who, with Benjamin
Brawley, saw his themes as "unnecessarily sordid and vulgar" and his
manner of treating them as a good example of "imperfect mastery of
technique."[37]

This, however, was mainly a cover for the belief that Hughes was only
catering to the pleasure of white faddists who had allegedly influenced
him in a bad way. Even Wallace Thurman, his fellow traveler on the bandwagon of *Fire,* thought as much when he charged that "urged on by a
faddistic interest in the unusual, Mr. Hughes has been excessively prolific,
and has exercised little restraint."[38]

The strongest and most direct charges, however, came from Benjamin
Brawley in his article "The Negro Literary Renaissance," published in
the *Southern Workman,*[39] and from Allison Davis who claimed that "the
severest charge one can make against Mr. Van Vechten is that he misdirected a genuine poet, who gave promise of a power and technique ex-
ceptional in any poetry,—Mr. Hughes."[40] Both of them drew immediate

responses, one from Carl Van Vechten and the other from Langston
Hughes.

Benjamin Brawley had implied that Van Vechten had influenced
Langston Hughes's first volume of poetry, *The Weary Blues,* which con-
tains a preface written by Carl Van Vechten. In his reply, therefore, Van
Vechten tried to show that that could not have been possible:

> *The Weary Blues* had won a prize before I had read a poem by Mr. Hughes
> or knew him personally. The volume, of which this was the title poem,
> was brought to me complete before Mr. Hughes and I ever exchanged
> two sentences. I am unaware even to this day, although we are the warm-
> est friends and see each other frequently, that I have had the slightest
> influence on Mr. Hughes in any direction. The influence, if one exists,
> flows from the other side, as any one might see who read my first paper
> on the *Blues,* published in *Vanity Fair* for August, 1925, a full year be-
> fore *Nigger Heaven* appeared, before, indeed, a line of it had been written.
> In this paper I quoted freely Mr. Hughes' opinion on the subject of
> Negro folk song, opinions which to my knowledge have not changed
> in the slightest.[41]

Unfortunately for his argument, however, the opening part of his
statement does not agree with established facts from other reliable
sources—including his own introduction to the book in question: *The
Weary Blues.* He met Langston Hughes and Countée Cullen for the first
time on 10 November 1924,[42] the very day Langston Hughes returned
from sea, and was introduced to him by Walter White at a party given
by the NAACP. He met and spoke with Langston Hughes again a year
later at the 1925 Awards dinner of *Opportunity* where the poem *The
Weary Blues* was awarded the first prize for poetry. Obviously, "the
volume, of which this was the title poem," was not given to him for on-
ward transmission to Alfred Knopf until later. Furthermore, the claim
that he had not written "a line" of his *Nigger Heaven* by August 1925 is
misleading, for in a letter dated 26 March 1925 Langston Hughes hoped
" 'Nigger Heaven' 's successfully finished. It is, isn't it?"[43]

Langston Hughes's rejoinder was stronger. Allison Davis, writing after
Van Vechten's denial of Benjamin Brawley's charge, had argued that if
the author of *Nigger Heaven* did not influence *The Weary Blues,* he "undoubtedly *did* influence" *Fine Clothes to the Jew,* Hughes's second

volume of poems which was dedicated to Carl Van Vechten.[44] In his letter to the editor of *The Crisis* Langston Hughes offered "a correction" based on verifiable facts. He had written many of the poems in both *The Weary Blues* and *Fine Clothes to the Jew* before 10 November 1924 when he met Van Vechten for the first time:

I would like herewith to state and declare that many of the poems in said book were written before I made the acquaintance of Mr. Van Vechten, as the files of THE CRISIS will prove; before the appearance of *The Weary Blues* containing his preface; and before ever he had commented in any way on my work. (See THE CRISIS for June, 1922, August, 1923, several issues in 1925; also *Buccaneer* for May, 1925.) Those poems which were written after my acquaintance with Mr. Van Vechten were certainly not about him, not requested by him, not misdirected by him, some of them not liked by him nor so far as I know, do they in any way bear his poetic influence.[45]

He returned to the matter in 1940 and explained that most of the poems that supposedly revealed Carl Van Vechten's influence on *Fine Clothes to the Jew* were not included in the earlier volume "because scarcely any dialect or folk-poems were included in the *Weary Blues*".[46] While what Hughes means by "folk-poems" is not clear, the emphasis in his statement is on the modifier "scarcely," because *The Weary Blues* does contain folk poems.

In any event, Langston Hughes could not have owed his interest in the blues and jazz to Carl Van Vechten. His pre-August 1925 correspondence with Van Vechten confirms the latter's claim with regard to the possibility of Hughes's having influenced his concept of the blues although they had different tastes.[47] Hughes's interest in the blues could be traced to the time when, at the age of nine, he heard the blues on Independence Avenue and on Twelfth Street in Kansas City.[48] With regard to jazz, he wrote one of his best jazz poems, *When Sue Wears Red,* at the age of seventeen. He met Carl Van Vechten at the age of twenty-two.

A careful study of his development as a writer shows that the credit for influence has often been misdirected. The three persons who most deserve it are frequently forgotten: (1) Paul Laurence Dunbar whose dialect poems he liked and tried to imitate as a child.[49] (2) Ethel Weimer, his English teacher at Central High School in Cleveland, who introduced him to the writings of Carl Sandburg, Amy Lowell, Vachel Lindsay, and Edgar Lee Masters.[50] (3) Carl Sandburg whose influence on his budding poetic temperament is evident in the form and content of some of his juvenilia[51] and who, obviously, helped to start him on the road which eventually led him to the stark realism—both in subject and style—that shocked some of his critics. Hughes described Sandburg as his "guiding star" in 1940; he had as a boy written a poem about him.[52]

Vachel Lindsay only helped to enlarge his audience since Hughes had already been published by *The Crisis* before he met and showed Lindsay his *Jazzonia, Negro Dancers,* and *The Weary Blues* at the Wardman Park Hotel in December 1925. As a matter of fact, the three poems had already been published in magazines before Lindsay saw them: *Jazzonia* in *The Crisis,* August 1923; *Negro Dancers* in *The Crisis,* March 1925; *The Weary Blues* in *Opportunity,* May 1925, after winning a prize. In any case, Hughes's work does not reveal as much influence of Vachel Lindsay as Countée Cullen's use of the African motif does, for instance.

Still more conspicuous is the absence of the influence of Hughes's famous patron on his work. Incidentally, Langston Hughes was introduced to her only in 1928.[53] At that time he had already published his first two volumes of poetry. He started work on his first novel, *Not Without Laughter,* in the summer of that year. Although the grant he received from her enabled him to complete and revise the novel, any influence she must have had on its form or content is not apparent. The relationship came to an end in December 1930 because Hughes could not satisfy her wish that he "be primitive and know and feel the intuitions of the primitive."[54]

Carl Van Vechten's interest in his writing must have been pleasing and encouraging to the young author. Given, however, Langston Hughes's strong sense of independence of opinion and of action, both as a child and as an adult, it is fairly reasonable to assume that his choice of subject and of manner of treatment could have been exactly as he had worked them out (before his acquaintance with Van Vechten) with or without the interest and encouragement of the author of *Nigger Heaven* or anyone else.

He was predisposed to identification with the common man—the black masses or, to use a more recent phrase, "the soul people." He was one of them. He looked through their eyes and felt through their senses. His art, therefore, was black self-expression.

OTHERS

Langston Hughes was not the only writer guilty of what Allison Davis contemptuously portrayed as the current Negro writers' practice of " 'confessing' the distinctive sordidness and triviality of Negro life, and making an exhibition of their own unhealthy imagination, in the name of frankness and sincerity."[55] We have seen Jean Toomer's self-confident celebration of the Negro folk in colors which, if extracted and examined by themselves through the Old Negro assimilationist microscope, can hardly be called "respectable." We have seen how, in spite of himself, Countée Cullen participated in the attempt to portray the Negro as he really was. His novel *One Way To Heaven* (1932) (beyond the scope of the present study) goes to a greater length in exposing the uncomplimentary side of the Negro.

Many other artists also participated in this attempt to let the Negro express himself without any conscious effort to please or to displease anyone—white or black. For instance, that was, collectively and individually, the basic aim of the young people who in the summer of 1926 founded *Fire*. A detailed analysis of all the young writers who took part in the revision of attitude towards the use of the Negro and Negro material in art, is not included in this study, since many of them, like Sterling Brown and to some extent Arna Bontemps, were not established until after 1926 and, indeed, after the depression of 1929. Suffice it therefore to look more closely at the more representative among them: Eric Walrond, Rudolph Fisher, and Zora Neale Hurston.

ERIC WALROND

Eric Walrond, like Claude McKay, was not a native-born black American. Yet his creative writings, like those of Claude McKay, are among the most representative works of the Harlem Renaissance. His volume of ten short stories, *Tropic Death* (1926), is a mosaic of elements of the life of West Indians—their joys, their sorrows, their superstitions—artistically presented without any apparent intention on the part of the author to please or to displease anyone. In spite of the author's obvious love of adjectives, he manages to place the reader right in the middle of the action and lets him form his own opinion. No action, no belief of the ordinary

West Indian is considered too sordid or too demeaning to be uncovered "to the wholesale gaze of the world at large."

Set in "a backwoods village in Barbadoes"[56] the first story, "Drought," brings out the pride and love of life of peasants engulfed in a drought. The situation is so severe that:

Turtle doves rifled the pods of green peas and purple beans and even the indigestible Brazilian *bonavis*. Potato vines, yellow as the leaves of autumn, severed from their roots by the pressure of the sun, stood on the ground, the wind's eager prey. Undug, stemless-peanuts, carrots— seeking balm, relief, the caress of a passing wind, shot dead unlustered eyes up through sun-etched cracks in the hard, brittle soil. The sugar corn went to the birds. Ripening prematurely, breadfruits fell swiftly on the hard naked earth, half ripe, good only for fritters. . . . Fell in spatters . . . and the hungry dogs, elbowing the children, lapped up the yellow-mellow fruit. [WTD, p. 18]

Yet Sissie regards as an insult to the integrity of her kitchen any attempt by her children to eat anything not cooked by her. [WTD, p. 21]

Another story, "Panama Gold," celebrates several aspects of folkways. Ella runs across to Lizzie's house to borrow "a pinch o' salt" with which to season the food she is cooking. The young Capadosia is punished by her mother (and promised more beating when her father returns) for turning "she back side" to Ella (when Ella asks her about her mother) "an' didn't even say ax yo' pardin." [WTD, p. 37] We hear the cooing of pigeons and the folk concept of what they say "at sunrise on a soap box coop on top the latrine:"

> A rooka ta coo
> A rooka ta coo
> My wife is just as good as you
> Good as you
> Good as you
>   [WTD, p. 44]

We watch Ella, the "mulatto with plenty of soft black hair," as she folksily balances a bucket of water on her head. "She didn't need a cloth twisted and plaited to form a matting for her head. . . . Her strides were typical of the West Indian peasant woman—free, loose, firm. Zim, zam, zim, zam. Her feet were made to traverse that stony gap. No stones defied her free, lithe approach. Left foot to right hand, right hand to left foot—and Ella swept down with amazing grace and ease. Her toes were broad; they encountered no obstacles. Her feet did not slip. The water did not splash. It was safe, firm, serene on top of her head." [WTD, pp. 56-57]

Even the embarrassing intraracial attitudes of West Indian blacks towards skin colors are spotlighted. Ella does not repulse Missah Poyah's advances because she does not like him as a person or because he has a wooden leg. Although she is convention-conscious and must have been knocked over by what she must have considered Missah Poyah's wrong approach (she mentally advises him to "go back an' lahn, dat not de way fi' cote" [WTD, p. 54], her main reason for rejecting the "wooden foot neygah man" [WTD, p. 53] is the color of his skin. "Gahd, he are black in troot'," she once told herself. [WTD, p. 50]

This intraracial prejudice based on the color of the skin is the leit-motiv of the third story, "The Yellow One." The bloody fight which results in the Yellow One's collapsing and passing out is motivated by black-skinned Hubigon's dislike for Jota Arosemena because he is yellow-skinned. *La madurita* herself—and she is the center of consciousness in most of the story—would not let black-skinned Negroes, whom she considers "ugly," come near her.

"The Wharf Rats" is a celebration of folk life. The folksiness of black diggers of the Panama Canal is highlighted when "exhausted, half-asleep, naked but for wormy singlets," they are shown humming "queer creole tunes" as they "play on guitar or piccolo, and jig to the rhythm of the *coombia*—a folk song "for *obeah.*" [WTD, p. 90] The description of their attachment to this folklore is worth quoting:

Over smoking pots, on black, death-black nights legends of the bloodiest were recited till they became the essence of a sort of Negro Koran. One refuted them at the price of one's breath. And to question the verity of the *obeah,* to dismiss or reject it as the ungodly rite of some lurid, crack-brained Islander was to be accursed pale-face, dog of a white. And the *obeah* man, in a fury of rage, would throw a machette at the heretic's head or—worse—burn on his doorstep at night a pyre of Maubé bark or green Ganja weed. [WTD, p. 90]

But folk life is not without its tragedies. Philip, one of the wharf rats,

is seized and eaten by a shark as he entertains Europeans with the West
Indian game of "cork." [WTD, pp. 110-14]

"The Palm Porch," with its central black-hating character, Miss
Buckner, also touches upon the anathematic subject: intraracial prejudice
based on the color of the skin. "One gathered from the words which
came like blazing meteors out of her mouth that Miss Buckner would have
liked to be white; but, alas! she was only a mulatto." [WTD, p. 125]
Her reaction to her 16-year-old daughter's elopement with a black man
is "It a dam pity shame"—not because the "shiny-armed black" has spent
some time in a jail but because he is not light-skinned. [WTD, p. 126]

The sixth story, "Subjection," is a facsimile of a colonized West
Indian community with all its peoples and attitudes: the docile men and
women who studiously keep off "de backra dem business," prostitutes,
women who must slave in order to feed their children, the baffled who
find comfort only in wine and religion, the power-drunk, trigger-happy
colonialist represented by the marine who slices off a boy's ear and
shoots Ballet to death because he dares to speak out.

In spite of this harrowing experience, the people's nearness to their
folk roots is evident not only in their idiom but also in their lifestyle.
Ballet eats his *conkee* from a banana leaf. The *obeah* cult is respected
and adhered to.

Adherence to obeah is also celebrated in "The Black Pin." A black
pin which Zink Diggs gives to Alfie sets a house on fire because "some
demon chemical, some liquid, some fire-juice, had been soaked into it
originally. *Obeah* juice." [WTD, p. 181] Its creator, however, is not above
its power. It almost ruins Zink Diggs completely when April returns it to
her by tossing it "upon a mound of fowl dung and wormy provisions
scraped together in the yard" and setting it on fire. [WTD, pp. 181-82]

With its focus on Seenie and her child, "The White Sanke" offers the
reader an insight into the life-style of a lowly West Indian community.
"The Vampire Bat" is a series of macabre episodes which, beyond the
demonstration of the power of *obeah,* celebrate the triumph of the weak
(blacks) over the strong (whites who exploit them economically and
sexually). For example, a black woman freezes the desire of a potential
rapist by plunging her umbrella into his eyes. A mulatto trader invokes
the magic of *obeah* against a vessel whose master has withheld part of
the goods he was supposed to deliver to him; the crew of the vessel "find

a rum soaked Negro corpse doubled up in the bottom" of a cask from which they are drinking. [WTD, p. 230] A white plantation owner picks up a black baby (supposedly illegitimate and abandoned) who turns into a vampire bat and kills him. The title story, "Tropic Death," focuses on still seamier aspects of the black West Indian life: disease, hunger, gangsterism, together with their effects on the community.

Although Eric Walrond is in no way at his best in all the stories, he consistently captures the folk soul by making his people talk most of the time in their appropriate dialects. The following is a dialogue between Alfred and his wife, "The Yellow One," who has just returned from getting water which Alfred had refused to go and get:

Alfred was sitting up, the unpacified baby in his arms.
" 'Im cry all de time yo' went 'way," he said, "wha' yo' t'ink is de mattah wit' 'im, he? Yo' t'ink him tummack a hut 'im?"
"Him is hungry, dat is wha' is de mattah wit' 'im! Move, man! 'Fo Ah knock you', yah! Giv' me 'im, an' get outa me way! Yo' is only a dyam noosant!"
"Well, what is de mattah, now?" he cried in unfeigned surprise.
"Stid o' gwine fo' de watah yo'self yo' tan' back yah an' giv' hawdahs an' worryin' wha' is de mattah wit' de picknee."
"Cho, keep quiet, woman, an' le' me lie down." [WTD, p. 62]

The self-confidence underneath the stories becomes significant when the assimilationist tendency of educated West Indians at that period is taken into consideration. Most of the subjects treated by Walrond are matters which a large part of the black literati of the West Indies and the United States would have liked to leave unrevealed.

RUDOLPH FISHER

Most of Rudolph Fisher's short stories are raw slices of life cut from a parcel of life not far from where Carl Van Vechten was to cut his *Nigger Heaven* later. Perhaps that was why, after the appearance of his novel *The Walls of Jericho* in 1928 *The Crisis* charged that "Mr. Fisher does not yet venture to write of himself and his own people; of Negroes like his mother, his sister and his wife."[57] Thinking mainly of his short story "High Yaller," Allison Davis had earlier placed him among writers whom he called Van Vechtenites."[58] Fisher's pre-August 1926 stories, therefore, are important to our study not only because of their Negro self-expressiveness, but also because they offer an insight into how easy it is to exaggerate the white influence—especially Carl Van Vechten's—on the young Harlem Renaissance writers.

Rudolph Fisher's "High Yaller," which won the first prize for fiction in *The Crisis* literary contest of 1925, is a realistic approach to an aspect of the emotional mulatto theme. There is no attempt on the part of the author to sell the near-white Evelyn Brown as an angel. Her inclination towards men of lighter color is made obvious and understandable. Once she can no longer bear the burden of the label "colored," she does the logical thing: she passes.

Commenting on "High Yaller," Charles Waddell Chesnutt said, "its atmosphere may be a correct reflection of Negro life in Harlem, with which I am not very familiar."[59] A self-confident portrayal of the less sophisticated Negro life by a member of the Negro race, "High Yaller" contains elements and intraracial problems which were as unacceptable to some black assimilationists as they were unnoticeable to the non-initiated observer. These include (1) the subconscious envy underneath the molestation of the so-called "high yaller"; (2) the secret desire of some of the darker Negroes to be fairer, as revealed in Jay's cynical remarks:

Point is, there aren't any more dark girls. Skin bleach and rouge have wiped out the stain. The blacks have turned sealskin, the sealskin are light-brown, the light-browns are all yaller, and the yallers are pink.[60]

(3) the unscrupulousness of some Negroes who thickened the color-line, as in Hank's, in the interest of their personal advancement; and (4) the Harlem parlance, including the "gutter-talk" of people like the boy whom Jay throws out of a room for being disorderly.[61]

The prize mentioned above was awarded to "High Yaller" in October 1925. Before then however, Walter White, starting from 10 February 1925 had tried unsuccessfully to place it with *American Mercury, Harper's* and the *Century* whose editors were his friends.[62] It will be difficult, therefore, to accuse Fisher of having written "High Yaller" to please white faddists.

"The City of Refuge," another story by Rudolph Fisher, also approaches Harlem life in a realistic manner and is, at least in one way, a forerunner of Van Vechten's *Nigger Heaven:* the heavenlike appearance of (the otherwise hell-like) Harlem when viewed from the outside. King Solomon Gillis, who thinks that he has come to a paradise, "sat meditating in a room half the size of his hencoop back home, with a single window opening into an airshaft."[63] In lieu of achieving the "two things in dis world," that he really wants—being a policeman, and getting a "gal"—he becomes Uggam's dupe and dope peddler and is arrested as such without his knowing his offence. Thus, viewed from the angle of the central character King Solomon Gillis, the title of the story, like *Nigger Heaven,* is meant to be an irony.

The uninspiring inside life of the otherwise heavenlike Harlem is also given some attention in "Vestiges: Harlem Sketches." The old preacher, Ezekiel Taylor, travels all the way from the South to Harlem in the hope of finding it a city of refuge; but what he finds is a "city of the devil— outpost of hell."[64] For her part, Majutah's grandmother sees it as a "city of Satan. . . . great, noisy, heartless, crowded place where you lived under the same roof with a hundred people you never knew; where night was alive and morning dead."[65]

However, the significance of "Vestiges" lies more in its use of folk material. Ezekiel Taylor, Deacon and Sister Gassoway, Majutah's grandmother, Anna's parents, the preacher and his congregation in "Revival" are all folk characters—types that had received very little attention before the birth of the New Negro (which, incidentally, is a nickname Rudolph Fisher gave his child in 1926).[66] Deacon Gassoway's dissatisfaction with the worship in Harlem gives us an idea of what a real folk worship should be:

"Yas, suh, Rev'n Taylor, dass jes' whut we goin' do. Start makin' 'rangments tomorrer. Martin an' Jim Lee's over to Ebeneezer, but dey doan like it 'tall. Says hit's too hifalutin for 'em, de way dese Harlem cullud folks wushup; Ain't got no Holy Ghos' in 'em, dass whut. Jes' come in an' set down an' git up an' go out. Never moans, never shouts, never even says 'amen.' Most of us is hyeh, an' we gonna git together an' start us a ch'ch of our own."[67]

Majutah's grandmother's "down-home ideas" offer us an insight into folkways and beliefs. The old woman "wouldn't consent to having a telephone in the flat—she thought it would draw lightning."[68] She prefers reading her Bible by the oil lamp to reading it by the electric light. She detests Harlem because, rebellious to the cherished folk life and values, it contains "brazen women . . . who swore and shimmied and laughed at the suggestion of going to church," women who wore red stockings and "dresses that looked like nightgowns," women who painted their faces and straightened their hair "instead of leaving it as God intended," women who like "Jutie—lied—often."[69] In fine, she feels uneasy in the face of the iconoclastic impulse of Harlem which has broken down the old folk culture, transforming "Jutie" into "Madge."

Anna's father, to some extent, shares the concern of Majutah's grandmother about the disintegration of folk values in Harlem. He is worried about the impact of "learnin' " on his daughter's attitude towards the Bible which she now doubts. The problem, he believes, is too much learning for "Sho they's sich a thing as too much learnin'! 'At gal's gittin' so she don't b'lieve nuthin'!"[70] A child should not go beyond high school in the interest of filial piety: ". . . Think of it—high school! When we come along they didn't even *have* no high schools. Fus' thing y' know she be so far above us we can't reach her with a fence-rail. Then you'll wish you'd a listened to me. What I say is, she done gone far enough."[71]

In addition to the folk ideas contained in this husband-wife argument, folk idioms color and dramatize the whole piece, helping to make it concrete and lifelike. Witness, for instance, the concreteness of one of the clauses in the above quotation: ". . . we can't reach her with a fence-rail." Or the folk wit in Anna's mother's one-sentence summary of her husband's life and attitudes: ". . . Y' got much cotton field in you, that's what!"[72]

The last of the sketches, "Revival," is a celebration of folk worship. The narrator achieves a considerable measure of objectivity by letting the reader observe the ceremony through the eyes of Pete and Lucky, two young men with different attitudes towards the folk practice. Nothing is recommended; nothing is condemned, as in most of Rudolph Fisher's stories. An aspect of black lifestyle is expressed.

The reception of Fisher's post-1926 works—notably his novel, *The Walls of Jericho*—was enhanced by the thirst for the Negro "stuff" which Carl Van Vechten's *Nigger Heaven* had almost raised to a choking point.

But the seeds that sprouted in his novel were tested in his short stories which also helped to tease upward that thirst intensified by *Nigger Heaven.*

ZORA NEALE HURSTON

Zora Neale Hurston's first publication in any journal with a considerable nationwide circulation was "Drenched in Light," a short story which appeared in *Opportunity* in December 1924. Before then, however, she had been published by little magazines, notably the *Stylus* of Howard University which in 1921 carried her poem *O Night,* and "John Redding Goes To Sea," a story which was reprinted in the January 1926 number of *Opportunity.* But all these are insignificant compared to her major works, both fiction and nonfiction, which were published in the 1930s. Nonetheless, she is relevant to our study. As insignificant as they are, her pre-1926 writings, when viewed against her personal character, show that in spite of personal friendships between black writers and white patrons and admirers, the early New Negro literature was essentially Negro self-expressing.

The story of Zora Neale Hurston is the story of a black woman who, from birth, was predisposed to identify more with whites than with blacks. Her parents had large quantities of white blood in their veins. A white man saw her into the world and, at the most formative stage of her life, gave her appropriate pieces of advice as to how to face life. For example, she should not "be a Nigger," because "Niggers lie and lie."[73] In elementary school she received favors from whites who loved her. When she was destitute a white woman befriended and got her a position with an actress—a position which really introduced her into the world of art. She recognizes the importance of her association with the actress in the following statement: I had been with her [the actress] for eighteen months and though neither of us realized it, I had been in school all that time. I had loosened up in every joint and expanded in every direction.[74]

On the other hand, her relations with the black world were unhappy. That world seemed to have been unfair to her, right from birth. Her father did not like her—at least she thought so—because she had been born a girl instead of a boy, "and while he was off from home at that."[75] When she lost her mother at the age of nine, she was exposed to the cruelties of relatives who objected to her ambition and lack of humility, believing that "a child in [her] place ought to realize [she] was lucky to have a roof over [her] head and anything to eat at all."[76] Even her own brother, Bob, wanted to make her his wife's slave.[77]

The result of this apparent foul play from the black world and the kindness from the white race was twofold: contempt for the Negro race and, since she was a member of that "mean" Negro race, respect for the white race whose feeling of superiority she gratified by acting out demeaning stereotyped traits attributed to the Negro. Thus "to many of her white friends," as Langston Hughes points out, "she was a perfect 'darkie,' in the nice meaning they give the term—that is a naive, childlike, sweet, humorous, and highly colored Negro."[78] In fact, her friend and employer, Fannie Hurst, speaks of "her gay unpredictability" and portrays her as being "uninhibited as a child."[79] Her own description of how jazz music affected her also reveals the extent to which she was willing to be accepted as "a perfect 'darkie' ":

It constricts the thorax and splits the heart with its tempo and narcotic harmonies. . . . I follow those heathen—follow them exultingly. I dance wildly inside myself; I yell within, I whoop; I shake my *assegai* above my head, I hurl it true to the mark *yeeeeooww*! I am in the jungle and living in the jungle way. My face is painted red and yellow and my body is painted blue. My pulse is throbbing like a war drum. I want to slaughter something—give death to what, I do not know.[80]

Paradoxically, her autobiography—especially the chapter entitled "My People! My People!"—does not hide her contempt for the black race.

Nevertheless, her creative writings are expressive of the Negro self. Her short story, "Spunk," which was awarded the second prize in the fiction division of the 1925 *Opportunity* literary contest, is a foretaste of her later works. Told from a dramatic third-person point of view, it places the reader right in the middle of the action carried out by men and women who closely resemble some of those in the Eatonville of the author's childhood, as described in her autobiography. The dialogues are colorful and more or less authentic, having been enriched with folk similes and metaphors. Witness, for instance, Elijah's description of Joe Kanty as he stands helplessly before Giant Spunk who claims his wife, Lena Kanty:

Lena looked up at him with her eyes so full of love that they wuz runnin'
over, an' Spunk seen it an' Joe seen it too, and his lip started to tremblin'
and his Adam's apple was galloping up and down his neck like a race horse.
Ah bet he's wore out half a dozen Adam's apples since Spunk's been on
the job with Lena.[81]

Or Spunk's instruction to Elijah and his companions that they should
carry and bury Joe Kanty whom he has killed in self-defence, when he
was making love to Lena and Joe attacked him from behind: "Take him
up an' plant him in 'Stoney lonesome.' "[82]

To strengthen the authenticity of the life portrayed, verifiable folk
beliefs are used to support the psychological motivation. Thus we have
the episode of the "big bob-cat," which Spunk believes to be the late
Joe Kanty who "done sneaked back from Hell!"[83] We also see the same
intensification of pyschological motivation with the folk belief in the
supernatural in Spunk's death. The giant accuses his dead victim of being
responsible for his own approaching death.[84]

We also have some other folk beliefs which, as details, intensify the
local color already captured. A good example of beliefs in this class is the
laying of Spunk "on the sawdust pile with his face to the East so's he
could die easy,"[85]—a belief which Zora Neale Hurston saw in practice
for the first time at her mother's deathbed.[86]

"John Redding Goes to Sea" is also a foretaste of Zora Neale Hurston's
later works. The storm in which John loses his life is almost a prototype
of the storm in *Their Eyes Were Watching God* (1937). John is more or
less a rough male version of Janie of *Their Eyes Were Watching God*.
Like Janie, he is motivated by a great desire to see the horizon, for "no
matter what he dreamed or who he fancied himself to be, he always
ended by riding away to the horizon."[87] Like Janie, his eyes are always
on the gate. Like Janie, he has a powerful imagination and a tree which
symbolically spurs him on to self-fulfillment.

The dialogues, like those in "Spunk" and Hurston's later works, are
folksy. The story itself is replete with black folk beliefs. Matty Redding
believes that her son's longing to leave home is due to the malice of a
witch. She explains: "The very night John wuz bawn, Granny seed ole
Witch Judy Davis creepin' outer dis yahd. . . . She put travel dust down
fuh mah chile, dat's whut she done, tuh make him walk 'way fum me.
An' evuh sence he's been able tuh crawl, he's been tryin' tuh go."[88]

The cry of a screech owl is seen as "a sho' sign uh death" by the
Reddings.[89] To drive the bird from the roof Stella (John's wife) "hur-
riedly thrust her hand into the salt-jar and threw some into the chimney
of the lamp." To neutralize the omen itself "Matty slipped out of her
blue calico wrapper and turned it wrong side out before replacing it. . . .
Alfred turned one sock."[90]

"Sweat" which, together with "Color Struck," was Hurston's contribution to *Fire* in 1926, is a story of an unfaithful husband who is killed by
a rattlesnake which he himself has planted in a hamper to kill his wife
so that he might be free to bring his mistress into their house. It is done
in folk idiom enriched with homespun similes, metaphors, and invectives.
Delia Jones, for example, urges herself to be patient: "Oh well, whatever
goes over the Devil's back, is got to come under his belly. Sometime or
ruther, Sykes, like everybody else, is gointer reap his sowing."[91] Clarke
renders the concept of philandering concrete by an extended metaphor
built around a homely object—sugarcane:

"Taint no law on earth dat kin make a man be decent if it aint in 'im.
There's plenty men dat takes a wife lak dey do a joint uh sugar-cane.
It's round, juicy an' sweet when dey gets it. But dey squeeze an' grind,
squeeze an' grind an' wring every drop uh pleasure dat's in 'em out.
When dey's satisfied dat dey is wrung dry, dey treats 'em jes lak dey
do a cane-chew. Dey throws 'em away. Dey knows whut dey is doin'
while dey is at it, an' hates theirselves fuh it but they keeps on hangin'
after huh tell she's empty. Den dey hates huh fuh bein' a cane-chew an'
in de way."[92]

The next piece, "Color Struck," however, is not as strong as either
"Spunk" or "Sweat." Nonetheless, it belongs to the literature of the
1920s. "Color Struck," which is subtitled "A Play in Four Scenes,"
deals with a subject which had not been, and was not to be, seriously
treated until Wallace Thurman in 1929 did so in his novel, *The Blacker
The Berry* . . . : the psychology of a young woman who is really black
as distinct from near-white or "yaller."

As usual, Zora Neale Hurston demonstrates her good knowledge of
folkways. The cakewalk is well dramatized; folk idiom is effectively used.
The play, however, could have been stronger if more attention had been
paid to the last scene which seems to anticipate the chapter "My People!
My People!" in the author's autobiography.

Certainly, taken as an isolated incident, Emmaline's eventual possession of "a very white" daughter with "long hair," is both possible and probable.[93] So also is her excessive self-hatred, as revealed in her final rejection of John, "a light brown-skinned man," who has "adored" her for twenty years. The problem however is that, as shown in the last scene, these two elements of the play do not develop smoothly from what has existed before them—in the first three scenes.

Like "Color Struck," "Muttsy," which was awarded one-half of second prize in the short-story section of the 1926 *Opportunity* contest, is artistically weak. The plot is overburdened with irrelevances whose main merit is that they demonstrate the narrator's intimate knowledge of black folkways. Yet, like "Color Struck" and, indeed, "Spunk," "Sweat" and "John Redding Goes to Sea", "Muttsy" expresses the folk spirit and heritage of the black race. Bluefront describes Pinkie's sharpness as follows: "Look heah, lil' Pigmeat, youse *some* sharp! If you didn't had but one eye ah'd think you wuz a needle—thass how sharp you looks to me."[94] Because his "right foot is itchin' " he believes that he is "gointer walk on some strange ground" with a loved one.

In her "sketch" of Zora Neale Hurston, Fannie Hurst wrote twenty words which adequately summarize the black writer's relation to her heritage: "In spite of herself her rich heritage cropped out not only in her personality but more importantly in her writings."[95] Helpless before an understandable subconscious urge to gratify the ego of her white friends, Zora Neale Hurston must have magnified her basic Negro traits of character. She was, however, formally trained as a folklorist. Thus the exaggeration which, in her writings, often took the form of folk idiom overloaded with folk similes, metaphors, and invectives was *more* evident in her person than in her works.

NOTES

1. *See* Chapter 3, p. 95.
2. Langston Hughes, *The Big Sea: An Autobiography* (New York: Hill and Wang, 1940), pp. 265-66.
3. Ibid.
4. Wallace Thurman, "Nephews of Uncle Remus," *Independent* 119, no. 4034 (24 September 1927): 297.
5. Wallace Thurman, "Negro Artists and the Negro," *New Republic* 52, no. 665 (31 August 1927): 37.

6. Langston Hughes, *The Weary Blues* (New York: Alfred A. Knopf, 1926), p. 34 (hereafter cited as HWB).

7. Countée Cullen, "Poet on Poet," *Opportunity* 4, no. 38 (February 1926): 73.

8. Langston Hughes, "The Negro Artist and the Racial Mountain," *Nation* 122 (23 June 1926): 694.

9. George S. Schuyler, "The Negro-Art Hokum," *Nation* 122 (16 June 1926): 662.

10. Ibid., pp. 662-63.

11. Ibid., 662.

12. Hughes, "The Negro Artist and the Racial Mountain," p. 692. The quotations throughout are taken from Hughes's article as published in the *Nation* 122 (23 June 1926): 692-94.

13. *See* J. Mord Allen, *Rhymes, Tales and Rhymed Tales* (Topeka, Kansas: Crane & Company, 1906).

14. For more detailed discussion of Dunbar and his contemporaries, *see* Chapter 2.

15. Hughes, *Big Sea,* pp. 210-13.

16. *See* Chapter 3, p. 95.

17. James Weldon Johnson, *Black Manhattan* (1930; reprint ed., New York: Arno Press and the New York Times, 1968), p. 228.

18. Langston Hughes, *Fine Clothes to the Jew* (New York: Alfred A. Knopf, 1927), n.p.

19. Sterling A. Brown, Arthur P. Davis, Ulysses Lee, eds., *The Negro Caravan* (1941; reprint ed., New York: Arno Press and the New York Times, 1969), p. 480.

20. Howard W. Odum and Guy B. Johnson, *The Negro and His Songs: A Study of Typical Negro Songs in the South* (Chapel Hill: University of North Carolina Press, 1925), p. 190.

21. LeRoi Jones, *Blues People* (New York: William Morrow and Co., 1963), p. 82. Jones's italics.

22. Letter, Hughes to Van Vechten, May 15, 1925, Yale University, The title of the blues sung by George is "Follow the Deal on Down." The following is one of its stanzas:

> I went to the gypsy's
> To get my fortune told
> Went to the gypsy's
> To get my fortune told
> Gypsy done told me
> Goddam your un-hard-lucky soul.

23. Janheinz Jahn, *Muntu: An Outline of the New African Culture,* trans. Marjorie Green (New York: Grove Press, 1961), p. 221. Emphasis added.

24. For the relationship between the blues and African folk songs, *see* Jones, *Blues People,* pp. 17-31.

25. Hughes, *Big Sea,* p. 215.

26. Hughes, *Fine Clothes to the Jew,* p. 21 (hereafter cited as HFC). Knopf, 1927), p. 21 (hereafter cited as HFC).

27. LeRoi Jones categorically calls it "a West African (Ashanti) ancestor dance." *Blues People,* p. 17.

28. Hughes, *Big Sea,* p. 10.

29. Langston Hughes, "Luani of the Jungle," *Harlem: A Forum of Negro Life* 1, no. 1 (November 1928): 10.

30. Ibid.

31. Ibid., p. 11.

32. Hughes, *Big Sea,* p. 105.

33. Hughes, *Big Sea,* p. 52.

34. Langston Hughes, *Selected Poems* (1959; reprint ed., New York: Vintage Books, 1974), p. 3.

35. Ibid.

36. Alain Locke, ed., *Four Negro Poets: The Pamphlet Poets* (New York: Simon & Schuster, n.d.), pp. 5-6.

37. Benjamin Brawley to *Opportunity* in "The Ebony Flute," *Opportunity* 5, no. 9 (September 1927): 277.

38. Thurman, "Nephews of Uncle Remus," p. 297.

39. Reported in *Opportunity* 5, no. 7 (July 1927): 212.

40. Allison Davis, "Our Negro 'Intellectuals'," *The Crisis* 35, no. 8 (August 1928): 269.

41. Van Vechten to Brawley in "The Ebony Flute," *Opportunity* 5, no. 7 (July 1927): 212-13.

42. Carl Van Vechten, "Introducing Langston Hughes to the Reader" in Hughes, *The Weary Blues,* p. 11. *See also* Hughes *Big Sea,* p. 271.

43. Hughes to Van Vechten, James Weldon Johnson Collection, Yale University, New Haven, Conn.

44. Davis, "Our Negro 'Intellectuals', p. 269. Davis's italics.

45. *The Crisis* 35, no. 9 (September 1928): 302.

46. Hughes, *Big Sea,* p. 271.

47. *See,* for example, Hughes's letter to Van Vechten on 15 May 1925. With regard to their different tastes, *see* Hughes's letter to Van Vechten on 4 June 1925 where he says: "I believe our tastes in Blues differ. You like best the lighter ones like Michigan Waters and I prefer

the moanin' ones like Gulf Coast and Nobody Knows the Way I Feel This Morning." James Weldon Johnson Collection, Yale University, New Haven, Conn.

48. *Kansas City Call,* 7 April 1939 in James A. Emanuel, *Langston Hughes* (New York: Twayne, 1967), p. 137.

49. Hughes, *Big Sea,* p. 28. *See also* p. 26.

50. Ibid., p. 28.

51. Ibid., p. 29.

52. Ibid.

53. Emanuel, *Langston Hughes,* p. 33.

54. Hughes, *Big Sea,* p. 325 (date based on James A. Emanuel's calculation). *See* Emanuel, *Langston Hughes,* p. 34.

55. Davis, "Our Negro 'Intellectuals'," p. 268.

56. Eric Walrond, *Tropic Death* (New York: Boni & Liveright, 1926), p. 13 (hereafter cited as WTD).

57. "The Browsing Reader," *The Crisis* 35, no. 11 (November 1928): 374.

58. Davis, "Our Negro 'Intellectuals'," p. 268.

59. "Words of the Judges," *The Crisis* 30, no. 6 (October 1925): 276.

60. Rudolph Fisher, "High Yaller," *The Crisis* 30, no. 6 (October 1925): 282.

61. Ibid., p. 283.

62. Charles F. Cooney, "Walter White and the Harlem Renaissance," *Journal of Negro History* 57, no. 3 (July 1972): 237-38.

63. Alain Locke, ed., *The New Negro* (1925; reprint ed., New York: Atheneum, 1969), p. 61.

64. Ibid., p. 75.

65. Ibid., p. 80.

66. "The Ebony Flute," *Opportunity* 4, no. 44 (August 1926): 261. *See* Chapter 2 of this study for the anticipation of this type of treatment of the folk.

67. Locke, ed., *The New Negro,* p. 78.

68. Ibid., p. 79.

69. Ibid., p. 80.

70. Ibid., p. 81.

71. Ibid.

72. Ibid.

73. Zora Neale Hurston, *Dust Tracks on a Road: An Autobiography* (1942; reprint ed., Philadelphia: J. B. Lippincott, 1971), p. 41. For a comprehensive study of Zora Neale Hurston's life *see* Robert E.

Hemenway, *Zora Neale Hurston: A Literary Biography* (Urbana: University of Illinois Press, 1977).

74. Hurston, *Dust Tracks on a Road,* p. 141.

75. Ibid., p. 27.

76. Ibid., p. 117.

77. Ibid., pp. 128-30.

78. Hughes, *Big Sea,* p. 239.

79. Fannie Hurst, "Zora Hurston: Personality Sketch," *Yale University Library Gazette* 35, no. 1 (July 1960): 18.

80. Zora Neale Hurston, "How It Feels To Be Colored Me," *World Tomorrow* 11, no. 5 (May 1928: 216.

81. Hurston, "Spunk" in Locke, *The New Negro,* p. 107.

82. Ibid., p. 108.

83. Ibid., p. 109.

84. Ibid., p. 110.

85. Ibid.

86. Hurston, *Dust Tracks on a Road,* p. 86.

87. Hurston, "John Redding Goes to Sea," *Opportunity* 4, no. 37 (January 1926): 16.

88. Ibid., pp. 16-17.

89. Ibid., p. 20.

90. Ibid.

91. Zora Neale Hurston, "Sweat," *Fire* 1, no. 1 (November 1926): 41.

92. Ibid., p. 42.

93. Zora Neale Hurston, "Color Struck: A Play in Four Scenes," *Fire* 1, no. 1 (November 1926): 7, 13.

94. Zora Neale Hurston, "Muttsy," *Opportunity* 4, no. 44 (August 1926): 247.

95. Hurst, "Zora Hurston: Personality Sketch," p. 18.

EPILOGUE

Critics are almost unanimous as to the latitude enjoyed by New Negro writers in their choice of subjects and in the treatment of the subjects chosen. Freed from what Charles S. Johnson described as "the stifling consciousness of being a problem,"[1] the young writers readily laughed at themselves and exposed to wide public light various in-group foibles and idiosyncrasies which were rarely mentioned before their arrival on the literary scene. What is often unacknowledged is the self-expressiveness of the Literary Awakening. Many critics cannot see how a movement whose every aspect was subjected to numerous patterns of white influence could be self-expressive. Some would like to know the self which was being expressed in view of the "double" (African/American) nature of the black American.

Certainly, the "doubleness" of the New Negro writers took considerable toll of the firmness of their tone. All the motifs of their literature (acceptance of Africa as custodian of part of the Afro-American ancestral roots, uncondescending use of the folk Negro as subject matter, recognition of all aspects of Negro life as worthy subjects for literature, an attempt to present the Negro as he really was without any falsification to please or irritate anyone, the rehabilitation of stereotypes) were conditioned by their conscious or subconscious feeling of "twoness" and the resultant ambivalence. Their racial awareness or cultivation of it was not like the race-consciousness manifested in Zionism—Alain Locke's implicit comparison of the Harlem Renaissance with Zionism notwithstanding.[2] The Zionist is committed to a single ideal and can proudly renounce any other one without any harm to his self. Conversely, the black American's renunciation of any element of his "twoness" is renunciation of his entire being. Therefore, his effort to assert his self must always be one of compromise. This situation, however, did not detract from the New Negro writers' objectives. Neither the ambivalence nor the multiplicity of the patterns of influence to which the Literary Awakening was subjected was able to depreciate its black Americanness.

The young authors were not islands in the mainstream of American literature. They were not impervious to literary currents around them. Yet there are situations in which a black American artist who is supposedly borrowing from a non-Negro culture can, in fact, be borrowing elements of the black cultural heritage which have infiltrated the amalgam of American cultures. The similarity between Léopold Sédar Senghor's poetry and St. John Perse's (Alexis Saint-Léger's) work shows how a Negro who apparently adopts European literary attitudes can, contrary to what critics think, be acting independently in choosing a black people's aesthetics. The Senegalese poet and scholar acknowledges and explains the resemblance by pointing out that St. John Perse's poetry itself bears a striking resemblance to *les textes des cosmogonies dogon* (the texts of *dogon* cosmogonies) and is not *tout à fait d'Europe* (completely European). In any case, Senghor already had in his desk drawers enough material for two volumes of poetry before he read, for the first time, St. John Perse's poetry which supposedly influenced him. His masters, he insists, are to be found among African folk poets.[3]

Albert C. Barnes no doubt exaggerated when he portrayed the American Negro art as "a sound art because it comes from a primitive nature upon which a white man's education has never been harnessed."[4] The Afro-American is not an African Negro clothed in impermeable Africanism. He is not, however, "merely a lampblacked Anglo-Saxon," contrary to George S. Schuyler's claim.[5] He is a colonized black. His self-assertion in the 1920s owed much to the sociopolitical situation which sought to rob him of his personship. The achievement of that assertion in literature was greatly enhanced by the participation of white writers who, as Alain Locke puts it, "helped in the bringing of the materials of Negro life out of the shambles of conventional polemics, cheap romance and journalism into the domain of pure and unbiased art."[6] Yet the literature derived much of its passion from his being black and colonized. This partially accounts for the similarity

between that literature and the writings of non-American blacks—
notably the young Africans and West Indians who founded the Paris-
based negritude in the 1930s.

Although some of these writers—Aimé Césaire, Léopold Sédar
Senghor, and Léon-G. Damas—have openly acknowledged their debts
to some of the New Negroes, the similarity can be attributed to two
main causes: (1) direct influence sustained by either racial identification or simply by what Ralph Ellison calls "identity of passions";[7]
(2) "parallelism" of literary attitudes[8] based *not* on cohabitation in
one geo-cultural environment or on intellectual contact but on what
Jean-Paul Sartre describes as "a *collective* memory" possessed by black
people "from one end of the earth to the other" in spite of the fact
that they are separated by differences in "languages, politics and the
history of their colonizers."[9]

The seeds of the Harlem Renaissance were sown at the very moment
the first African set foot on American soil. Their flowering was not
pure because the movement was not mainly segregative but basically
assimilationist. Their fruit, nevertheless, was expressive of the black
American.

NOTES

1. *Ebony and Topaz: A Collectanea* (New York: National Urban
League, 1927), p. 12.

2. Alain Locke, *The New Negro* (1925; reprint ed., New York:
Atheneum, 1969), p. 14. For a revealing discussion of Black American
Nationalism and Zionism, *see* Edwin S. Redkey, *Black Exodus: Black
Nationalist And Back-to-Africa Movements, 1890-1910* (New Haven:
Yale University Press, 1969), pp. 302-4.

3. Léopold Sédar Senghor, *Poèmes* (Paris: Editions du Seuil, 1964;
1973), pp. 153-56.

4. Albert C. Barnes, "Negro Art and America" in Locke, ed., *The
New Negro*, p. 19.

5. "The Negro-Art Hokum," *Nation* 122 (16 June 1926): 662.

6. Locke, *The New Negro*, p. 49.

7. Ralph Ellison, *Shadow and Act* (1953; reprint ed., New York:
Vintage Books, 1972), p. 263. Ellison is essentially right when he sees
the "identity of passions" more in shared colonial experience than in
"pigmentation." He is, however, wrong when he is unable to find any

"cultural value" in the experience, even though the colonized have parts of their roots—parts which set them apart from their colonizers— among peoples whose cultures reveal more similarities than differences.

8. This is the point of view of Léon-G. Damas who, shortly before his death, tried to play down the idea of direct influence. Interview with Léon-G. Damas, Washington, D.C., 5 August 1975.

9. Jean-Paul Sartre, "Black Orpheus" in *The Black American Writer: Poetry and Drama,* ed., C. W. E. Bigsby, vol. 2. (Baltimore, Md.: Penguin Books, 1969), p. 32.

SELECTED BIBLIOGRAPHY

Achebe, Chinua. *Things Fall Apart.* 1958, Reprint. London: Heinemann, 1976.

Alain Locke Papers. Washington, D.C. Howard University. Moorland-Spingarn Research Center.

Anderson, Sherwood. *Winesburg, Ohio.* 1919. Reprint. New York: Viking Press, 1960.

Arnold, Matthew. *Four Essays on Life and Letters.* Edited by E. H. Brown. New York: Appleton-Century, 1947.

Black Opals, 1927-1928.

Bone, Robert A. *The Negro Novel in America.* Rev. ed. New Haven: Yale University Press, 1965.

Bontemps, Arna. *100 Years of Negro Freedom.* New York: Dodd, Mead & Co., 1961.

Bontemps, Arna, ed. *The Harlem Renaissance Remembered.* New York: Dodd, Mead & Co., 1972.

Brawley, Benjamin, ed. *Early Negro American Writers.* 1935. Reprint. New York: Dover Publications, 1970.

——. *The Negro Genius.* New York: Dodd, Mead & Co., 1937.

Bridgman, Richard. "Melanctha." *American Literature: A Journal of Literary History, Criticism, and Bibliography* 33, no. 3 (November 1961): 350-59.

Brinnin, John Malcolm. *The Third Rose: Gertrude Stein and Her World.* Boston: Little, Brown and Co., 1959.

Brisbane, Robert H. "His Excellency: The Provincial President of Africa." *Phylon* 10, no. 3 (Third Quarter 1949): 257-64.

Bronz, Stephen H. *Roots of Negro Racial Consciousness: The 1920s: Three Harlem Renaissance Authors.* New York: Libra Publishers, 1964.

Brown, Sterling. *Negro Poetry and Drama and Negro in American Fiction.* 1937. Reprint. New York: Atheneum, 1969.

Brown, Sterling A.; Davis, Arthur P.; Lee, Ulysses, eds. *The Negro Caravan.* 1941, Reprint. New York: Arno Press and the New York Times, 1969.

Campbell, James Edwin. *Echoes From The Cabin and Elsewhere.* Chicago: Donohue & Henneberry, 1895.

Carmichael, Waverley Turner. *From the Heart of a Folk: A Book of Songs.* Boston: Cornhill Co., 1918.

Carolina Magazine, 1927-1929.

Chesnutt, Charles W. *The Conjure Woman.* 1899. Reprint. Ann Arbor: University of Michigan Press, 1969.

Chicago Bee, 24 December 1927.

Chicago Defender, 6 September 1924.

Clarke, John Henrik, ed. *Harlem: A Community in Transition.* 1964. Reprint. New York: Citadel Press, 1969.

Collection of the Manuscript Division. Washington, D.C., Library of Congress.

Collier, Eugenia. *The Four-Way Dilemma of Claude McKay.* CAAS Occasional Paper no. 6. Atlanta, Ga.: Atlanta University, n.d.

Connelly, Marc. *The Green Pastures.* New York: Farrar & Rinehart, 1930.

Cooney, Charles F. "Walter White and the Harlem Renaissance." *Journal of Negro History* 57, no. 3 (July 1972): 231-40.

Cooper, Wayne and Reinders, Robert C. "Claude McKay in England, 1920." *New Beacon Reviews.* Collection One. Edited by John La Rose. London: New Beacon Books, 1968.

Cooper, Wayne F., ed. *The Passion of Claude McKay: Selected Poetry and Prose, 1912-1948.* New York: Schocken Books, 1973.

Cotter, Joseph S. *Caleb, The Degenerate: A Play in Four Acts.* Louisville: Bradley & Gilbert Co., 1903.

———. *Negro Tales.* New York: Cosmopolitan Press, 1912.

———. *A White Song and a Black One.* Louisville: Bradley & Gilbert Co., 1909.

Courlander, Harold. *A Treasury of African Folklore.* New York: Crown Publishers, 1975.

Courlander, Harold and Leslan, Wolf. *The Fire on the Mountain and Other Ethiopian Stories.* New York: Holt, Rinehart and Winston, 1950.

Cowley, Malcolm. *Exile's Return: A Literary Odyssey of the 1920s.* 1934. Reprint. New York: Viking Press, 1956.

The Crisis: A Record of the Darker Races. Articles are cited from this journal for the years 1910-1933.

Cronon, E. D. *Black Moses: The Story of Marcus Garvey and the Universal Negro Improvement Association.* Madison, Wis.: University of Wisconsin Press, 1955.

Cronon, David, ed. *Marcus Garvey.* Englewood Cliffs, N.J.: Prentice-Hall, 1973.

Cruse, Harold. *The Crisis of the Negro Intellectual.* New York: William Morrow and Company, 1967.

Cruse, Harold Wright. "An Afro-American's Cultural Views." *Présence Africaine* 17 (December 1957-January 1958): 31-43.

Cullen, Countée. *Black Christ and Other Poems.* New York: Harper & Brothers, 1929.

———. *The Medes and Some Poems.* New York: Harper & Brothers, 1935.

———. *On These I Stand: An Anthology of the Best Poems.* New York: Harper & Row, 1947.

———. "Surrounded by His Books Countée Cullen Is Happy." Interview with Countée Cullen. *Christian Science Monitor,* 23 October 1925.

Cullen, Countée, ed. *Caroling Dusk: An Anthology of Verse by Negro Poets.* New York: Harper & Brothers, 1927.

cummings, e. e. *The Enormous Room.* 1922. Reprint. New York: Liveright, 1970.

Cunningham, Virginia. *Paul Laurence Dunbar and His Song.* New York: Dodd, Mead & Co., 1947.

Dadié, Bernard B. *Le Pagne Noir: Contes Africains.* Paris: Présence Africaine, 1955.

Dandridge, Raymond Garfield. *The Poet and Other Poems.* Cincinnati: Raymond G. Dandridge, 1920.

Davis, Daniel Webster. *Weh Down Souf.* Cleveland: Helman-Taylor Co., 1897.

Dayrell, Elphinstone. *Folk Stories from Southern Nigeria, West Africa.* 1910. Reprint. New York: Negro Universities Press, 1969.

Du Bois, W. E. B. *The Amenia Conference.* New York: Amenia, 1925.

———. *Darkwater: Voices from Within the Veil.* 1920. Reprint. New York: Schocken Books, 1969.

———. *Dusk of Dawn: An Essay Toward an Autobiography of a Race Concept.* 1940. Reprint. New York: Schocken Books, 1968.

———. "The Evolution of Negro Leadership." *Dial* 31, no. 362 (16 July 1901).

———. *The Souls of Black Folk.* 1903. Reprint. New York: Washington Square Press, 1970.

———. "Strivings of the Negro People." *Atlantic Monthly* 80 (August 1897): 194-98.

Dunbar, Paul Laurence. *The Complete Poems of Paul Laurence Dunbar.*

New York: Dodd, Mead & Co., 1913.
——. *The Sport of the Gods.* 1902. Reprint. London: Collier-Macmillan, 1970.
Ellison, Ralph. *Shadow and Act.* 1953. Reprint. New York: Vintage Books, 1972.
Emanuel, James A. *Langston Hughes.* New York: Twayne, 1967.
Fauset, Jessie Redmond. *There is Confusion.* 1924. Reprint. New York: AMS Press, 1974.
Firbank, Ronald. *The Complete Ronald Firbank.* Norfolk, Conn.: New Directions Book, 1961.
Fire!! A Quarterly Devoted to the Younger Negro Artists 1, no. 1 (November 1926).
Foster, William Z. *The Negro People in American History.* New York: International Publishers, 1954.
Fox, Stephen R. *The Guardian of Boston: William Monroe Trotter.* New York: Atheneum, 1970.
Frank, Waldo. *Holiday.* New York: Boni and Liveright, 1923.
Franklin, John Hope. *From Slavery to Freedom: A History of American Negroes.* New York: Alfred A. Knopf, 1947.
Frazier, E. Franklin. "Garvey: A Mass Leader." *Nation* 123, no. 3189 (18 August 1926): 147-48.
Freud, Sigmund. *On Creativity and the Unconscious.* Edited by Benjamin Nelson. New York: Harper & Row, 1958.
Fullinwider, S. P. *The Mind and Mood of Black America.* Homewood, Ill.: Dorsey Press, 1969.
Glasgow, Ellen. "The Soul of Harlem." *Bookman* 64, no. 4 (December 1926): 509-10.
Gloster, Hugh M. *Negro Voices in American Fiction.* 1948. Reprint. New York: Russell & Russell, 1965.
Green, Paul. *Five Plays of the South.* New York: Hill and Wang, 1963.
Harlan, Louis R. "Booker T. Washington and the White Man's Burden." *American Historical Review* 71, no. 2 (January 1966): 449.
Harlem: A Forum of Negro Life 1, no. 1 (November 1928).
Hemenway, Robert E. *Zora Neale Hurston: A Literary Biography.* Urbana: University of Illinois Press, 1977.
Heyward, DuBose. *Mamba's Daughters.* New York: Literary Guild, 1929.
——. *Porgy.* New York: Doran, 1925.
Hoffmann, Frederick J. *The Twenties: American Writing in the Postwar Decade.* Rev. ed. New York: Free Press, 1949.
Holloway, John Wesley. *From the Desert.* New York: Neale Publishing Co., 1919.

Horace. *Epistle to the Pisones*. Translated by Norman J. DeWitt. In *Drama Survey* 1, no. 2 (October 1961).

Hornblow, Arthur. *A History of the Theatre in America: From Its Beginning to the Present Time*. Philadelphia: J. B. Lippincott Co., 1919.

Howells, W. D. "Life and Letters." *Harper's Weekly*, 27 June 1896, p. 630.

———, ed. *Voices from the Harlem Renaissance*. New York: Oxford University Press, 1976.

Huggins, Nathan Irvin. *Harlem Renaissance*. New York: Oxford University Press, 1971.

———, ed. *Voices from the Harlem Renaissance*. New York: Oxford University Press, 1976.

———. *Fine Clothes to the Jew*. New York: Alfred A. Knopf. 1927.

———. "The Negro Artist and the Racial Mountain." *Nation* 122 (23 June 1926): 692-94.

———. *Not Without Laughter*. 1930. Reprint. London: Collier-Macmillan, 1969.

———. *Selected Poems*. 1959. Reprint. New York: Vintage Books, 1974.

———. *The Weary Blues*. New York: Alfred A. Knopf, 1926.

Hurst, Fannie. "Zora Hurston: Personality Sketch." *Yale University Library Gazette* 35, no. 1 (July 1960): 17-21.

Hurston, Zora Neale. *Dust Tracks on a Road: An Autobiography*. 1942. Reprint. Philadelphia: J. B. Lippincott, 1971.

———. "How It Feels to Be Colored Me." *World Tomorrow* 11, no. 5 (May 1928): 215-16.

Interview with Mercer Cook, Washington, D.C., 6 August 1975.

Interview with Léon G. Damas, Washington, D.C., 5 August 1975.

Issacs, Harold R. "Five Writers and Their African Ancestors." *Phylon* 21, nos. 3; 4 (1960): 243-65; 317-36.

Jacques-Garvey, Amy, ed. *Philosophy and Opinions of Marcus Garvey*. 1923. Reprint. New York: Atheneum, 1969.

Jahn, Janheinz. *Muntu: An Outline of the New African Culture*. Translated by Marjorie Green. New York: Grove Press, 1961.

James Weldon Johnson Memorial Collection, Beinecke Rare Book and Manuscript Library, Yale University, New Haven, Connecticut.

Johnson, Abby Arthur and Johnson, Ronald Maberry. *Propaganda and Aesthetics: The Literary Politics of Afro-American Magazines in the Twentieth Century*. Amherst: University of Massachusetts, 1979.

Johnson, Charles S. *Ebony and Topaz: A Collectanea*. New York: National Urban League, 1927.

Johnson, James Weldon. *Along This Way.* 1933. Reprint. New York:
    Viking Press, 1968.
——. *The Autobiography of An Ex-Coloured Man.* 1912, 1927. Reprint.
    New York: Hill and Wang, 1960.
——. *Black Manhattan.* 1930. Reprint. New York: Arno Press and the
    New York Times, 1968.
——. *Fifty Years and Other Poems.* 1917. Reprint. Boston: Cornhill
    Publishing Co., 1921.
——. *God's Trombones.* 1927. Reprint. New York: Viking Press, 1969.
——, ed. *The Book of American Negro Poetry.* 1922, 1931. Reprint.
    New York: Harcourt, Brace & World, 1959.
Jones, LeRoi. *Blues People.* New York: William Morrow and Co., 1963.
Jordan, Winthrop D. *White Over Black, American Attitudes Toward the
    Negro, 1550-1812.* Chapel Hill: University of North Carolina Press,
    1968.
Kellner, Bruce. *Carl Van Vechten and the Irreverent Decades.* Norman:
    University of Oklahoma Press, 1968.
Kent, George. *Blackness and the Adventure of Western Culture.* Chicago:
    Third World Press, 1972.
Knopf, Alfred A. "Reminiscences of Hergesheimer, Van Vechten, and
    Mencken." *Yale University Library Gazette* 24, no. 4 (April 1950):
    145-73.
Lawrence, D. H. *Phoenix.* Edited by Edward D. McDonald. New York:
    Viking Press, 1936.
Les Arts à Paris 8 (October 1923).
Leuders, Edward. *Carl Van Vechten.* New York: Twayne, 1965.
——. *Carl Van Vechten and the Twenties.* Albuquerque: University of
    New Mexico Press, 1955.
Levy, Eugene. *James Weldon Johnson: Black Leader Black Voice.*
    Chicago: University of Chicago Press, 1973.
Lindsay, Vachel. *Collected Poems.* Rev. ed. 1913. Reprint. New York:
    Macmillan Co., 1973.
Littlejohn, David. *Black on White: A Critical Survey of Writing by
    American Negroes.* New York: Grossmann, 1966.
Locke, Alain. "Beauty Instead of Ashes." *The Nation,* 126 (April 18,
    1928), 432-34.
——. ed. *The New Negro.* 1925. Reprint. New York: Atheneum, 1969.
Locke, Alain, ed. *Four Negro Poets: The Pamphlet Poets.* New York:
    Simon & Schuster, n.d.
Locke, Alain, and Gregory, Montgomery, eds. *Plays of Negro Life: A
    Source-Book of Native American Drama.* 1927. Reprint. Westport,
    Conn.: Negro Universities Press, 1970.

Loti, Pierre. *Le Mariage de Loti.* Paris: Calmann Levy, Editeur, 1888.

Luhan, Mabel Dodge. *Intimate Memories.* New York: Harcourt, Brace and Co., 1936.

McIlhenny, E. A. *Befor' de War Spirituals: Words and Melodies.* Boston: Christopher Publishing House, 1933.

McKay, Claude. *A Long Way From Home.* 1937. Reprint. New York: Harcourt, Brace & World, 1970.

———. *Banana Bottom.* New York: Harper & Brothers, 1933.

———. *Banjo: A Story Without a Plot.* 1929. Reprint. New York: Harcourt Brace Jovanovich, 1957.

———. *Constab Ballads.* London: Watts & Co., 1912.

———. *Harlem Shadows.* New York: Harcourt, Brace and Co., 1922.

———. *Home to Harlem.* New York: Harper & Brothers, 1928.

———. "My Green Hills of Jamaica." (Typescript, dated 1946, in Claude McKay Papers, Schomburg Collection, New York Public Library.

———. *Selected Poems of Claude McKay.* New York: Harcourt, Brace & World, 1953.

———. *Songs of Jamaica.* Kingston, Jamaica: Aston W. Gardner, 1912.

Maran, René. *Batouala: An African Love Story.* Translated by Alexandre Mboukou. Rockville, Md.: New Perspective, 1973.

———. "Contribution of the Black Race to European Art." *Phylon* 10, no. 3 (1949): 240-41.

Matthews, Carl S. "Documents: Marcus Garvey Writes from Jamaica on the Mulatto Escape Hatch." *Journal of Negro History* 59, no. 2 (April 1974): 170-76.

Meier, August. *Negro Thought in America, 1880-1915.* Ann Arbor: University of Michigan Press, 1970.

The Messenger. 1917-1927.

Miller, Kelly. "After Marcus Garvey—What of the Negro?" *Contemporary Review* 131 (1927): 492-500.

———. *Race Adjustment: Essays on the Negro in America.* New York: Neale Publishing Co., 1908.

New Era, 1916.

Newman, Frances. "Love in Many Guises." *Bookman* 64, no. 4 (October 1926): 226-28.

Odum, Howard W., and Johnson, Guy B. *The Negro and His Songs: A Study of Typical Negro Songs in the South.* Chapel Hill: University of North Carolina Press, 1925.

O'Neill, Eugene. *The Emperor Jones, Anna Christie, The Hairy Ape.* New York: Modern Library, 1949.

———. *The Plays of Eugene O'Neill.* New York: Random House, 1948.

Opportunity: A Journal of Negro Life. 1923-1933.

Peterkin, Julia. *Black April*. Indianapolis: Bobbs-Merrill Co., 1927.
———. *Green Thursday: Stories*. New York: Alfred A. Knopf, 1924.
———. *Scarlet Sister Mary*. Indianapolis: Bobbs-Merrill Co., 1928.
Pickens, William. "The Emperor of Africa: The Psychology of Garveyism." *Forum* 70 (August 1923): 1790-99.
Redding, Saunders. *To Make A Poet Black*. 1939. Reprint. Chapel Hill: University of North Carolina Press, 1968).
Redkey, Edwin S. *Black Exodus: Black Nationalist and Back-to-Africa Movements, 1890-1910*. New Haven: Yale University Press, 1969.
Riley, Roberta. "Search for Identity and Artistry." *CLA Journal* 17, no. 4 (June 1974): 480-85.
Saint Louis Argus, 3 February 1928.
Sandburg, Carl. *Complete Poems*. New York: Harcourt, Brace and Co., 1950.
Sartre, Jean-Paul. "Black Orpheus." In *The Black American Writer: Poetry and Drama*, edited by C. W. E. Bigsby, vol. 2. Baltimore, Md.: Penguin Books, 1969.
The Schomburg Collection, New York Public Library, New York.
Schuyler, George S. "The Negro-Art Hokum." *Nation* 122 (16 June 1926): 662-63.
Senghor, Léopold Sédar. *Poèmes*. Paris: Editions du Seuil, 1964; 1973.
Sitwell, Osbert, Sir. "New York in the Twenties." *Atlantic*, February 1962, pp. 38-43.
Spencer, Samuel R., Jr. *Booker T. Washington and the Negro's Place in American Life*. Boston: Little, Brown and Co., 1955.
Stein, Gertrude. *Things as They Are*. Pawlet, Vt.: Banyan Press, 1950.
———. *Three Lives*. 1909. Reprint. New York: Vintage Books, 1936.
Stowe, Harriet Beecher. *Uncle Tom's Cabin*. 1851-1852. Reprint. New York: New American Library, 1966.
Talley, Thomas W. *Negro Folk Rhymes: Wise and Otherwise*. New York: Macmillan Co., 1922.
Talley, Truman Hughes. "Marcus Garvey—The Negro Moses?" *World's Work* 41, no. 2 (December 1920): 153-66.
Thurman, Wallace. "Harlem Facets." *The World Tomorrow* 10, no. 11 (November 1927): 465-67.
———. "Negro Artists and the Negro." *New Republic* 52, no. 665 (31 August 1927): 37-39.
———. "Negro Poets and Their Poetry." *Bookman* 67, no. 5 (July 1928): 555-61.
———. "Nephews of Uncle Remus." *Independent* 119, no. 4034 (24 September 1927): 296-98.

Toomer, Jean. *Cane.* 1923. Reprint. New York: Liveright, 1975.

Toomer Collection. Yale University, New Haven, Conn.

Toomer Papers, Manuscript Division, Fisk University Library, Nashville, Tenn.

Toronto Star Weekly, 25 March 1922.

Turner, Darwin T. "An Intersection of Paths." *Phylon* 17, no. 4 (June 1974): 463.

———. *In a Minor Chord: Three Afro-American Writers and Their Search for Identity.* Carbondale: Southern Illinois University Press, 1971.

Twain, Mark. *The Adventures of Huckleberry Finn.* 1884. Reprint. New York: Collier Books, 1962.

Van Vechten, Carl. *Nigger Heaven.* 1926. Reprint. New York: Harper, Colophon, 1971.

———. *Notes for an Autobiography.* Compiled for the Colophon edition in June 1930.

Vincent, Theodore G., ed. *Voices of a Black Nation, Political Journalism in the Harlem Renaissance.* San Francisco: Ramparts Press, 1973.

Wagner, Jean. *Les poètes noirs des Etats-Unis.* Paris: Nouveaux Horizons, 1965.

Walrond, Eric. *Tropic Death.* 1926. Reprint. New York: Collier Books, 1972.

Washington, Booker T. "Cruelty in the Congo Country." *Outlook* 78 (8 October 1904): 375-77.

———. "Industrial Education in Africa." *Independent* 60, no. 2989 (15 March 1906): 616-19.

———. *Up from Slavery.* 1901. Reprint. New York: Bantam Books, 1963.

Waters, Ethel. *His Eyes Is on the Sparrow.* 1950. Reprint. New York: Pyramid Books, 1967.

Weisberger, Bernard A. *Booker T. Washington.* New York: New American Library, 1972.

Wiggins, Lida Keck. *The Life and Works of Paul Laurence Dunbar.* New York: Kraus Reprint, 1971.

Williams, Kenny J. *They Also Spoke: An Essay on Negro Literature, 1787-1930.* Nashville, Tenn.: Townsend Press, 1970.

INDEX

Achebe, Chinua, 167
Afraid, 166, 168
Aframerican. *See* Afro-Americans
Africa, conceptual description, 10, 128, 168
African: art, 98; artifacts, 4, 34; chiefs, 4; civilizations, 5, 164; deracinated (*see* Deracinated African) folklore, 4; idols and masks, 4; motif in the New Negro writings, 148-50, 159, 166, 174; musical habits, 166; Negro, 34, 194; tom-toms, 166; writers, 195
Africanization: Jesus, 147; Medea's ancestry, 147
Africans and Afro-Americans: affinity to nature, 129; common roots, 129, 150, 169; communication through songs, 129
Afro-Americans: ancestral heritage, 168-69; double consciousness, 43, 67, 126; factors that affect, 129-30; immortality of folk superstitions, 130; intraracial classifications, 47, 125, 134; lamp-

blacked Anglo-Saxon, 158; musical effect on Europe, 5; reconciliation with past, 136; soul, 130-31, 138, 150; work songs, 162; writing in English, 153
Afro-Jamaican folk culture, 79
Afro-slave, emasculation of, 132
Alexander, Lewis, 111
The Alexander Pushkin Poetry Prize, 93
All God's Chillun Got Wings, 18
Allen, Devere, 92
Allen, Frederick, 92
Allen, J. Mord, 159
Alpha Kappa Alpha Sorority, story competition, 98
Amazons of Dohomey, 10
American: citizenship, 168; black participation in, 114; civilization, crisis in, 1; culture, Negro jazz, 164-65. *See also* Jazz
American Mercury, 180
American Negro jazz, 164-65
Anderson, Regina, 29, 92
Anderson, Sherwood, 8, 101, 140-43

About the Author

CHIDI IKONNÉ is Assistant Professor and Acting Chairman of the Afro-American Studies Department at Harvard University. His articles have appeared in *Phylon, Research in African Literatures, Journal of African Studies,* and other publications.